TM

References for the Rest of Us! ®

BESTSELLING BOOK SERIES FROM IDG

Are you intimidated and confused by computers? Do you find that traditional manuals are overloaded with technical details you'll never use? Do your friends and family always call you to fix simple problems on their PCs? Then the ...*For Dummies*® computer book series from IDG Books Worldwide is for you.

...*For Dummies* books are written for those frustrated computer users who know they aren't really dumb but find that PC hardware, software, and indeed the unique vocabulary of computing make them feel helpless. ...*For Dummies* books use a lighthearted approach, a down-to-earth style, and even cartoons and humorous icons to diffuse computer novices' fears and build their confidence. Lighthearted but not lightweight, these books are a perfect survival guide for anyone forced to use a computer.

> "I like my copy so much I told friends; now they bought copies."
>
> — Irene C., Orwell, Ohio

> "Quick, concise, nontechnical, and humorous."
>
> — Jay A., Elburn, Illinois

> "Thanks, I needed this book. Now I can sleep at night."
>
> — Robin F., British Columbia, Canada

Already, millions of satisfied readers agree. They have made ...*For Dummies* books the #1 introductory level computer book series and have written asking for more. So, if you're looking for the most fun and easy way to learn about computers, look to ...*For Dummies* books to give you a helping hand.

TM

IDG BOOKS
WORLDWIDE

4/98

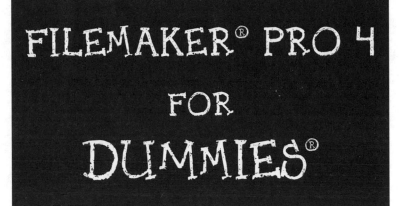

FILEMAKER® PRO 4
FOR
DUMMIES®

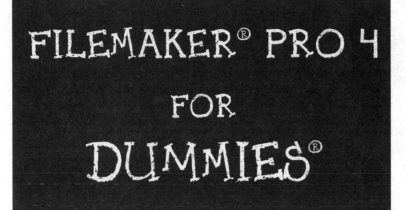

FILEMAKER® PRO 4 FOR DUMMIES®

by Tom Maremaa

IDG Books Worldwide, Inc.
An International Data Group Company

Foster City, CA ♦ Chicago, IL ♦ Indianapolis, IN ♦ New York, NY

FileMaker® Pro 4 For Dummies®

Published by
IDG Books Worldwide, Inc.
An International Data Group Company
919 E. Hillsdale Blvd.
Suite 400
Foster City, CA 94404
www.idgbooks.com (IDG Books Worldwide Web site)
www.dummies.com (Dummies Press Web site)

Library of Congress Catalog Card No.: 97-80698

ISBN: 0-7645-0210-7

Printed in the United States of America

10 9 8 7 6 5 4 3 2

1O/TQ/QX/ZY/IN

Distributed in the United States by IDG Books Worldwide, Inc.

Distributed by Macmillan Canada for Canada; by Transworld Publishers Limited in the United Kingdom; by IDG Norge Books for Norway; by IDG Sweden Books for Sweden; by Woodslane Pty. Ltd. for Australia; by Woodslane Enterprises Ltd. for New Zealand; by Longman Singapore Publishers Ltd. for Singapore, Malaysia, Thailand, and Indonesia; by Simron Pty. Ltd. for South Africa; by Toppan Company Ltd. for Japan; by Distribuidora Cuspide for Argentina; by Livraria Cultura for Brazil; by Ediciencia S.A. for Ecuador; by Addison-Wesley Publishing Company for Korea; by Ediciones ZETA S.C.R. Ltda. for Peru; by WS Computer Publishing Corporation, Inc., for the Philippines; by Unalis Corporation for Taiwan; by Contemporanea de Ediciones for Venezuela; by Computer Book & Magazine Store for Puerto Rico; by Express Computer Distributors for the Caribbean and West Indies. Authorized Sales Agent: Anthony Rudkin Associates for the Middle East and North Africa.

For general information on IDG Books Worldwide's books in the U.S., please call our Consumer Customer Service department at 800-762-2974. For reseller information, including discounts and premium sales, please call our Reseller Customer Service department at 800-434-3422.

For information on where to purchase IDG Books Worldwide's books outside the U.S., please contact our International Sales department at 650-655-3200 or fax 650-655-3297.

For information on foreign language translations, please contact our Foreign & Subsidiary Rights department at 650-655-3021 or fax 650-655-3281.

For sales inquiries and special prices for bulk quantities, please contact our Sales department at 650-655-3200 or write to the address above.

For information on using IDG Books Worldwide's books in the classroom or for ordering examination copies, please contact our Educational Sales department at 800-434-2086 or fax 317-596-5499.

For press review copies, author interviews, or other publicity information, please contact our Public Relations department at 650-655-3000 or fax 650-655-3299.

For authorization to photocopy items for corporate, personal, or educational use, please contact Copyright Clearance Center, 222 Rosewood Drive, Danvers, MA 01923, or fax 978-750-4470.

is a trademark under exclusive license to IDG Books Worldwide, Inc., from International Data Group, Inc.

About the Author

Tom Maremaa is an award-winning technical writer who has written about computers for at least 15 years. When not writing about the Macintosh operating system for Apple Computer, Tom enjoys reading the works of James Joyce and Thomas Pynchon.

ABOUT IDG BOOKS WORLDWIDE

Welcome to the world of IDG Books Worldwide.

IDG Books Worldwide, Inc., is a subsidiary of International Data Group, the world's largest publisher of computer-related information and the leading global provider of information services on information technology. IDG was founded more than 25 years ago and now employs more than 8,500 people worldwide. IDG publishes more than 275 computer publications in over 75 countries (see listing below). More than 90 million people read one or more IDG publications each month.

Launched in 1990, IDG Books Worldwide is today the #1 publisher of best-selling computer books in the United States. We are proud to have received eight awards from the Computer Press Association in recognition of editorial excellence and three from *Computer Currents'* First Annual Readers' Choice Awards. Our best-selling *...For Dummies*® series has more than 50 million copies in print with translations in 38 languages. IDG Books Worldwide, through a joint venture with IDG's Hi-Tech Beijing, became the first U.S. publisher to publish a computer book in the People's Republic of China. In record time, IDG Books Worldwide has become the first choice for millions of readers around the world who want to learn how to better manage their businesses.

Our mission is simple: Every one of our books is designed to bring extra value and skill-building instructions to the reader. Our books are written by experts who understand and care about our readers. The knowledge base of our editorial staff comes from years of experience in publishing, education, and journalism — experience we use to produce books for the '90s. In short, we care about books, so we attract the best people. We devote special attention to details such as audience, interior design, use of icons, and illustrations. And because we use an efficient process of authoring, editing, and desktop publishing our books electronically, we can spend more time ensuring superior content and spend less time on the technicalities of making books.

You can count on our commitment to deliver high-quality books at competitive prices on topics you want to read about. At IDG Books Worldwide, we continue in the IDG tradition of delivering quality for more than 25 years. You'll find no better book on a subject than one from IDG Books Worldwide.

John Kilcullen
John Kilcullen
CEO
IDG Books Worldwide, Inc.

Steven Berkowitz
Steven Berkowitz
President and Publisher
IDG Books Worldwide, Inc.

Eighth Annual
Computer Press
Awards ≥1992

Ninth Annual
Computer Press
Awards ≥1993

Tenth Annual
Computer Press
Awards ≥1994

Eleventh Annual
Computer Press
Awards ≥1995

IDG Books Worldwide, Inc., is a subsidiary of International Data Group, the world's largest publisher of computer-related information and the leading global provider of information services on information technology. International Data Group publishes over 275 computer publications in over 75 countries. More than 90 million people read one or more International Data Group publications each month. International Data Group's publications include: **ARGENTINA:** Buyer's Guide, Computerworld Argentina, PC World Argentina; **AUSTRALIA:** Australian Macworld, Australian PC World, Australian Reseller News, Computerworld, IT Casebook, Network World, Publish, Webmaster; **AUSTRIA:** Computerwelt Osterreich, Networks Austria, PC Tip Austria; **BANGLADESH:** PC World Bangladesh; **BELARUS:** PC World Belarus; **BELGIUM:** Data News; **BRAZIL:** Annuário de Informática, Computerworld, Connections, Macworld, PC Player, PC World, Publish, Reseller News, Supergamepower; **BULGARIA:** Computerworld Bulgaria, Network World Bulgaria, PC & MacWorld Bulgaria; **CANADA:** CIO Canada, Client/Server World, ComputerWorld Canada, InfoWorld Canada, NetworkWorld Canada, WebWorld; **CHILE:** Computerworld Chile, PC World Chile; **COLOMBIA:** Computerworld Colombia, PC World Colombia; **COSTA RICA:** PC World Centro America; **THE CZECH AND SLOVAK REPUBLICS:** Computerworld Czechoslovakia, Macworld Czech Republic, PC World Czechoslovakia; **DENMARK:** Communications World Danmark, Computerworld Danmark, Macworld Danmark, PC World Danmark, Techworld Denmark; **DOMINICAN REPUBLIC:** PC World Republica Dominicana; **ECUADOR:** PC World Ecuador; **EGYPT:** Computerworld Middle East, PC World Middle East; **EL SALVADOR:** PC World Centro America; **FINLAND:** MikroPC, Tietoverkko, Tietoviikko; **FRANCE:** Distributique, Hebdo, Info PC, Le Monde Informatique, Macworld, Reseaux & Telecoms, WebMaster France; **GERMANY:** Computer Partner, Computerwoche, Computerwoche Extra, Computerwoche FOCUS, Global Online, Macwelt, PC Welt; **GREECE:** Amiga Computing, GamePro Greece, Multimedia World; **GUATEMALA:** PC World Centro America; **HONDURAS:** PC World Centro America; **HONG KONG:** Computerworld Hong Kong, PC World Hong Kong, Publish in Asia; **HUNGARY:** ABCD CD-ROM, Computerworld Szamitastechnika, Internetto online Magazine, PC World Hungary, PC-X Magazin Hungary; **ICELAND:** Tolvuheimur PC World Island; **INDIA:** Information Communications World, Information Systems Computerworld, PC World India, Publish in Asia; **INDONESIA:** InfoKomputer PC World, Komputek Computerworld, Publish in Asia; **IRELAND:** ComputerScope, PC Live!; **ISRAEL:** Macworld Israel, People & Computers/Computerworld; **ITALY:** Computerworld Italia, Macworld Italia, Networking Italia, PC World Italia; **JAPAN:** DTP World, Macworld Japan, Nikkei Personal Computing, OS/2 World Japan, SunWorld Japan, Windows NT World; **KENYA:** PC World East African; **KOREA:** Hi-Tech Information, Macworld Korea, PC World Korea; **MACEDONIA:** PC World Macedonia; **MALAYSIA:** Computerworld Malaysia, PC World Malaysia, Publish in Asia; **MALTA:** PC World Malta; **MEXICO:** Computerworld Mexico, PC World Mexico; **MYANMAR:** PC World Myanmar; **NETHERLANDS:** Computer! Totaal, LAN Internetworking Magazine, LAN World Buyers Guide, Macworld Netherlands, Net, WebWereld; **NEW ZEALAND:** Absolute Beginners Guide and Plain & Simple Series, Computer Buyer, Computer Industry Directory, Computerworld New Zealand, MTB, Network World, PC World New Zealand; **NICARAGUA:** PC World Centro America; **NORWAY:** Computerworld Norge, CW Rapport, Datamagasinet, Financial Rapport, Kursguide Norge, Macworld Norge, Multimediaworld Norge, PC World Ekspress Norge, PC World Nettverk, PC World Norge, PC World ProduktGuide Norge; **PAKISTAN:** Computerworld Pakistan; **PANAMA:** PC World Panama; **PEOPLE'S REPUBLIC OF CHINA:** China Computer Users, China Computerworld, China InfoWorld, China Telecom World Weekly, Computer & Communication, Electronic Design China, Electronics Today, Electronics Weekly, Game Software, PC World China, Popular Computer Week, Software Weekly, Software World, Telecom World; **PERU:** Computerworld Peru, PC World Profesional Peru, PC World SoHo Peru; **PHILIPPINES:** Click!, Computerworld Philippines, PC World Philippines, Publish in Asia; **POLAND:** Computerworld Poland, Computerworld Special Report Poland, Cyber, Macworld Poland, Networld Poland, PC World Komputer; **PORTUGAL:** Cerebro/PC World, Computerworld/Correio Informático, Dealer World Portugal, Mac*In/PC*In Portugal, Multimedia World; **PUERTO RICO:** PC World Puerto Rico; **ROMANIA:** Computerworld Romania, PC World Romania, Telecom Romania; **RUSSIA:** Computerworld Russia, Mir PK, Publish, Seti; **SINGAPORE:** Computerworld Singapore, PC World Singapore, Publish in Asia; **SLOVENIA:** Monitor; **SOUTH AFRICA:** Computing SA, Network World SA, Software World SA; **SPAIN:** Communicaciones World España, Computerworld España, Dealer World España, Macworld España, PC World España; **SRI LANKA:** Infolink PC World; **SWEDEN:** CAP&Design, Computer Sweden, Corporate Computing Sweden, Internetworld Sweden, it.branschen, Macworld Sweden, MaxiData Sweden, MikroDatorn, Natverk & Kommunikation, PC World Sweden, PCaktiv, Windows World Sweden; **SWITZERLAND:** Computerworld Schweiz, Macworld Schweiz, PCtip; **TAIWAN:** Computerworld Taiwan, Macworld Taiwan, NEW VISION/Publish, PC World Taiwan, Windows World Taiwan; **THAILAND:** Publish in Asia, Thai Computerworld; **TURKEY:** Computerworld Turkiye, Macworld Turkiye, Network World Turkiye, PC World Turkiye; **UKRAINE:** Computerworld Kiev, Multimedia World Ukraine, PC World Ukraine; **UNITED KINGDOM:** Acorn User UK, Amiga Action UK, Amiga Computing UK, Apple Talk UK, Computing, Macworld, Parents and Computers UK, PC Advisor, PC Home, PSX Pro, The WEB; **UNITED STATES:** Cable in the Classroom, CIO Magazine, Computerworld, DOS World, Federal Computer Week, GamePro Magazine, InfoWorld, I-Way, Macworld, Network World, PC Games, PC World, Publish, Video Event, THE WEB Magazine, and WebMaster; online webzines: JavaWorld, NetscapeWorld, and SunWorld Online; **URUGUAY:** InfoWorld Uruguay; **VENEZUELA:** Computerworld Venezuela, PC World Venezuela; and **VIETNAM:** PC World Vietnam.
5/7/98

Dedication

To Mimi, for teaching me, as usual, about things *other* than computers.

To all my friends at IDG Books Worldwide for their support and encouragement.

To Apple Computer, for making the Macintosh the best darn computer in the whole wide world.

To Microsoft, for making Windows 95 and Windows NT a pleasure to learn and use.

Thank you, one and all.

Author's Acknowledgments

First, I want to thank Mike Kelly at IDG Books for thinking of me to write this book. Mike got the ball rolling and was, as always, great to work with.

My very special thanks go to my project editor, Kyle Looper, without whom I could not have finished this book. Kyle was simply excellent in developing the outlines and shaping the content of each chapter (and hanging in there with me to produce what I had to produce). Special thanks also to Diane Giangrossi, who copyedited each chapter with such brilliance and insight that it made me rethink how I use the English language.

I also appreciate all the efforts from the folks at IDG Books Worldwide, both in Editorial and Production. You're terrific.

At Claris Corp, I want to thank Kevin Mallon and Tony Campitelli, both of whom went out of their way to get me what I needed to produce this book.

Publisher's Acknowledgments

We're proud of this book; please register your comments through our IDG Books Worldwide Online Registration Form located at http://my2cents.dummies.com.

Some of the people who helped bring this book to market include the following:

Acquisitions, Development, and Editorial

Project Editor: Kyle Looper

Acquisitions Editor: Michael Kelly

Media Development Manager: Joyce Pepple

Associate Permissions Editor: Heather Heath Dismore

Copy Editor: Diane L. Giangrossi

Technical Editor: John Wilson

Editorial Manager: Colleen Rainsberger

Editorial Assistants: Paul E. Kuzmic, Darren Meiss

Production

Project Coordinator: Regina Snyder

Layout and Graphics: Lou Boudreau, Linda M. Boyer, Maridee V. Ennis, Angela F. Hunckler, Jane E. Martin, Drew R. Moore, Anna Rohrer, Brent Savage

Proofreaders: Betty Kish, Christine Berman, Rachel Garvey, Janet M. Withers

Indexer: Sherry Massey

General and Administrative

IDG Books Worldwide, Inc.: John Kilcullen, CEO; Steven Berkowitz, President and Publisher

IDG Books Technology Publishing: Brenda McLaughlin, Senior Vice President and Group Publisher

Dummies Technology Press and Dummies Editorial: Diane Graves Steele, Vice President and Associate Publisher; Mary Bednarek, Director of Acquisitions and Product Development; Kristin A. Cocks, Editorial Director

Dummies Trade Press: Kathleen A. Welton, Vice President and Publisher; Kevin Thornton, Acquisitions Manager

IDG Books Production for Dummies Press: Michael R. Britton, Vice President of Production and Creative Services; Beth Jenkins Roberts, Production Director; Cindy L. Phipps, Manager of Project Coordination, Production Proofreading, and Indexing; Kathie S. Schutte, Supervisor of Page Layout; Shelley Lea, Supervisor of Graphics and Design; Debbie J. Gates, Production Systems Specialist; Robert Springer, Supervisor of Proofreading; Debbie Stailey, Special Projects Coordinator; Tony Augsburger, Supervisor of Reprints and Bluelines;

Dummies Packaging and Book Design: Robin Seaman, Creative Director; Jocelyn Kelaita, Product Packaging Coordinator; Kavish + Kavish, Cover Design

♦

The publisher would like to give special thanks to Patrick J. McGovern, without whom this book would not have been possible.

♦

Contents at a Glance

Cartoons at a Glance

By Rich Tennant

Table of Contents

Part V: Things That Didn't Quite Fit Elsewhere 289

Introduction

• •

*T*here's nothing quite like the thrill of your first roller-coaster ride. You climb slowly to the top, hearing the click-click of the gears on the track, not knowing what to expect. You begin to feel edgy. Then suddenly from the top you plunge downward, feeling the vertical drop, the G-force against your body and face. Man, you're in for a ride. Perhaps the ride of your life.

Taking that ride can be the best or worst experience of your life, right? Taking a ride through the twists and turns of computer software can be the same thing: either the best or the worst experience you've had. Hey, this is no time to read a book, you may be thinking. Just take the plunge and suffer the consequences. Well, think again. If your ride is FileMaker Pro, you may need a little guidance along the way, a helping hand, some sage advice to keep you on the track.

FileMaker Pro 4 For Dummies is your reading and riding companion for what, I hope, will be the best software experience of your life. This book is here to help you navigate the rough spots on the course, to help you get through the sharp turns and heavy vertical drops. It knows that you may have other, more important things on your mind than wading through the 400-page manual that came in the box with FileMaker Pro. It can help you get up to speed rapidly with the program, to build things you can be proud of.

This book has the basics as well as the intermediate stuff, along with step-by-step instructions, detailed explanations, and illustrations for things that defy normal description. Icons mark text with special interest or meaning. Sidebars protect you from technical slop. This book may not protect you from the normal perils of the ride, but it can buffer the experience a bit and make it enjoyable.

About This Book

You don't have to sit down and read this baby from cover to cover. You can if you want to, but it's not necessary. This isn't a historical novel or a three-act play. The book is meant to be read out of sequence, if that's useful to you. You may pick up a chapter here, a chapter there, and pretty soon the knowledge from both will mesh together. That's the idea behind the book. Sometimes, we learn best when we learn out of sequence.

This book is organized in parts, with each part focusing on a broad facet of the program. Within parts, individual chapters approach different aspects of the topic. The chapters are littered with icons and cluttered with technical sidebars. Read what you must; then put the knowledge to work for you and the book back on the shelf.

Conventions Used in This Book

Because you read this book out of sequence, looking for tips, useful help, shortcuts, anything that helps you find things out fast and become more productive with FileMaker Pro, you ought to know about some conventions used in this book. These are standard in ...*For Dummies* books and I use them here. Among these conventions:

- ✔ The ⇨ (command arrow) indicating that you should click on a menu, followed by that menu item.
- ✔ Monospaced fonts for what you see on your screen.
- ✔ Underlined words indicating hyperlinks.

What You're Not to Read

There are bound to be topics in a book like this that delve deeper into the inner workings of FileMaker Pro than you might really be interested in reading. These are flagged for you by a Technical Stuff icon or an icon appropriate to the book's topic that indicates the same idea. You don't have to read any text that's identified by these icons in order to understand the subject at hand. You can skip over that text, or return it to another time. It's your call.

Foolish Assumptions

Because one book can't cover everything, I assume that you know the basics of working with the Macintosh or Windows. These basics include choosing menu items, using a mouse, knowing mouse terms (click, double-click, click and drag), and manipulating windows (moving, resizing, and closing). And you can navigate around okay. If you need additional Macintosh or Windows help, I wholeheartedly suggest David Pogue's *Macs For Dummies* or Andy Rathbone's *Windows 95 For Dummies,* both published by IDG Books Worldwide, Inc.

I'm also assuming that if you're a Mac user, you'll be tolerant and understanding when the book talks about things related to Windows — and vice versa. The beauty of FileMaker Pro is that it's seamlessly cross-platform: The interface on the Mac is virtually identical to the interface in Windows. Almost by default, if you get up to speed on the Mac version of the program, you'll be equally up to speed on the Windows version. Mac and Windows folks can coexist peaceably in the FileMaker Pro world.

How This Book Is Organized

To make reading easier, the book is broken up into parts, chapters, and smaller things. The parts are boundaries for larger topics that the book covers. The chapters focus on a portion of a greater topic. They contain the fascinating information as well as the worrisome detail. The following sections tell you what to expect.

Part I: The Nitty-Gritty

In this part, you get down to the basics. You roll up your sleeves and check the blueprints for the database house you want to build. You also check out the blueprints or templates that others have used to build their database houses. At times, you may even work without your computer, just plain old paper and pencil to sketch out the design of the house. You get an idea here, in Part I, of the tools at your disposal and what you've got to work with. When you're ready, you can take a deep breath and start to build.

Part II: Doing It

You've doubtless heard that Nike commercial where the message is to *Just Do It*. Well, in this part, you're doing it, all right. You're in the thick of things, designing and building the FileMaker Pro database of your dreams. You're working with the tools that are available, and you're starting to make things happen.

Part III: Off to Work We Go

Those of you who do not have to build a FileMaker Pro database from scratch should start here. Managing a database; entering, deleting, and finding records; and working on a FileMaker Pro database at the office is the stuff of Part III. Some of this is fun, some is not. In this part, we try to whistle while we work.

Part IV: Advanced Stuff, OK?

Life moves forward, not backward. So will you as you pick up speed with FileMaker Pro. You'll be ready to learn some advanced stuff, or what I call advanced stuff. It's really not that hard, once you get into it. Publishing your database on the Web, for example, is straightforward and kind of fun. You'll like it, if you give yourself license to try it. Same goes for scripting the actions of buttons in your database. As for relational stuff, well, that's another matter. . . .

Part V: Things That Didn't Quite Fit Elsewhere

Here's a collection of goodies that just didn't fit in other chapters. You'll find some gems here in this part. You'll know them when you see them. Trust me. The chapter about America Online will nudge your life in the database forward.

Part VI: The Part of Tens

Finally, the part that makes a ...*For Dummies* book the special literary experience it is: the Part of Tens. Hear about keyboard shortcuts, cool things to click on in FileMaker Pro, and other amazing things that add up to the magic number ten.

Appendix

The Appendix is all about the installation of FileMaker Pro on your computer. It's a short chapter, as you might expect. Installation is really a piece of cake. If you can point and click with your mouse, and read text in dialog boxes, then you don't really need to read this appendix; FileMaker Pro's on-screen installation guidance is that easy.

Icons Used in This Book

Because all words and no pictures make books dull, the text is spiced with lots of cool icons.

This icon points out the easy way, or, at least, an easier way to use one of FileMaker Pro's features.

This icon highlights important information that you should try to remember. These friendly little reminders can make your FileMaker Pro experience that much more useful.

This icon alerts you, in a friendly, ...*For Dummies* kind of way, to the little things and sometimes the big, ugly, monstrous things too that can trip you up along the way to database creation.

This icon flags technical information that you may or may not want to read. It's not for everybody. It won't hurt you to read it (I don't think), and it may even increase your FileMaker Pro acumen.

Where to Go From Here

You've got to start somewhere. Check out the Cartoons at a Glance page. Just starting is, in itself, important. I suggest Chapter 1. That roller coaster is climbing to the top now. I hear the click-click of the gears on the track. Are you ready to roll?

Part I
The Nitty-Gritty

The 5th Wave   By Rich Tennant

KYLE AND TODD'S SOFTWARE Co.

"That's right. Daddy will double your salary if you make him more FileMaker Pro templates."

In this part . . .

Suddenly, you're entering another world — a world of databases, where fields aren't the fields you knew as a young child growing up in Iowa. Does it look vaguely familiar? No. Do you know anybody there? No. Is this the land of Oz, or what?

Well, you're in the driver's seat. Buckle up and get ready for a ride. You'll be driving the FileMaker Pro database engine, a high-performance, yet easy-to-drive beast that roars like a mighty lion when you touch the accelerator.

Chapter 1

I've Got It — Now What Do I Do?

*T*his chapter is your ticket to ride. Enter here, please, and get ready to check out the superhighways of the database world. The ride may be bumpy, even a little scary at times, especially if you're a beginner. But I promise, at the very least, to make it fun. Not necessarily a thrill a minute, but fun. You're about to drive a machine with a powerful engine — FileMaker Pro. If you're an intermediate driver, or you need to manage an existing FileMaker Pro database right away, you may want to jump ahead to Part III, especially Chapter 15, which deals with adding, deleting, and editing your records, as well as some other cool things. If you're a beginner, read on and fasten your seat belts.

Driving the FileMaker Pro Engine

Whenever people think of databases, they think of those old metal filing cabinets loaded with manila folders, stuffed to the brim like fat pigs, right? (On my first job at *Popular Computing* magazine, I actually had one of those metal beasts topple over and nearly fall on my head — which is one reason why I avoid them now at all costs.) Now try to imagine all those files and folders that contain your company's most intimate secrets stored electronically on a single floppy disk or a computer hard drive. Neat, huh?

Start your engines, ladies and gentlemen! You don't have to be nerdy or geekish to drive the FileMaker Pro engine, just willing to find out a few things about the instrumentation in the cockpit. I'm your copilot.

To begin with, I'm not going to try to sell you on the glories of FileMaker Pro. That's not my job. Besides, you probably know about them already. The program does have some features, however, that I really like — things that I think you'll find useful as well:

- You can add pictures, sound, and even movies to the records in your database.

- You can work across a network that links both Macs and PCs with FileMaker Pro; the Macintosh and Windows versions of FileMaker Pro are *cross-platform compatible*. That phrase is a fancy way of saying that Macs and PCs running FileMaker Pro can share the same files. That capability is cool if you're in a small business or a mixed-environment office — in other words, where you've got Macs and PCs, sitting on desks side by side, that need to talk to each other.

- You can import and export databases that were created in other file formats. FileMaker Pro lets you bring in that data, translate it, convert it, and add it to your existing databases.

- In FileMaker Pro 3 and 4, you can take advantage of relational capabilities, something you couldn't do in earlier versions of the program. Don't run out of the room screaming now. *Relational capabilities* is nothing but a fancy way of saying that you can match files, or "relate" them, from one database to another so that the same information appears simultaneously in both. Good stuff, indeed.

- In FileMaker Pro 4, you can actually publish your database on the Web, using the tools provided by FileMaker Pro's Web Companion. Now that's definitely a jump forward in the database world, particularly if you've got a catalog of goodies that you're itching to make accessible on your Web site. Stick around, and I explain how you can do it.

After you get the hang of working with FileMaker Pro, you'll appreciate these things. Remember that I told you so.

Don't be put off, incidentally, by the suffix *Pro* in FileMaker Pro. You don't have to be a professional, or a nerdy rocket scientist for that matter, to work happily and easily with this program.

Before you know it, you'll be able to

- Create nifty databases with lots of information, including invoices, mailing labels, reports, contact lists, order forms, and so on.

- Search through all that information and get the particulars of what you need to know.

Overcoming the database fear

Right away, the biggest fear you have to overcome is the notion that you're working with some Frankenstein monster of a database. I'm thinking here of a database that's huge, an electronic behemoth that contains, for example, over 100,000 records — and that you will be lost trying to navigate it. Whenever I talk to people about databases, that's what pops into their heads.

This scenario is highly unlikely. What's more likely is that you'll be working with a few thousand records or fewer. Now, I know that number sounds large, too, but it really isn't. It's quite manageable with FileMaker Pro.

The beauty of 1,000 records is that you can practically run a business with a database of that size. You can build a client list, invoice the clients on that list, produce labels to ship products to those clients or customers, generate reports on what you have sold or shipped, and so on. All this with a minimum of fuss and bother, using FileMaker Pro.

The thing I like about FileMaker Pro is that it lets you work on a human scale. Unless you're a glutton for punishment, you won't be building or working with 100,000 records. So you can eliminate that fear right now, okay?

  ✔ Update the information in your database, analyze it, and print it out when you want to.

Heck, I ran a small business for three years with FileMaker Pro, shipping products, invoicing customers, printing out reports — and I'd never worked with a database program before.

Starting Up FileMaker Pro

Roll up your sleeves now and get cranking on FileMaker Pro. If you've walked into a room containing a computer that has the FileMaker Pro program installed, here are the steps to take to start up FileMaker Pro:

1. **Sit down and relax.**

   Make sure that your monitor, chair, mouse, and workspace are comfortable and to your liking. Make any necessary adjustments.

2. **Turn on your computer and monitor.**

   You may also want to turn on other devices, such as your printer, modem, fax machine, and so on. Just remember that these machines are at your disposal, not the other way around. Repeat after me: *Machines are here to serve me.*

3. Locate that icon.

When the Macintosh or Windows Desktop appears on-screen, look on your hard drive for the FileMaker Pro icon shown in Figure 1-1. In Windows, it's probably in the Claris subfolder of the Program files folder, or you can get to it by clicking Start⇨Programs⇨FileMaker Pro 4⇨ FileMaker Pro. On the Mac, the icon will be in your FileMaker Pro 4 folder on your hard disk, ready and waiting.

Figure 1-1:
The
FileMaker
Pro 4 icon.

FileMaker Pro

4. Just double-click the FileMaker Pro icon to launch the program.

By the way, I'm assuming that you already have at least a minimum understanding of what's required to operate your Mac or Windows computer. For example, *double-click* and *point* and *drag* are mouse actions, the Command key — the one with the Apple logo and the daisy or ⌘ on it if you're driving a Mac — is an all-purpose keyboard shortcut key, just as the Ctrl key is on your Windows PC. If you need to refresh your Macintosh or Windows skills, I suggest David Pogue's *Macs For Dummies,* 5th Edition or Andy Rathbone's *Windows 95 For Dummies,* 2nd Edition, both published by IDG Books Worldwide, Inc.

If you haven't installed FileMaker Pro, consult the Appendix for a helping-hand approach to installing the software.

If FileMaker Pro doesn't start, make a note of any error message that appears and exit the program. Shut down your computer and restart it. Then try to launch FileMaker Pro again. If it still doesn't work, jot down any error messages and consult your computer guru. Your computer may need more resources — more random-access memory (RAM), for example — to run the program successfully.

A successful launch

After you launch FileMaker Pro, you see the Open dialog box, as Figure 1-2 shows.

Figure 1-2:
The Open
dialog box.

Now you can open an existing file or create a new file.

If you click New, a dialog box appears that lets you name the new database and save it where you want. Figure 1-3 shows what the dialog box looks like.

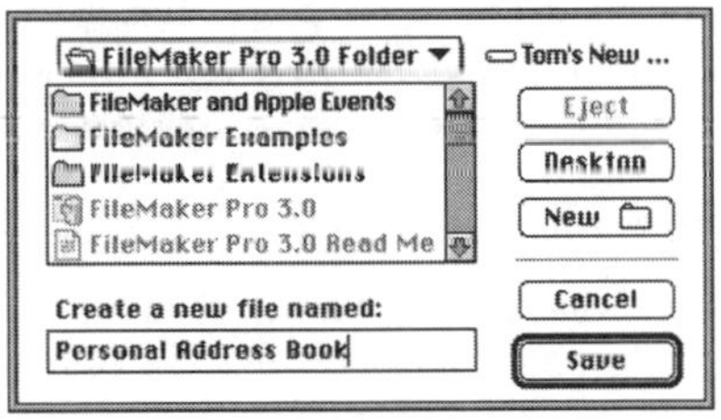

Figure 1-3:
The Create
a New File
dialog box.

If you click your mouse in the Create a New File Named box and type in something like **Personal Address Book**, that's what appears on-screen. Every time you want to create a new file, that's what you do. Piece of cake, so far. Just click the New button, and you're off and running.

A quick look around the scene

After you name your database, your screen looks like Figure 1-4, which shows the Define Fields dialog box. You're in the driver's seat, and this dialog box is one part of your FileMaker Pro dashboard, with some of its instrumentation in place. Pretty cool, don't you think? The FileMaker Pro engine is revved up and ready to go. Table 1-1 gives you a brief explanation of the controls that you work with.

Table 1-1	FileMaker Pro Screen Items
Screen Item	*Description*
File Name	The name of the file that you've entered in the New dialog box — for example, Personal Address Book.
Field Name	The blinking cursor appears here first. Enter the name of the field that you want to define in your database. The name can be up to 60 characters — no longer than that. A good idea is to use a name that represents the kind of data you want to add to your database — for example, Name, Address, or Phone Number, if you're creating a personal address book.
Type (of field)	Radio buttons to click. You have eight types of fields to choose from: Text, Number, Date, Time, Container, Calculation, Summary, and Global.
Create	Click this button after you have entered the name and the type of the field you want. It works like an Enter button so that the information you've entered now appears on-screen in the box above the Field Name.
View By	This item lets you view the fields in your database by creation order, field name, field type, or custom order. When you click one of these items, it sorts the fields that you've defined in your database accordingly.
Done	After you've completed entering the names and types of fields, you simply click the Done button, and the Define Fields dialog box disappears. All the names and fields then appear on each record in your database.

Don't worry just yet about the other icons and buttons and menu items on your first big screen. You see an item, for example, called Layout #1 in the upper-left corner and, just below that, an icon that looks like a mini-Rolodex with a number below it. You can also see a Records item, with an Unsorted item below that. You can't access these items until you've gone through the process of defining the fields that you want in your FileMaker Pro database. You can't access the menu items on your screen just above the menu bar of your file, except for the Edit menu. What this lack of access means is that you can edit the stuff in your Define Fields dialog box, doing the usual cut, copy, and paste, but you can't use the File, Mode, Select, Format, Script, and Window menus, all of which are grayed out (in other words, not accessible). Hang tight; be patient.

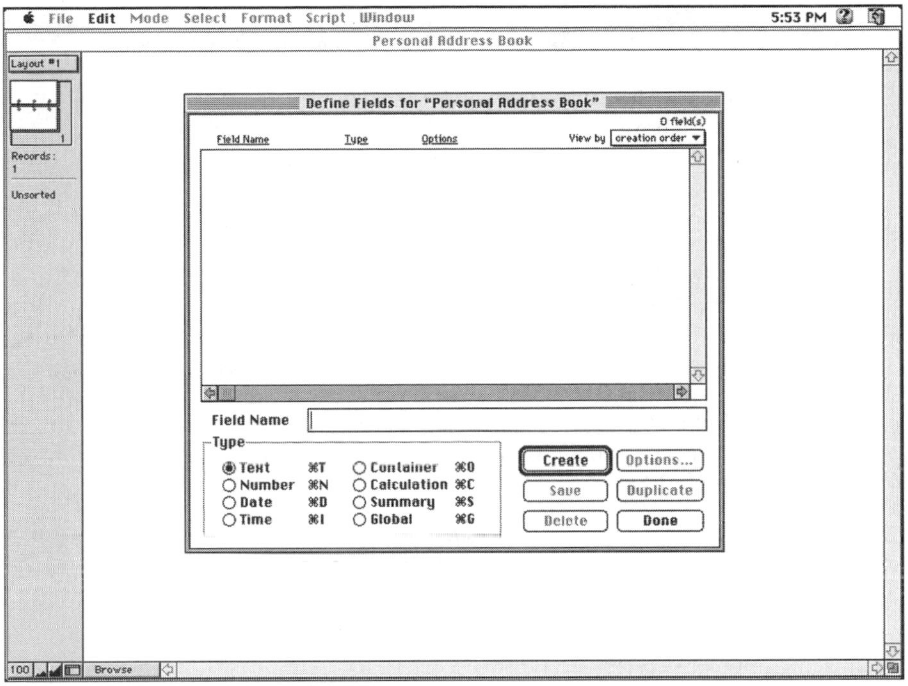

Figure 1-4:
The first big
screen —
the Define
Fields
dialog box.

A few good concepts

A little bit of understanding, just knowing a few good concepts, can go a long way. To figure out how databases work, you need to put on your thinking cap for a moment. Things aren't really *that* complex. In the database world, you need to know three good terms: *file, record,* and *field.* Sound familiar? Well, they're throwback terms to the days when databases consisted of heavy metal filing cabinets, with drawers you pulled open by a little metal handle. Those drawers most often were filled with manila folders containing scraps of paper (usually in odd sizes) held together by paper clips. We've come a long way since then, but unfortunately, the old filing cabinet metaphor still lives in the electronic age. So that's where you've got to start, okay?

Think of your *database* as simply all the information you've put into that manila file folder. Think of a *file* as a collection of your records, or sheets of paper in that folder. And then think of a *record* as a single sheet of information with lots and lots of fields. *Fields* are those neat rectangular storage bins in a database record where you can enter names, addresses, and phone numbers, as well as pictures, movies, and sounds.

Time to Define Those Fields of Data

Before you can really do stuff with FileMaker Pro, you've got to define the fields. That's the essence of FileMaker Pro — defining fields. A good database lives or dies by the fields you've defined.

What you're doing when you *define* fields is, essentially, categorizing the data that you're putting into your FileMaker Pro database. You're saying, for example, "Okay, I have a piece of data called *last name,* and I'm going to define it as a string of text — not a picture, number, or formula, just plain old text — and I'm going to carve out a little field where I can store all the last names in my database. Naturally, to make things easy for myself, I'm going to name that field last name. Every record in my database will have a field called last name, unless I specify otherwise. And each time I enter data into my records, I'm going to enter the last names of the people into that last name field."

Fields are the places where you enter all the data you need for your database. Just think of fields as long, rectangular boxes on-screen — boxes you can stretch and move around — that let you store names, street addresses, phone numbers, pictures, sounds, dates, and all the other neat stuff that makes up your database.

Fields are really cool; they're like elastic storage bins of information. And they're resizable, so you can stretch them out to the sizes you want. More about fields in Chapter 8.

There it is: If you're creating a new database, the Define Fields dialog box should be staring at you on-screen. It's clean and simple, which is part of the beauty of FileMaker Pro. It's also pretty intuitive — that is, it doesn't take a rocket scientist to figure it out. Fields are your way of specifying exactly the field types you want in your little database and, at the same time, specifying the order in which you want the fields to appear. Simple as that. No sweat, yet.

Take a closer look at the Define Fields dialog box in Figure 1-5.

That's a typical-looking Define Fields dialog box. Follow these simple steps to create something similar:

1. **Type the name of your first field in the Field Name box.**

   You can make that name up to 60 characters, but try not to use a long name, if possible. Shorter, more precise names are always better.

Define Fields for "Personal Address Book"

8 field(s)

Field Name	Type	Options	View by	creation order ▼
⬦ Last Name	Text			
⬦ First Name	Text			
⬦ Street	Text			
⬦ City	Text			
⬦ State	Text			
⬦ Zip Code	Text			
⬦ Phone Number	Text			
⬦ Photo	Container			

Field Name [   ]

Type

- ⦿ Text ⌘T
- ○ Number ⌘N
- ○ Date ⌘D
- ○ Time ⌘I
- ○ Container ⌘0
- ○ Calculation ⌘C
- ○ Summary ⌘S
- ○ Global ⌘G

[Create] [Options...]
[Save] [Duplicate]
[Delete] [Done]

Figure 1-5:
That Define
Fields
dialog box,
up close
and
personal.

2. **Click the appropriate radio button for the type of field you want.**

   At this point, if you're looking at the Define Fields dialog box and wondering what the heck all those other radio buttons are for, well, not to worry. You may be wondering when, for example, the Summary button or the Calculation button is more appropriate to click than the Number button. Chapter 8 explains all those buttons. For the moment, just stick with the steps here to get the ball rolling so you can define those text fields. Believe me: You define a lot of fields as text fields in any FileMaker Pro database you build or work on.

3. **Now click Create and move on to your next text fields, which contain specific textual information.**

   You define each new field just as you did your first field. Some frequently used database fields include last name, first name, street, city, state, zip code, phone number, and perhaps even a graphic illustration. Note that you define zip codes and phone numbers also, even though they're numeric, as Text fields.

4. **Click Done or press Esc.**

   You're rolling. You've got fields defined in your records. Neat.

FileMaker Pro is the most intuitive database program ever designed. But sometimes, it may do things that surprise you. For example, if you create a little personal address book, you would think that the zip codes and phone numbers you want in that database would be defined as Number fields. Right? Wrong. FileMaker Pro wants you to define them as Text fields, and for good reason. If they're defined as Number fields, you can use them to do calculations. That doesn't make much sense for a zip code, does it? Or, I guess, a phone number. . . .

Getting Ready to Go Forth and Populate

Suppose that you created a new file named Personal Address Book and went about defining the following fields: last name, first name, street, city, state, zip code, phone number, and photo. You find a file with all those neatly defined fields, as in Figure 1-6.

Now you're ready to populate those fields with data. In database language, the data you enter into those fields is known as a *value*. Values contain the information in those fields you've defined.

The beauty of your database, of course, is that values can be a variety of things, from names and dates to formulas and calculations. Imagine that old filing cabinet with a scientific calculator stuck in every manila folder. Things can really get awesome when you start tapping into the true power of FileMaker Pro.

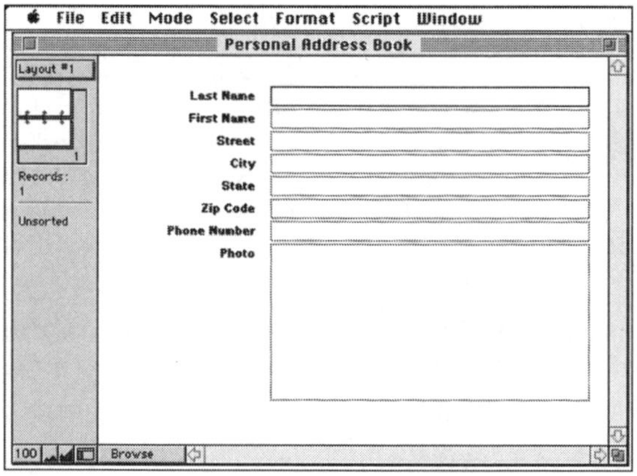

Figure 1-6:
A database
record,
ready to be
populated
with
information.

You've defined the fields, and now you're ready to rock 'n' roll. Here's how:

1. Choose Mode⇨Browse.

A check appears to the left of the Browse menu item. That check simply means that you're in Browse mode, and while you're there, you can view your records. You can do more than browse, however; you can also enter the data you want in your database and edit the data that already exists in your database as records. The key word here is *enter*. That's what you want to do to get the ball rolling.

FileMaker Pro is good about letting you know exactly what mode you're in while you're looking at your screen. Right there, at the bottom left of your screen, you find the button marked Browse (assuming, of course, that you activated the Browse mode in the preceding step). It's actually a pop-up menu, or mode selector, which, when you click it, gives you a choice of FileMaker Pro's four standard modes: Browse, Find, Layout, and Preview. Each mode provides you with a different way of working with your data, as well as a different view of it. Though I'm not a big fan of the word *mode* because it's fraught with ambiguity, we're stuck with it here in the world of FileMaker Pro. In any case, you may want to think of these modes as four cool views of your data, plus, along with each view, the tools you need to manipulate that data. Enough said.

2. **Click the area to the right of the field names.**

   A set of empty boxes appears. Enter the values — that is, the names, streets, and zip codes — you want for each person in your database. Go to it and begin populating those entry boxes!

3. **When you come to the Photo field, choose File↵Import/Export↵ Import Picture.**

   From there, you can import a picture or illustration in a variety of file formats (EPSF, GIF, MacPaint, PICT, and TIFF) into your record, as shown in Figure 1-7.

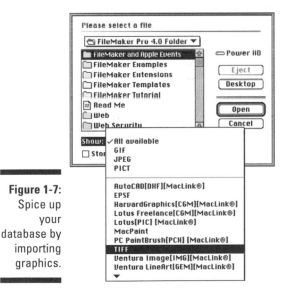

Figure 1-7:
Spice up
your
database by
importing
graphics.

Amazingly enough, your FileMaker Pro database can include data other than just plain text, numbers, and mathematical formulas. Imagine having pictures of your family or members of your school class or the people in your office right there, along with names and addresses, in your database. Little snapshots that you've scanned in and then imported. Cool, no? It gets even better when you think of adding a QuickTime movie to your database. That's like having a mini-movie attached to your records. For more details about importing movies and pictures, check out Chapter 19.

One way of getting photos for your database is to use a digital camera, like an Apple Quicktake. Because the pictures are in a digital format, you don't have to develop or scan them. Just take the picture and drop it in.

Magic! Your database record appears happily populated at the center of the screen, as Figure 1-8 shows, and you're ready to add a new record.

Figure 1-8:
A database
record,
complete
with values
entered in
fields, and
even a
photo.

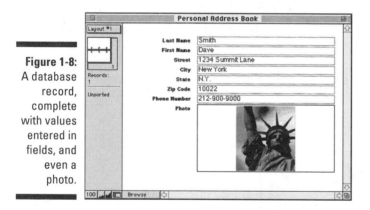

Adding Another Record and Plugging In More Values

Now what do I do? That should be the title of this section. In the database world, after you figure out what to do first, the next steps are often a matter of just repeating the same thing a second, and a third, and a fourth time . . . until you've got what you want.

Creating one record in, for example, a personal address book is pretty straightforward after you get the hang of things and feel comfortable defining fields. Creating another record is, not surprisingly, just more of the same. Here are the steps to take:

1. **Choose Mode⇨New Record or use the keyboard shortcut ⌘+N on the Mac or Ctrl+N in Windows.**

Using a keyboard shortcut, such as ⌘+N or Ctrl+N, to create a new record is a good habit to get into. It's easy to remember and saves you the time of going to the Mode menu, pulling it down, and selecting New Record. A couple of keyboard shortcuts can take you a long way indeed, particularly if, as a reflex, you know what you're doing automatically. Incidentally, that same ⌘+N or Ctrl+N shortcut, when you're in Layout mode, gives you — presto! — a new layout.

2. **Enter the data you want into the boxes next to the fields you've defined.**

Just press Enter (not Return on the Mac) when you've completed the entries. Figure 1-9 shows what the screen looks like after you've entered another record.

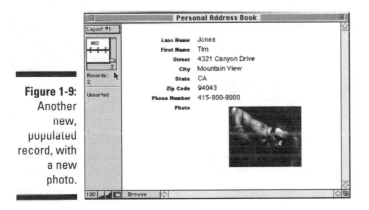

Figure 1-9: Another new, populated record, with a new photo.

Layout Design Time

After you enter data in your file and build up a collection of records, you're ready for the next big step — layouts. Don't panic. You don't have to be a computer artist here. Laying out is actually fun stuff. You get to apply your designing skills (elementary or nonexistent) to your database.

You want to lay out the data in your personal address book so that it looks good and is easy to read and review. That's the important thing. Image is not everything in the world of databases, but a little design flair goes a long way.

Each time you define the fields you want in your new file, FileMaker Pro automatically offers you its standard layout. That's what you use for your data entry and what you find up there on the left corner of your screen as Layout #1. But — and here's the best part — you can also change that standard layout, or create an entirely new layout.

Here's how: Choose Mode⇨Layout, or click the mode selector at the bottom left of your screen and click Layout. Figure 1-10 shows you what the Layout screen looks like.

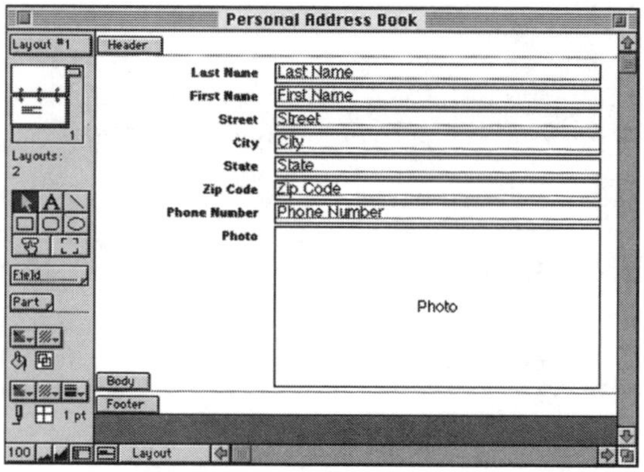

Figure 1-10:
Layout #1:
the
standard
layout with
lots of tools
(those
buttons on
the left side
of your
screen).

In the standard layout, you've got three parts in the main body of the screen: header, body, and footer. And you have a ruler running vertically and horizontally on-screen, along with a set of graphic tools to the left. You also have fields and their names.

The header determines the information that appears on the top of every page. The body is, obviously, the information that appears between the header and the footer. And the Footer is what appears on the bottom of each page. Check out Chapter 12 for more specific information on all the things you can do with headers, footers, and body parts in your layouts.

Things look cool so far. No problem. But what if you want to try another design for your personal address book? What if you want columns for the first and last names in your book and a separate column for zip codes? Here's how you can do that:

1. Choose Mode⇨New Layout or press ⌘+N or Ctrl+N.

   A dialog box like the one in Figure 1-11 appears.

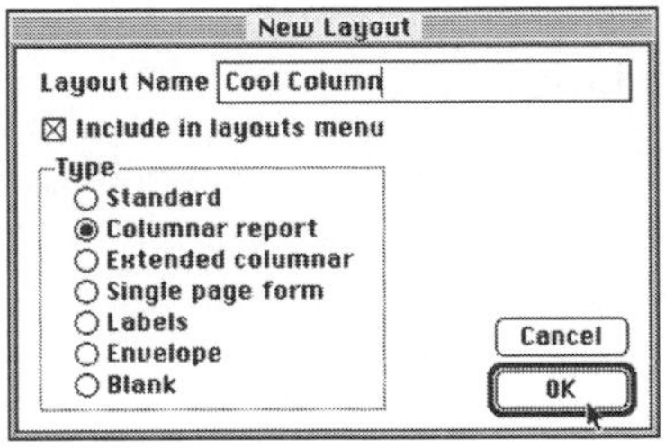

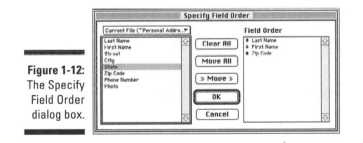

Figure 1-11:
The New
Layout
dialog box.

2. **Type a unique name, such as** Cool Column, **in the Layout Name box.**

   You give each layout a unique name to help you remember the differences between different layouts in your database.

3. **Click the format that you want to use and then click OK.**

   In this example, I clicked Columnar Report.

What's a *columnar report,* anyway, you may well ask? Simple. It's a layout that sets up the fields in a row from left to right and puts the field names in the header, right above each column. That way, when you browse through your records in a columnar report, you can see them in a continuous list — that is, more than one record at a time.

After you click OK to select your new layout, the Specify Field Order dialog box comes up, as in Figure 1-12.

Figure 1-12:
The Specify
Field Order
dialog box.

In the Specify Field Order dialog box, you can do just what the name of the dialog box suggests: place your fields in the order in which you want them to appear. Here's what you do:

1. **Click the field you want to appear first in your columnar report — for example, the Last Name field in the Personal Address Book — and click Move.**

   Now that Last Name field moves into the Field Order list.

2. **Now click the next field you want to appear — in this example, the First Name field — and click Move.**

   This field takes its correct place in the Field Order lineup.

3. **Now, to follow through with the example of the Personal Address Book, click the Zip Code field and click Move.**

4. **Click OK.**

There you are! You've got a new columnar report layout. Check out the status area on the screen — that is, that button just above the Book icon, which, when you click it, gives you a pop-up menu telling you that you're in either the layout named Cool Column as shown in the example in Figure 1-11, or Layout #1. You see, if you click that status area menu, that you now have two layouts in your file. FileMaker Pro also tells you how many layouts you have directly below the mini-Rolodex (Book icon), as Figure 1-13 shows.

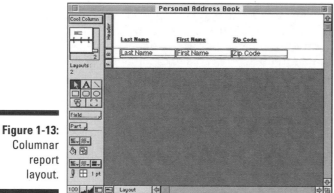

Figure 1-13:
Columnar
report
layout.

Getting Fancy with Your Layouts

If you want to, you can adjust the size of the fields in your layouts, stretching and positioning them where appropriate on the page. For example, depending on the data in your personal address book, you may want to keep the fields narrow and more compact so you can browse through your database more easily. FileMaker Pro provides you with a neat set of tools to manipulate field sizes in your layouts, letting you pick up and move around the fields to create the look and feel of the database you want. You can do all kinds of formatting, too, on particular fields. Chapter 13 explains these tools and more.

One of the most powerful features of FileMaker Pro is sitting right there among the layout tools, just below the Rectangle tool. It's the Specify Button tool, shown in Figure 1-14.

Figure 1-14:
The coolest
button ever
invented
for your
FileMaker
Pro layouts.

—The Specify Button tool

This button certainly makes life easier for anybody who's designing a new layout. The tool seems so obvious that you wonder why nobody ever thought about it before. Well, actually somebody did, but you had to go to the Scripts menu to find it, and then you weren't always sure how to use it.

Once you start using this Specify Button tool, you can't stop. It's that much fun because you get to drop a button on a record in your FileMaker Pro database and define what you want the button to do when somebody clicks it. Each button you specify performs a script for you with a great deal of choices, as you can see from the list in Figure 1-15. Check out Chapter 22 for details on choosing scripts that get your buttons to perform tasks for you.

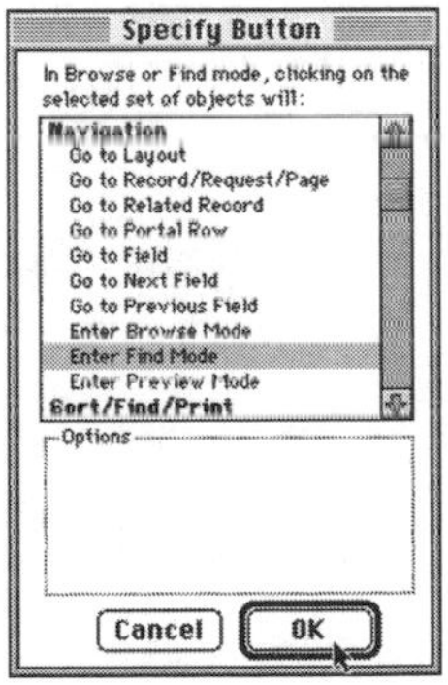

Figure 1-15:
Some
things you
can get a
button to do
for you.

Specify Button

In Browse or Find mode, clicking on the selected set of objects will:

Navigation
Go to Layout
Go to Record/Request/Page
Go to Related Record
Go to Portal Row
Go to Field
Go to Next Field
Go to Previous Field
Enter Browse Mode
Enter Find Mode
Enter Preview Mode
Sort/Find/Print

Options

Cancel   OK

Buttons are one of the coolest things in FileMaker Pro. I promise you that once you start, you'll go button crazy like every other FileMaker Pro user. You can drop a button on your layout anywhere and, basically, attach a little script to it telling it to perform some pretty complicated (as well as pretty simple) tasks. Nothing like washing the dishes or taking out the garbage, but you can get a button to open up specific records for you, sort the records, dial a phone number, move you from Browse mode to Find mode with just a mouse click, do a complex calculation, and so on. Buttons are there to help you simplify the navigational maneuvers that you or anybody else using your FileMaker Pro database has to go through just to find your way around a large collection of files and records.

Ready to Browse

Browsing your database can be almost as much fun as creating it. If you've created a personal address book, for example, you'll want to browse through it and use it as a handy information source, which you can modify and update on a regular and timely basis. Figure 1-16 shows a personal address book with a columnar layout waiting for you to start browsing. Neat, huh?

To browse the records in your database, just point and click as follows:

1. **Choose Mode⇨Browse, or click the mode selector and click Browse.**

2. **If you want to get another view, such as the view in the example of the Cool Column, just click the status area button above the mini-Rolodex (Book icon). You can also switch to Layout #1 in that pop-up menu or toggle between the views.**

Figure 1-16:
Cool
Column
view. You
got it!

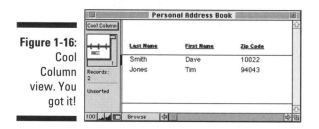

3. **Now click the upper page of the Book icon to view the first record in your database.**

You can move through the records in your database by clicking the Book icon.

When you're hot, you're hot. The ride was kind of fun, wasn't it?

Printing This Puppy

Obviously, having a neatly printed copy of the records in your database is a good idea. You've got some choices now as far as printing is concerned. When you choose File⇨Print, the dialog box in Figure 1-17 appears — if you have an Apple LaserWriter printer.

```
┌────────────────────────────────────────────────────┐
│ Personal LaserWriter LS                7.2  [ Print ]│
│                                             ┌───────┐│
│ Copies: [1]   Pages: ● All ○ From: [  ] To: [  ]     │
│                                             [Cancel] │
│                                             [ Help ] │
│ Paper Source: ● Multipurpose Tray  ○ Paper Cassette  │
│ Number pages from: [1]                               │
│ Print: ● Records being browsed                       │
│        ○ Current record                              │
│        ○ Blank record, showing fields [as formatted] │
│        ○ Script: [ All scripts      ]                │
│        ○ Field definitions                           │
└────────────────────────────────────────────────────┘
```

Figure 1-17:
The Print
dialog box.

You just enter the number of copies you want to print and the range of pages — that is, if you want to print all pages or just from one particular page to another particular page. Paper source is usually Multipurpose Tray. And you can specify from what numeral you want to start the page numbering. The first page can actually be numbered 5, if you like.

FileMaker Pro gives you some other options, too. If you want to print a report, you can click Records Being Browsed. If you want to print the record currently selected in Browse, you can click Current Record. You can also print a blank record, a field definition, or a script that you've created.

In any case, after you've decided what you want to print, the number of copies, pages, and so on, just click the Print button. And wait to see the printed version of your efforts.

Printing the stuff in your database is a good habit to get into. You'll have hard-copy backups of your data, in case you need them or have a problem with the electronic version. And with pen or pencil, you can mark up those hard copies, like a good editor does with blue pen or an architect with pencil, T-square, and ruler, if you see things in your layout or database design that you want to change.

Quitting FileMaker Pro

Call it a day. After you've put in a hard day's work, you want to quit FileMaker Pro before turning off your computer.

Don't worry about saving your work — it's already been saved for you. FileMaker Pro has been doing that automatically behind the scenes the whole time you've been busy at the keyboard or pointing and clicking with your mouse. In fact, the File menu doesn't even have a Save option. Is that truly amazing, or what?

Of course, not all software programs behave quite this way, saving for you as you go along. But because your records and the data stored in them are so valuable, and because a system crash or power failure could wipe out new work in an instant, the wizards at Claris decided to make saving a no-brainer. Frankly, it may take a little getting used to, but I think it's cool.

If you don't like FileMaker Pro's automatic saving feature, you can always change it by choosing Edit⇨Preferences⇨Application. From the dialog box, click the Memory tab. Now you have two choices: saving during idle times (which is the default option), or saving during specified intervals. Take your pick!

To quit FileMaker Pro, just choose File⇨Quit on the Mac or File⇨Exit in Windows. That's all. Your work for the day has been happily saved wherever you've decided to put it in your Macintosh or Windows folders. Tomorrow, it'll be ready and waiting for you to open again.

Chapter 2

Designing Your Database with (Or without) Your Computer

● ●

In This Chapter

▶ Designing a database is like putting your life in order

▶ Going where other FileMaker Pro users have gone before

▶ If you're stuck. . . .

▶ Calling all rebels, calling all artists. . . .

● ●

So you think you're ready to design your database, but you're not sure how to set it up — well, this chapter is for you. But tell you what: I'm going to commit a heresy. As much as I love working on computers, I'm now asking you to turn yours off. That's right. Quit FileMaker Pro and shut down your computer. Why? Read on to find out.

Thinking Creatively 101

Setting up a database is like putting your life in order — whether it's your personal or business life — so that you can function most efficiently. Sometimes, that's easier said than done. The main thing is that you've got to make good choices — creative choices.

To get the most out of FileMaker Pro — before you start defining all those fields and before you start entering data in them — I want you to start stretching your creative muscles a bit. I've got some warm-up exercises that ought to go a long way toward helping you do that. So here goes.

Step 1: Dreaming of the ideal workspace

After you've turned off your computer, find a quiet place where you can think freely and concentrate.

Find a pen or pencil and go to your sketch pad or yellow legal pad on which you can draw. (I can hear the voices of protest already: "What? Me, draw?" Listen, we all started out drawing in school before we ever wrote a single sentence or added a number in a column. Everybody can draw — at least a little.)

Now give yourself license to picture in your mind's eye an image of the ideal workspace. This workspace is the place at your office, home, or school where you've got everything — every piece of information, every item you need to get the job done — right there at your fingertips. What does that ideal workspace look like? I bet you have a pretty good idea. Sketch it out on paper now. Draw it as best you can. Then put it away (you come back to it later).

Step 2: Collecting raw data

Now go back into your (real) workspace and look around you. What have you got on your desk besides your Mac or Windows computer? If your desk is anything like mine, it's far from perfect. Undoubtedly, you have lots of little pieces of paper scattered about, including

- Business cards
- Letters
- Bills
- Manila folders
- Pink notepads for phone messages
- A couple of odd-sized calendars
- Stick-on notes
- Envelopes, mailers, stamps
- A whole lot more paper items

And these bits and pieces contain all the information — or data — you need to successfully make your way through your typical day. This data may include phone numbers, addresses, dates, and so on.

Nothing is inherently wrong with all these bits of paper, even if they're messy and scattered about your workspace. They are the raw data of your business, home, or school, maybe even your life. Don't think about what might happen if any of this raw data gets lost or misplaced.

TIP

What do I put in my database?

In the course of working with FileMaker Pro, many people have designed a whole range of databases for business and home use. The ones I like best are the ones that start at home. Just creating a FileMaker Pro database that keeps an inventory of valuable household items can be both fun and useful. Or make a database that stores and manages the information in your favorite collection of compact discs or home videos — how about that?

No set rules govern what you can or cannot store in your database. The only rule I can think of — and it isn't really a rule — is that the information you collect should be important to you. You want to preserve that information, navigate through it easily to find and retrieve what you want, and add new pieces of information so that you can grow your database.

The funny thing about raw data that I've noticed over the years is the way it stares at you, or rather, you stare at it — without moving. And also how all that raw data just accumulates. We go blithely from order to informational disorder according to the laws of entropy, I guess. Well, that's life in the Information Age.

But for the moment, just leave all those bits and pieces of raw data scattered about. The more disorganized the better, okay? My motto is "Think globally, act locally — on your desktop."

Step 3: Prioritizing your time

Now shift gears for a moment and turn to the subject of time. I'm not thinking of Time in the philosophical sense, or Time as the fourth dimension in Einstein's view of the universe. I'm just thinking of plain old, ordinary, everyday time. Tick, tock. Tick, tock.

I want you to take a leap of faith and become your own time cop, as it were. No, this isn't a science-fiction movie with Jean-Claude van Damme. If you can take a moment, make a short list of your A, B, C, and D priorities in time. A is the thing you must do, the thing you need to spend the most time doing. B is less important. C is lower down in priority, and D lower still. For example, scouting for new customers may be an A priority for your business, while doing the actual work may be a B priority, and billing your customers may be a C priority.

Bear with me on this concept. I'm going somewhere with it.

Step 4: Linking your data and priorities

Now, after you've had a chance to stare at your own raw data and make a list of your A, B, C, and D time priorities, you're ready for the next big step. And it's pretty straightforward, when you think about it. You're going to merge the last two steps: collecting your raw data and prioritizing your time. Literally, I mean that you mark each item of data with an A, B, C, or D priority stamp.

After you do this step — which is really a kind of mapping between the two steps, between data items and priority items — you have a better idea of what your FileMaker Pro database should include. You can think of these data items — the names, addresses, and phone numbers on business cards, for example — as fields. Once you start thinking of fields as being slots for data as well as time stamps, you're on your way to designing a database that will work for you.

If you look closely enough, almost every piece of raw data — from invoices to shipping labels — has some element of time associated with it. You just have to keep your eyes open for it. Even a simple business card that's passed on to you may have an element of time and priority attached to it. For example, if you're like me, you sometimes scribble a note on the back of the card saying that you should call this person by such-and-such date. So that card becomes a priority for you. In your database, fields ought to encompass the priorities you have assigned to your data.

If you think about it, what FileMaker Pro is doing for you, albeit at lightning speed, is managing your data according to the rules of time and priority that you've specified.

Step 5: Finding the visual metaphor

In Step 1, you put aside those early sketches you made of the ideal workspace. Now's the time to retrieve them. You need them for the next step.

But be realistic: You may not be able to realize your dream of the ideal workspace just yet — or even afford it — but you can achieve the next best thing with FileMaker Pro.

A database can pretty much look like anything you want it to look like. No rules exist, per se. Your FileMaker Pro database can be plain vanilla, or espresso and cream with a cherry on top.

The key is to find a visual image or metaphor that you're comfortable with — in other words, one that doesn't bore you to death. If you make a drawing of a dull gray metal filing cabinet with drawers containing dozens of manila folders, you may have something (as a visual metaphor) that's perfectly functional but boring as all heck.

Remember that you're combining data and time into a visual representation. You want it to be exciting. Why can't your FileMaker Pro files live in an exciting world? A visually exciting world is one that you look forward to entering, browsing, and exploring every day. So the metaphor needs to be "livable" — and, of course, exciting. Enough said.

Well, not quite enough said on the topic of finding the right metaphor. I want to share another perspective with you. Think of building a house as a metaphor. You could have a mental picture of what it is and start cutting and nailing, but chances are that it won't look too great when you're done. (That depends on how skillful you are with hammer and nails, I would add.) You need a plan or blueprint to iron out the details prior to construction. The same thinking applies to building a database. You need to analyze the requirements, the information or data that you need to collect, and the way that information needs to be reported, and then build the database from those specifications. Then you can make it pretty and add buttons and all that graphic stuff.

Here are seven important sets of questions to ask yourself when thinking about the design of your database:

- ✔ What's the picture you have of the world in which your data lives? Is it a dull gray metal filing cabinet? Probably not. If not, how would you like to see your collected data stored? Do you have in mind a container or set of containers?

- ✔ What are the most important things — the things of highest priority — that happen in this world of data? And when do they happen? For example, do you receive lots of phone calls? And do you need to keep track of them?

- ✔ How would you navigate through this world? What buttons, arrows, or pointers would you use? In other words, how would you find your way around this database world?

- ✔ How do the pieces of data in this world connect to other pieces of data? Is the information related in some way? What are the relationships you want to establish?

- ✔ Who is going to use the data in your world? Will the data be made available to other people besides yourself? What do you think will be some of their concerns in working with your database?

> ✓ How are you going to build on or add to the information in this world? How do you see your database expanding and growing?
>
> ✓ Who is going to maintain the database? In other words, who's responsible for its care and feeding?

Keep asking yourself these questions, even if you can't come up with answers right away. Then let your sketch pad do the talking, and start recording the visual images of your database world that pop into your head. Before you know it, you've come up with a killer design. You know it when you see it.

Part II of this book provides you with the tools and techniques for actually creating your database step-by-step. But before you get familiar with the tools in Part II, you need to spend the time coming up with answers to the preceding questions. Believe me: It's time well spent.

If You're Stuck. . . .

If you're stuck, sleep on it. You may not get the idea or visual metaphor for your FileMaker Pro database right away. Keep thinking about that ideal workspace and what it should look like. Talk to friends and see what they suggest. And pretty soon, as if by magic, things will start cooking for you.

Chapter 3

Customizing Your FileMaker Pro Database

In This Chapter

▶ Making FileMaker Pro work for you

▶ Setting preferences is a good thing

▶ Checking your Mac's memory

This chapter, as you can probably guess from the title, is all about customizing your FileMaker Pro database. You may well ask, "Now why on Earth would I want to do that?" For one thing, your database will behave, when you open and close it, more or less the way you want it to. Customizing your database doesn't mean that you'll get it to serve you tea and crumpets at four o'clock in the afternoon, but it does mean that you can set certain preferences in FileMaker Pro, giving you more control of your program's behavior and how it displays things for you and makes connections, for example, to a computer network.

Database customization is something that users typically do as an afterthought. You build a database, add fields and records to it, modify the layout, print it, and then get around to setting the preferences. Some people never do that — and then wonder why the database they built doesn't quite perform up to their expectations.

My recommendation is to do your customizing before you get too bogged down in building your FileMaker Pro database. It's simple, straightforward stuff. All you really have to do is go into the Preferences menu and walk through a series of dialog boxes, adjusting and modifying the settings for your application as well as for your files. It's definitely worth the effort — sooner rather than later.

Customizing as behavior modification, or making FileMaker Pro do exactly what you want

Customizing is the process by which you set the default behavior of each of your FileMaker Pro databases. For example, if you want FileMaker Pro to save your work automatically as you go along, you can do that by clicking the appropriate radio button in the Memory Preferences dialog box. If you want to use smart quotes (a feature that changes straight quote marks to curly ones) in any text you enter in your fields, you can establish that as the default behavior of your database. FileMaker Pro will obey your wish. If you want your database to open with a password, you can specify that action in a preference dialog box. What you're really doing by customizing your database is choosing among a range of preferences that determine how things should or should not behave in your database.

FileMaker Pro provides you with a range of preferences to select for your database, including preferences on the Layout, Memory, Modem, Dialing, and Plug-ins. In addition, you can specify document preferences that determine what happens, for example, when a user opens and closes your database, or you can use another preference to enable FileMaker Pro's spell checking when you enter text into a Text field. If you're planning to publish your database on the Web (see Chapters 20 and 21 for details), you also have the option with FileMaker Pro 4 of setting your preferences for FileMaker Pro's Web Companion, where you can specify how you want folks to view, search, and sort the information in your database on the Web. If you don't choose the preferences you want, FileMaker Pro reverts to its default settings for each of those preferences — in other words, the settings that were already there when you first launched the program.

Now, the important thing to keep in mind is that you can set different preferences for each database you build. Just because you set the preferences for one database a particular way — for example, saying how you want it to open or whether you need a password — doesn't mean that all your databases must behave the same way. In fact, you may want to change or modify the behavior — the settings in FileMaker Pro's preferences — for each database according to how you use it or who has access to it.

The Power to Customize

If you've already created a FileMaker Pro database, something like the personal address book in Chapter 1, you're well on your way to the next step, which is customization. It isn't some fancy procedure, just a matter of deciding on your preferences. And the best way to do that is to check out the dialog boxes that come up when you choose the Edit⇨Preferences menu item (see Figure 3-1) and then, from submenus, click Application, or Document, or Web Companion. If you click Application or Document, a General Preferences dialog box opens.

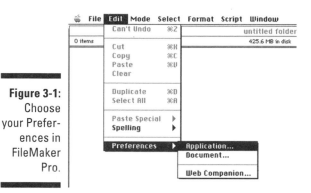

Figure 3-1:
Choose
your Prefer-
ences in
FileMaker
Pro.

Some important things to remember about setting preferences in FileMaker Pro are:

✔ Your document preferences — that is, the ones you set in the General Document Preferences dialog box (see "Setting general document preferences" later in this chapter) — apply only to the file you're currently working on at that specific time.

✔ Other preferences you set apply to any file that you open.

✔ Your preferences don't change until you go into each Preferences dialog box and change them again. In other words, what you have stays until you change it.

Setting Those Many Preferences

When you choose Edit⇨Preferences⇨Application, you see the General Application Preferences dialog box shown in Figure 3-2. But don't think that this dialog box contains your only preferences in FileMaker Pro. If you pull down the General menu in the upper-left corner of the dialog box, you find other preferences, too: Layout, Memory, Modem, Dialing, and Plug-ins. You don't have to set all these preferences right away. But check out what's there and what happens with each setting so that when you come back to the settings later, you'll be ready to make the choices you want to enhance the power of your FileMaker Pro database.

Setting general application preferences

In the General Application Preferences dialog box, you find a set of choices. Walking through them one by one to see what's available to you is a good idea. Put on your thinking cap. Now's the time to start choosing.

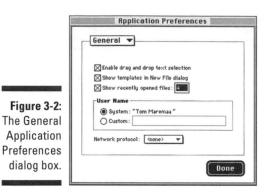

Figure 3-2:
The General
Application
Preferences
dialog box.

If you click the box that says Enable Drag and Drop Text Selection, you can use drag and drop to move text without having to use the Macintosh or Windows Clipboard. It's a handy option — not essential but handy. If you are running Mac OS 7.5 and are in Layout mode, you can drag and drop the selection onto your Macintosh Desktop. The selection appears as an icon labeled Picture Clipping. You can then drop that picture clipping into another place in your FileMaker Pro layout.

Notice on the Mac the box that says Show Templates in New Dialog; you may find that option a bit confusing. What are they talking about? Is it English? A good example of such a dialog box appears in Figure 3-3. What happens here is that FileMaker Pro shows you a list of template files when you launch the program or when you choose File⇨New. Templates can be the lifeblood of anybody working with FileMaker Pro (check out Chapter 4, if you don't believe me). This option is useful if you're working with a number of templates and want quick access to them. But for now, if you have only one or two databases that you're working with, you probably don't need to click this box.

Under User Name, you have two radio buttons to choose from: System and Custom. If you click System, FileMaker Pro uses the system's user name (that is, whoever is using your Macintosh or Windows computer), which it finds from your Macintosh's Chooser or in the Sharing Setup control panel. Clicking Custom lets you enter your own name or the name of the person who is currently using the file. I like using the Custom preference rather than letting FileMaker Pro default to the System name. You get to keep track of who's doing what.

On the Network Protocol pop-up menu, you can choose a network connection, or leave it as <none> if you're not on a network. The protocols on a Mac that you can choose from are AppleTalk, MacIPX, and TCP/IP. If you're on a network, check with your System Administrator or the person in charge of managing your network before you click any of the boxes. If you're a single user of FileMaker Pro, these protocols aren't relevant. Just leave the box displaying <none>.

If you do make any changes to your network connections, the changes don't take effect until you quit FileMakerPro and then start it up again.

Figure 3-3:
The Show
Templates
in New
dialog box.

Setting general document preferences
==================================

To open the General Document Preferences dialog box, simply choose Edit⇨Preferences⇨Document. In the dialog box, you have a set of check boxes that let you specify a whole range of behaviors for your FileMaker Pro database.

Two more things to remember about document preferences are that they affect only the database file you're currently working on and that you can set different document preferences for each file you create.

Figure 3-4 shows you the Document Preferences dialog box.

If you're working with a shared file — that is, one that's shared on a network with other people — the shared file has the same document preferences for everybody who works on it. You can change the document preferences, but only if you have the master password or if the file isn't password protected. For more about password protection and working on a network, see Chapter 18.

For starters, you see the choice of whether to use *smart quotes* — curly apostrophes ('') and quotation marks (" ") that can make your document look very professional and businesslike. Most fonts support smart quotes, but if you happen to use a font that doesn't, FileMakerPro substitutes plain marks (' ") for the smart quotes. If you deselect this choice, FileMakerPro uses plain marks.

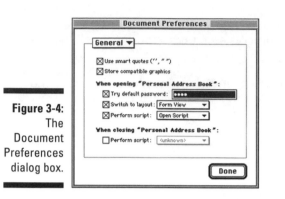

Figure 3-4:
The
Document
Preferences
dialog box.

Under When Opening <database file>, you have three choices to think about:

- **Try Default Password:** When you choose this option and enter a password of your choice, FileMaker Pro automatically enters that password when you open the file. If the password isn't valid, FileMaker Pro tells you to type another password. If you want to bypass the default password and enter a different one, all you have to do is press the Option key while you're opening the file.

  Passwords aren't essential to working with your files, unless you want to restrict access to them. It's a handy option to exercise, however, if you don't want other folks to open your files.

- **Switch to Layout:** If you choose this option and then choose a layout from the pop-up menu — presto! — you get the layout you've specified when you open the file. This option is very useful and saves you time, particularly if you know that you have to modify the layout of a particular file, or if you have a main menu layout as the front-end, or startup, screen for your file. With this option selected, you go right to the layout you want.

  If you don't choose this option, FileMaker Pro opens the last layout displayed when you closed the file, or it opens a layout you designated in a startup script (see the Perform script option coming up next).

- **Perform Script:** This option is a more advanced feature of FileMaker Pro. Scripting is the ultimate form of customizing your database. By writing a certain script, you can make FileMaker Pro perform all kinds of neat tricks. For example, when opening or closing a file, you can define a startup script that tells FileMaker Pro to hide the status area, to set a certain window size, or to find all records and sort them alphabetically. Chapter 22 explains these possibilities and more.

Setting layout application preferences

To open the Layout Application Preferences dialog box, simply choose Edit⇨Preferences⇨Application. Click Layout from the General drop-down menu, and a dialog box pops open.

Figure 3-5 shows you the Layout Application Preferences dialog box.

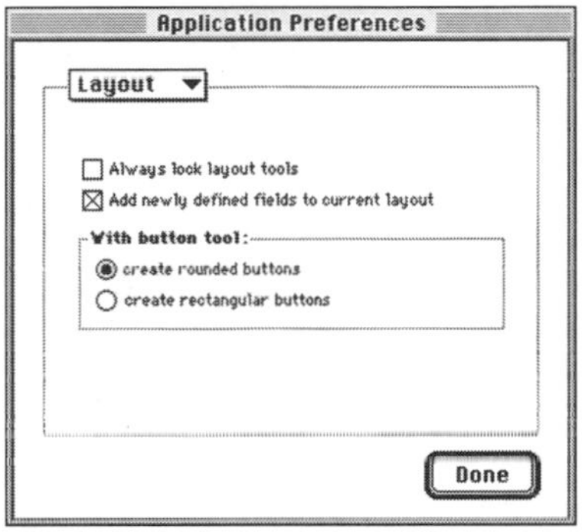

Figure 3-5:
The Layout
Application
Preferences
dialog box.

You work with layouts a lot in FileMaker Pro, and, in Layout Application Preferences dialog box, you can make some important, though not irrevocable, choices:

- **Always Lock Layout Tools:** If you check this box, you can keep a layout tool selected — that is, ready to use — until you choose a different tool or press Enter. If you don't select this option, FileMaker Pro resets the cursor as the Pointer tool after you use a tool, whether you're finished with the tool or not, but not if you double-click the tool. Actually, this setting is the same as double-clicking a tool.

- **Add Newly Defined Field to the Current Layout:** If you check this box, you're saying that FileMaker Pro can add a new field to the layout that's currently displayed on-screen. For example, if you define a new field as Text, that field appears on the layout as a dotted rectangle into which you can enter text. You're telling FileMaker Pro to repeat this procedure each time you define a particular field. FileMaker Pro adds new fields to current layouts as you create them in the Define Fields dialog box.

- **With Button Tool:** You have two layout preferences to choose from with regard to the Button tool, which sits there in the Tool panel to the far left of your layout. The Button tool lets you drop a button on your FileMaker Pro layout. Now why the heck would you want to do that? Well, it's simple: You can use buttons to perform a broad range of actions for you, such as finding, sorting, and browsing records. What a button can do for you is incredible. Chapter 22 explains all that.

The difference between your choices here is purely a matter of taste. If you don't like the looks of a certain type of button with a certain layout, you can always change this preference. Create Rounded Buttons gives you buttons with rounded edges, whereas Create Rectangular Buttons gives you buttons that have corners.

Setting memory application preferences

To open the Memory Application Preferences dialog box, simply choose Edit⇨Preferences⇨Application. Click Memory from the General drop-down menu, and a dialog box pops open.

Figure 3-6 shows you the Memory Application Preferences dialog box.

In the Memory Application Preferences dialog box, the default setting is the Save during idle time button under Save Changes to Disk. You don't have to change this unless you want to specify saving your changes during certain intervals. I like to work with this option set in FileMaker Pro, because I know my files are being saved automatically, and not in specified intervals. But you should note the following warning.

This option is not a good idea if you use a notebook computer, because saving during idle time can run down your power supply.

Figure 3-6:
The
Memory
Application
Preferences
dialog box.

```
┌──────────── Application Preferences ────────────┐
│  ┌─────────────┐                                │
│  │ Memory  ▼   │                                │
│  └─────────────┘                                │
│   ┌─Save changes to disk:──────────────────┐    │
│   │ ◉ during idle time.                     │    │
│   │ ○ every │10 minutes ▼│ or when necessary.│    │
│   └─────────────────────────────────────────┘    │
│   File cache is always on.  Current size is 2587K.│
│                                                  │
│                                    ┌──────┐      │
│                                    │ Done │      │
│                                    └──────┘      │
└──────────────────────────────────────────────────┘
```

Setting plug-ins application preferences

The last application preference you have is plug-ins. To open the Plug-in Application Preferences dialog box, simply choose Edit⇨Preferences⇨Application. Click Plug-ins from the General drop-down menu, and a dialog box pops open. This option is the same in Windows as it is on the Mac.

Figure 3-7 shows you the Plug-ins Application Preferences dialog box.

If you click the Web Companion check box in that dialog box, you enable the plug-in named Web Companion, which allows access to your database on the Web. But that's only the beginning. For more details on publishing your database on the Web using FileMaker Pro 4, check out Chapters 20 and 21. For the moment, don't worry too much about setting this preference, or about setting the Web Companion preference, which is the last menu item below Application and Document. Again, Chapters 20 and 21 explain it all.

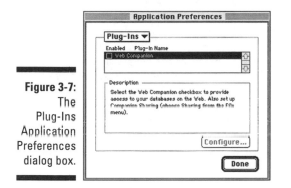

Figure 3-7:
The
Plug-Ins
Application
Preferences
dialog box.

Setting Mac Memory Requirements

The Memory Requirements dialog box isn't listed in either Application or Document Preferences, but I think it should be considered in this chapter because, by setting it just as you would other preferences, you can get the best possible performance out of FileMaker Pro. By *memory,* I'm talking about the amount of system memory on Macintosh that FileMaker Pro needs to do its job.

Of course, most software programs like as much memory as you can possibly allocate to them. FileMaker Pro is not what's sometimes called a *memory hog* — a program that requires globs of memory just to wake up in the morning. FileMaker Pro is quite reasonable, I think, in its memory demands.

Setting the FileMaker Pro memory partition on your Mac

The suggested memory size for FileMaker Pro 4 is 4096K or 4MB of RAM. That's how much RAM FileMaker Pro 4 needs to work happily on your system. By *happily*, I mean without getting any out-of-memory errors, or having to close out of the program because you're running low on memory.

The minimum requirement for RAM is 1024K, but I don't suggest working with so little memory, if you can help it. The general rule is to use as much RAM as you can afford. You'll be glad that you did. On a Mac system with 16MB of RAM, your System and Finder, along with Fonts and Extensions, typically take up about 8MB of RAM, leaving you with 8MB of RAM to run FileMaker Pro 4 and perhaps one other software program, such as Microsoft Word. If you've got more than 16MB of RAM on your Macintosh system, try increasing the amount of memory allocated to FileMaker Pro 4 by another 4MB. Otherwise, on a system with 16MB of RAM, stick with 4MB of memory for FileMaker Pro 4.

The program asks for 4096K (or 4MB) of RAM to do its magic. Be sure that you let it have that memory, or that you make an adjustment if you have less than 4MB of RAM that you can allocate to FileMaker Pro on your Macintosh.

1. **Click the FileMaker Pro icon so that it's highlighted.**

2. **In the Macintosh Finder on the Desktop, choose File⇨Get Info.**

   A Get Info box for FileMaker Pro 4 appears on-screen (see Figure 3-8).

3. **Check the Memory Requirements information fields at the bottom-right corner of the box.**

4. **If the Preferred size setting is less than 4096K, double-click inside the box and enter** 4096.

Figure 3-8:
The Get Info box for FileMaker Pro 4.

```
▤▤▤▤ FileMaker Pro Info ▤▤▤▤
       FileMaker Pro

  Kind : application program
  Size : 2.7 MB on disk (2,868,170 bytes
         used)
 Where : Power HD : FileMaker Pro 4.0
         Folder :

 Created : Tue, Jul 22, 1997, 2:00 PM
Modified : Tue, Jul 22, 1997, 2:00 PM
 Version : FileMaker Pro 4.0v1x25
           (7/22/97) © Claris Corp.
Comments :


┌─── Memory Requirements ───
│ Suggested size :   4096   K
│ Minimum size :     1024   K
☐ Locked  Preferred size :    4096   K

Note : Memory requirements will increase by
       2,490K if virtual memory is turned off in
       the Memory control panel.
```

Chapter 4

Checking Out Those Templates (A Breather — Whew!)

●●●

In This Chapter

▶ What are templates, anyway?

▶ Working with templates

▶ Introducing some cool templates

▶ Finding even more cool templates

●●●

*T*his chapter is something of a departure from the other chapters in this book. You have my permission now (as if you really need it!) to take some time off from your work on getting up-to-speed with FileMaker Pro. Becoming familiar with the FileMaker Pro interface and toolset, designing your own database, thinking in relational terms — that's hard work, indeed. You're entitled to a break. But don't get me wrong: This break isn't a license to goof off.

By devoting quality time to this chapter — and taking the guided tour of templates (at the very least) — you're going to find yourself knowing and understanding things about FileMaker Pro that you didn't know and understand before. It's as simple as that.

Are you ready for a breather from the work ethic? And for some fun? Well, stick around.

A Guided Tour through Template City

Imagine not having to come up with your own database design. Imagine having the luxury of studying the work of other FileMaker Pro designers and learning from their examples (and mistakes).

Welcome to the magical world of templates! Let me be your guide.

What are templates, anyway? Well, to answer my own question, they're simply prebuilt FileMaker Pro files. They're files that have already been created with the power tools that come with FileMaker Pro. Templates have fields that are already defined and formatted, along with cool layouts and even cooler buttons that let you move from one file to another.

The neat thing about templates, I think, is that they can help you master the art of building your own database in FileMaker Pro more quickly. You get to see how somebody else has done it, plain and simple. (Of course, oftentimes you don't get to see all the sweat that went into a particular database, just the end product.)

In any case, templates are there for you — hundreds of them, if not thousands — as FileMaker Pro enabling tools. They show what you can do to build the forms you need for your own business, school, or personal use. Most are pretty standard: business letters, fax sheets, order and invoice forms, contact lists, and so on. But with a little tweaking and adjustment, you can often use them to create your own custom forms. Later in this chapter, I show you how you can customize a template and adapt it to your own database needs.

I like to collect as many templates as I can, just so I can check out what other people are doing with FileMaker Pro.

Whether your FileMaker Pro template was created on a Mac or a PC running Windows doesn't matter. That's because FileMaker Pro is designed to read your template files without having to modify them according to the Macintosh or Windows operating systems. This cross-platform capability is neat because it means that FileMaker Pro can share your files and templates across a computer network, one where Macs and PCs are hooked up and connected to each other. So if somebody you know creates a template running FileMaker Pro under the other platform, be happy. You can still use it and work with it on your computer.

Rules of the Game

Here are some general rules for using templates that I think you ought to follow:

1. **Be sure to make a backup copy of any template folder or directory you want to check out. Keep the original in a separate folder or on a floppy disk.**

2. **Open an existing template and check out the list of layouts in the Layout pop-up menu.**

   By doing so, you see the nuts and bolts of each template, how it was assembled and finally put together. The Layout menu is a dynamite source for ideas and inspiration.

3. **Click the buttons on each template and see what happens.**

   If the buttons are smartly designed and linked right, you find yourself moving from one template to another with the greatest of ease.

4. **After you have checked out a template and decided you want to modify it for your own purposes, be sure to make a clone of the template.**

   Clones? What am I talking about here? Bear with me because this clone thing is important stuff and can save you a great deal of time in working with a template.

5. **Choose File➪Save a Copy As.**

   Figure 4-1 shows you the menu item. This step looks pretty obvious, doesn't it? Actually, it's not, because in working with FileMaker Pro, you begin to forget about saving the work in your files. FileMaker Pro saves automatically for you, so you can tend to forget that, in fact, you do have options for saving.

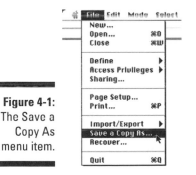

Figure 4-1:
The Save a
Copy As
menu item.

6. **In the Create a Copy dialog box that appears, click the Type menu and pull it down to Clone (No Records).**

   You can see this dialog box for making a clone in Figure 4-2.

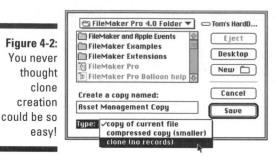

Figure 4-2:
You never
thought
clone
creation
could be so
easy!

Now, a *clone* is simply a copy of the original template, but without any of the information or data that was in it. This empty copy makes adding or deleting fields, putting in your own graphic images or pictures, and moving pieces around in your layout much easier. In other words, once you have a clone, you're ready to customize this puppy so that it works right for your needs.

After you create a clone of a template, be sure to give it the name identical to your original template. Because template files are usually linked together with buttons and lookup fields that take you from one file to another, you confuse the heck out of them if you give them different names.

If you save your clone with the same name, you have to save it in a different folder or directory; otherwise, the clone replaces the original file. Watch out for that!

A Bundle of Templates

FileMaker Pro comes bundled with a whole library of templates and example files. At last count, I found three separate folders loaded with templates, including as many as 23 templates for business, 13 for home, and 8 for education. Check them out — they're useful both for learning the fundamentals of the program and in helping you build your own databases with FileMaker Pro.

When you launch the program, you get the screen shown in Figure 4-3, which lets you create a new file based on one of the existing FileMaker Pro templates. Before clicking the radio button that lets you perform that action, you may want to get more information about the templates that come with the program and how to use them.

Figure 4-3:
The New
Database
dialog box,
where by
clicking a
radio button
you can
create a
new file
based on a
template.

If you click the Template Info button at the bottom of the dialog box, you see the screen shown in Figure 4-4. This FileMaker Pro database provides you with a brief introduction to templates and buttons that launch business, education, or home templates that you can adapt and modify for your own purposes.

To navigate your way through this nifty library of templates, you can also open the Templates folder and select the category you want to peruse. In Figure 4-5, I've opened the Home folder and inside that folder selected Video Database as the FileMaker Pro template I want to check out. You have lots of other templates to choose from, depending on what you think may be useful for your home, business, or education needs.

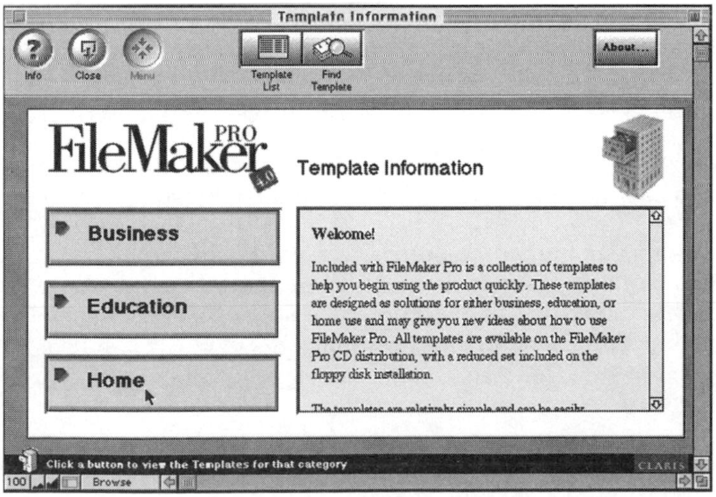

Figure 4-4:
Launching a
business,
education,
or home-use
template is
as easy as
clicking a
button
in the
database.

Figure 4-5:
A Video
database
template
selected
from among
the Home
templates in
FileMaker
Pro.

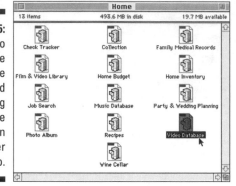

Buttons and Dialogs template

You may think that the Buttons and Dialogs template is an odd template to find in your Templates folder. But it's one of the most useful in designing and building a FileMaker Pro database that works for you. Buttons . . . and more buttons — what do you do with them? They're your navigational markers in a FileMaker Pro database: You use buttons to point to other records. Life in your database world is much easier, believe me, when you can point and click your way around from one record to another. Figure 4-6 shows a screen from one of a set of navigational buttons in the Buttons and Dialogs template, which you can find in the FileMaker Pro Examples folder.

How do you get these buttons? Getting them is easy, really. All you have to do is choose Mode⇨Layout to bring yourself instantly to the layout tools that appear in Figure 4-6. Then to use any of these buttons in your database, simply copy the button, using the standard Copy command in the Edit menu, and paste it, again with the standard Paste command, into one of your records. The buttons are prebuilt and designed for you, like little widgets that you can drop onto your records.

In order to do this copying and pasting of buttons, however, your record has to be in Layout mode; you can't perform the copy-and-paste from Browse.

After you paste the button onto your record, you can pick it up with the Pointer tool and position it wherever you want. You can also resize it and change its colors and fill patterns. With the Text tool, you can type a name on the button to label it. Chapters 9 and 10 cover the complete toolset at your disposal.

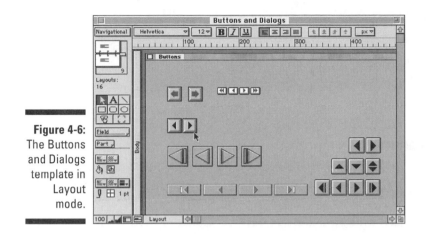

Figure 4-6:
The Buttons
and Dialogs
template in
Layout
mode.

But what good is just a plain old button sitting there in one of your records? I'm glad you asked. Now the fun really begins because you can get that button to do a multitude of tasks for you by assigning a little script to the button. Scripts with buttons? Check out Chapter 22 for more details. But here are the highlights:

1. **You click the button to highlight it.**

2. **Choose Format⇨Button, as Figure 4-7 shows.**

The Specify Button dialog box shown in Figure 4-8 opens with a long list of choices you can scroll down: everything from Do Nothing to Finding Records, from Sorting Records to Dialing a Phone Number, with many choices in between. They're just some of the actions you can get any button, no matter what its size or its position on your layout, to perform. Clicking a button and instantly having it do the action you have prescribed for it is a very handy feature, indeed. In Figure 4-8, I've selected Next from the choices in the pop-up menu as the action I want for my button depicted in the layout. That means that if a user clicks the button with the navigational arrow, the button moves the user to any number of "next" possibilities: next record, next layout, and so on.

The thing to remember here is that you don't have to spend a lot of time designing your own buttons or dialog boxes with the layout tools in FileMaker Pro. You've got a neat set of them already available in the Buttons and Dialogs template.

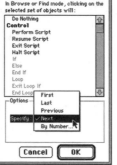

Figure 4-7:
The Button
menu item
selected in
the Format
menu.

Figure 4-8:
The Specify
Button
dialog box
with the
Next item
selected in
the pop-up
menu.

Contacts template

The Contacts template, which you can find in the Integrated Solutions folder
in the FileMaker Pro Examples folder, is pretty much self-explanatory — or is
it? For one thing, the Contacts template keeps track of all the relevant
information you need on people with whom you're in contact. It's perfect for
business, school, or home, particularly if you do a great deal of phone work
and need to look up home and business numbers and fax numbers. Figure
4-9 shows you the Data Entry screen for the Contacts template.

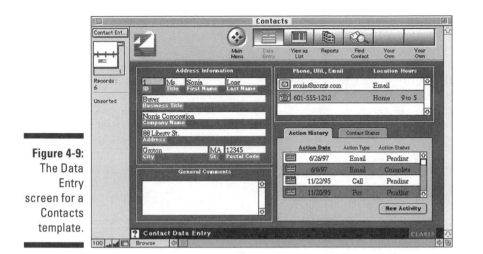

Figure 4-9:
The Data
Entry
screen for a
Contacts
template.

The Contacts template includes a set of layouts and forms for a whole range of activities related to contacts. For example, by clicking the Status button just above the Book icon, you open a pop-up list of items that includes Data Entry Form, Contacts by Type, Contacts by Date, and Contacts by Status. Each one of these items is a separate file that you can use after you begin to populate your Contacts database with names, addresses, phone numbers, and other information. It's all been set up for you; that's the beauty of this template.

Button-mania

If you're connected to America Online, CompuServe, Prodigy, or another online service, you can probably find a forum that's devoted to Claris products. Check it out, because you'll find a folder filled with several nifty FileMaker Pro databases built by ordinary people (not computer programmers). Many of these databases are shareware products, meaning that if you use them, you need to send the author of the product a fee (something typically in the range of $10 to $25).

I mention this forum because one of the hottest items online is — you guessed it — buttons. And I mean buttons in all sizes, shapes, and configurations. Some are straight giveaways; others are shareware. In any case, when you can add lots of prebuilt, predesigned buttons to your collection, they really help in designing your own database.

Check out the buttons at the top of the screen. They help you navigate from one file to another. Just by clicking each respective button, you can move from the Data Entry form to Reports, View as List, or Find Contact. These forms have all been set up for you, with the appropriate layouts and positioning for the fields in each file. In other words, each button already has a script written for it to perform. You can also add new buttons of your own creation to perform the kinds of actions you want for your own customized version of this template. For example, you can add a button that, when a user clicks it, performs a sort of the records in your database. Neat, huh?

Expense Report template

The Expense Report template is pretty cool because it keeps track of your expenses, including the dates and calculated totals, and generates a report of those expenses. Then it provides you with the balance in your account. Figure 4-10 shows you the Enter Expenses layout of the template. Note the buttons on the top of the screen — View as Form, View as List, Reports, New Record, Delete Record, and Find Record. The design is clean and uncluttered, and you can build on it or adapt it to your own business or personal needs.

Again, the buttons here act just like other buttons in your templates. By clicking them, you go directly to the different forms.

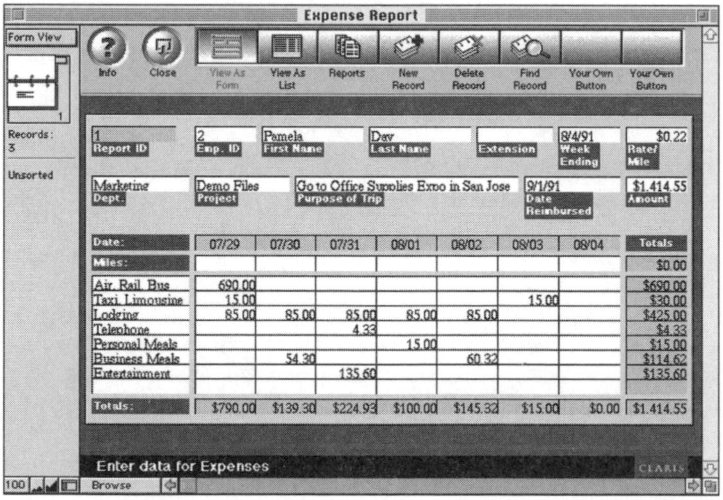

Figure 4-10: The Data Entry screen for the Expense Report template.

Invoices template

The Invoices template, shown in Figure 4-11, is another cool template. It's ideal if you're shipping a product to a particular customer base and you need to create mailing labels, packing slips, monthly income reports, and so on. Any business lives and dies by invoicing. How else can you get paid? When I had my own software company, I used a modified version of this template to bill customers and distributors. Nothing fancy here, just the essentials. This one template alone, if modified to your business, can save you a great deal of time and money. Figure 4-12 shows you the Shipping Information portion of the template, with a little truck button at the bottom.

When you click the truck button in the Invoices templates, you see the screen shown in Figure 4-13, which provides you with the shipping details for the product that you've invoiced. This example is certainly an effective use of buttons. You may want to study this template and then modify it to suit your own needs. Count your blessings that such a template exists and that others exist as well, all built by FileMaker Pro experts.

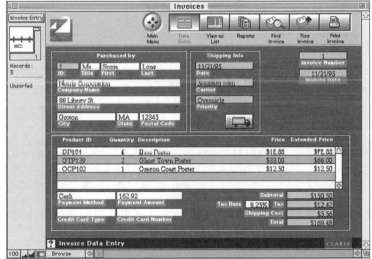

Figure 4-11:
The Data Entry screen for the Invoices template.

Figure 4-12:
Check out
the truck
button
in this
selected
portion
of the
Invoices
template.
Neat things
happen
when you
click it.

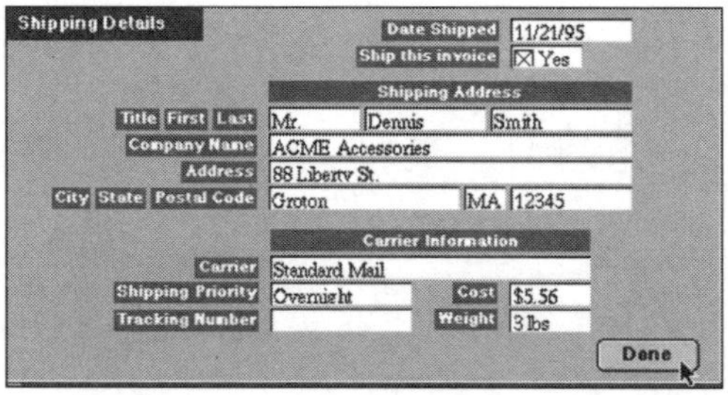

Figure 4-13:
The
Shipping
Details Data
Entry
screen for
the Invoices
template.

Products template

The Products template lets you enter information about your company's product offerings by product list, price, and vendor. Every company, whatever its size, must constantly update its product and price lists for its customers. It's a lot easier to do this in FileMaker Pro than a word-processing program, especially if you have a good template with some calculation fields that compute the values of your updated price list.

If you have to maintain a product and price list, use this template and modify it for your company's needs. FileMaker Pro even lets you create in this template a product catalog that contains pictures or graphic images. Your customers will love you for that. See what the Data Entry screen looks like in Figure 4-14.

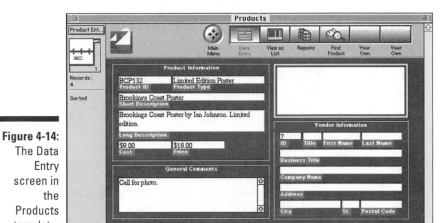

Figure 4-14:
The Data
Entry
screen in
the
Products
template.

A Bonanza of Other Templates

A veritable bonanza of templates is out there, with many templates in the public domain that you can readily adapt and modify to your own database needs, whether they involve a business, school, or home. Many are available on various online services, particularly America Online, which has a good forum on Claris and Claris products. The keyword you type is **Claris**. Check the FileMaker Pro folders and see what's been uploaded lately.

TIP

What to look for in a template

The thing to look for in a good template — if you collect and download a few from the different online services and electronic bulletin boards — can be summed up in one word: *simplicity.* You can build on a simply designed template much more easily than one that's loaded with too many buttons, fields, layouts, and features. What works for one FileMaker Pro template designer may not always work for you. Look for designs you can add to, without letting things get too complicated or unwieldy.

Nothing is worse than a database that's confusing in design, sluggish in performance (because it's bloated with features and files), and difficult to navigate. You've got to avoid cumbersome and overwhelming designs at all costs. Again, simplicity is the operative word.

Getting Good Ideas by Template Touring

Templates are good fodder for design ideas. Study them. Brood on them. Check out the buttons and see where you fly.

Remember that each template reflects the needs and priorities of a particular business, school, or home. No two businesses or homes are alike, and neither are two templates.

If you've taken the time to check out the screens from the templates in this chapter, perhaps even studied them in detail, you're ready for the next step — either to modify an existing template or to build one from scratch on your own. The choice, of course, is ultimately yours.

Modifying a Template, or the Joy of Sculpting

To modify an existing template, follow the steps outlined earlier in this chapter under the heading "Rules of the Game." Nothing is really complicated here: You just want to save the template as a clone, meaning that you get to start fresh because all the data populating the template's fields is removed.

What you want to do next, after you've saved the template as a clone, is a bit more dramatic: You want to strip the template down to its essentials. By *essentials,* I mean the fields and buttons that you think you really need for your business, school, or home use.

You ought to think through this process of simplifying the template. And when you're ready, just remove the fields you know you don't need (you can always replace them later). Check the Define Fields dialog box and see what fields make sense for your database and what you truly need. The idea here is to start with a template that's lean and mean and build on it.

Then print out a copy of the new template. Take a look at it away from your computer and mark it up with pen and pencil accordingly. You can see things that are extraneous, fields that you don't really need. Next time through, remove these fields from the template. Let others review the hardcopy version of your new template and mark it up. Eventually, you reach a good starting point from which to build a database that's right for you.

Chapter 5

The Relational Boogie

Relational databases are *not* electronic filing systems for old and current love interests. Nor are relational databases made especially to store genealogies. A *relational database,* simply defined, is a database that draws information from one or more additional database files, kind of a sharing of information thing. This is one way to set up your databases. The other choice is to stay with a *flat-file,* or self-contained, database in which all the database information resides in the same file.

Relational databases are just plain better at doing some things than flat-file databases, but relational databases are also more complex to think about and set up. Most tasks, on the other hand, require nothing more than the simple, flat-file alternative. In this chapter, I try to show you how to know the difference.

"Wait a minute," I'm hearing you say. "This stuff sounds hard." Don't panic. Stick with me — this chapter is an easy-does-it introduction to the relational boogie, guaranteed not to throw your back out. I demonstrate the tougher dance steps in Chapter 22.

Choosing a Model: Flat-File versus Relational

FileMaker Pro gives you a choice between two models. (No, not Cindy Crawford or Tyra Banks — I said models, not supermodels.) This choice is between *conceptual models,* which are ways to think about and construct your FileMaker Pro databases. Your choice is between the flat-file model and the relational model.

The first choice is building a database that's basically a collection of records — what's called in the nerdy world of computers a *flat-file database,* which is a database that contains all the records in one file and where all records in the file are alike. Most databases fall into this category. You have a laundry list of things you want to store and retrieve — for example, phone numbers, the names of items in your compact disc collection, the titles of books in your library, a list of household valuables. . . . Well, you get the idea.

Probably 90 percent of the databases that you build, work on, and live with are in this category. (How did I get the figure of 90 percent? I used the tried-and-true method of statistical analysis known as Making a Wild Guess.) This type of database is fine. FileMaker Pro is there to deliver your needs, and most database needs, if the truth be told, are not overwhelming. You need to store, access, look up, and retrieve the information you've put in fields. Typically these fields, when you add them up, contain lists — lots and lots of lists.

Now, your second choice is to go *relational.* Like building a personal or business relationship, you can choose to match the information in your records in one file with the information in your records in another file. The relational thing, if you'll pardon the metaphor, is a kind of matchmaking. You're matching the data in one file with the data in another. Am I making sense?

In technical terms, a relational database lets you define an expression that establishes a relationship between values (that is, the data you've entered in your fields) in fields that you've matched up. In fancier terms, this relationship can also be called a *link* or a *join expression.* The relationship essentially has three components: the name of the matching field, which is specified in a master file; the related filename; and finally, the name of the matching field in a related file.

Relational advantages

Going relational has a few distinct advantages:

- ✔ You can edit and revise that relationship — that is, define and redefine how the data from one file matches the data from another.
- ✔ Your data is stored in only one file at a time — in other words, you don't duplicate the information in multiple files. You aren't repeating the same information two or more times.
- ✔ Your database is organized more logically and consistently. You can see the connections from one file to another.

Relational disadvantages

I don't want to paint a completely rosy picture of going relational. The process has some disadvantages:

✔ In planning and designing your database, you need to think everything through very carefully with an eye toward establishing relationships between matching fields and files.

✔ You have to wrestle, early on, with a more extensive set of questions. What information will my database contain? What files do I need? What fields will be in each of my files? And — this is the big *and* — what data in my files is common to, or matches with, other data in my files? (More than a little brainwork is required here.)

✔ After you've decided to do the relational thing, going through your files, doing the match-ups, and using the tools you've got in FileMaker Pro takes extra work.

Bear in mind that you don't have to make the Big Choice right away. You should know what your options are, and setting your thinking wheels in motion early on certainly helps. But if you decide to use a flat-file database rather than a relational one and later change your mind, your world won't end. You can always modify your flat-file database to be relational down the road. You've got that flexibility in terms of choices. FileMaker Pro doesn't paint you into a corner.

If you start to get the feeling that a database that you have set up is duplicating information from other files, it's a good bet that your file would work better as a relational database. If you find that many of the fields (the storing places for information in your databases that usually have names like First Name, Address, and so on) that you have set up are blank in many records, relational is the way to go.

Doing the Relational Boogie, Part 1

In this part of the book, I want to introduce you to the nitty-gritty of what you need to know if you're going to work successfully with FileMaker Pro. I want to save the actual doing for Part II, when you can roll up your sleeves and get down to business. But here, in this chapter, I think I've whetted your appetite for the relational thing, so I want to show you, at least partially, what some of the steps are in this relational dance. You may want to try them out. It's a seven-step boogie.

In this dance routine, I use the Personal Address Book that I create in Chapter 1 as an example. That file appears in Figure 5-1.

This little FileMaker Pro address book is about as simple as a file gets. I have fields defined for Last Name, First Name, Street, City, State, Zip Code, Phone Number, and even a Photo for fun. So far, the file has only three records. Eventually, I want to add more records with photos of the different folks in my address book.

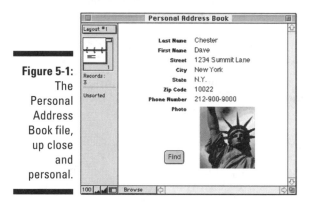

Figure 5-1:
The
Personal
Address
Book file,
up close
and
personal.

But wait a minute. This FileMaker Pro address book isn't the only file that I've created for names and addresses. I have another FileMaker Pro file called Contacts, which I use for business purposes. It's loaded with fields for Last Name, First Name, City, State, Main Phone Number, Fax Number, Zip Code, and so on.

Now obviously, some folks from my business Contacts file ought to be in my Personal Address Book. Why not establish a relationship between the two files? If I do, I'm thinking, it ought to save me time because I won't be duplicating the same information in two separate files. The last names in one file, for example, can be related to the last names in the other file. In addition, I can look up the last names of people in my Contacts file — without even opening the Contacts file — by just typing their names in the Last Name field of my Personal Address Book. So you may be thinking, too, why not go for it? Okay, here's going for it:

1. **Open a FileMaker Pro database by choosing File⇨Open and selecting the database you want.**

2. **Choose File⇨Define⇨Relationships.**

   The relational strategy in this example is to match the Last Name field (as well as other fields I choose) in the Personal Address Book file with the last name in the Last Name field in the Contacts file. You can use your own files if you want; for this particular dance, any partner will do.

When using FileMaker Pro relationally, defining the relationship is important because you need to set up master and related files early on so that you know how you're establishing the connection and where you can look up the information (that is, in the master file). This example makes the Personal Address Book file the master file and Contacts the related file.

The Define Relationships dialog box appears, as Figure 5-2 shows for my Personal Address Book. Be prepared to name that relationship and define what the relationship is — namely, which file you want your master file to be related to.

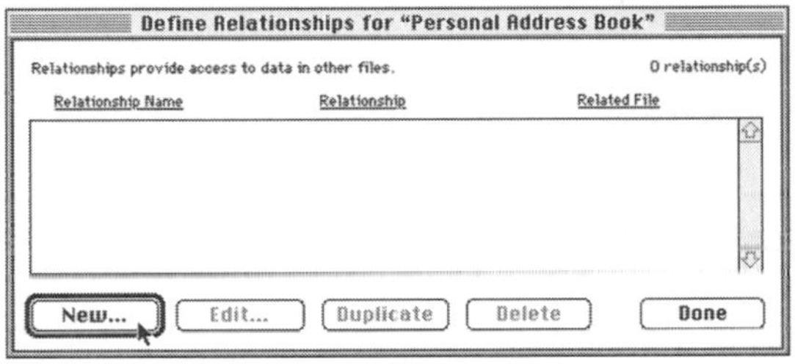

Figure 5-2:
The Define Relationships dialog box; click New to swing into action.

```
┌────────────────────────────────────────────────────────────────┐
│         Define Relationships for "Personal Address Book"          │
│ Relationships provide access to data in other files.  0 relationship(s) │
│ Relationship Name          Relationship          Related File     │
│                                                              ⬆     │
│                                                                    │
│                                                              ⬇     │
│ ( New... )  ( Edit... )  ( Duplicate )  ( Delete )      ( Done )  │
└────────────────────────────────────────────────────────────────┘
```

3. Click the New button.

After you click New, FileMaker Pro asks you to specify a file that you want to relate to your master file. In the example that Figure 5-3 shows, I've selected Contacts from my Templates folder.

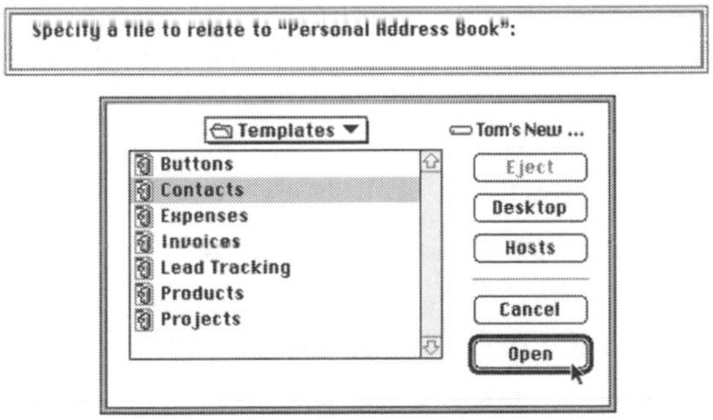

Figure 5-3:
Specifying a file to relate to my Personal Address Book.

Specify a file to relate to "Personal Address Book":

```
┌──────────────────────────────────────────────┐
│   📁 Templates ▼        ▭ Tom's New ...        │
│ ▩ Buttons          ⬆                           │
│ ▩ Contacts                  ( Eject )          │
│ ▩ Expenses                  ( Desktop )        │
│ ▩ Invoices                  ( Hosts )          │
│ ▩ Lead Tracking                                │
│ ▩ Products                  ( Cancel )         │
│ ▩ Projects         ⬇        (( Open ))         │
└──────────────────────────────────────────────┘
```

4. Click the related file — in this case, Contacts — and click Open.

The Edit Relationship dialog box opens, as Figure 5-4 shows.

Figure 5-4:
The Edit
Relationship
dialog box,
where you
match data
between
files.

```
┌─────────────────────────────────────────────────────────┐
│                    Edit Relationship                      │
│ Relationship Name  Contacts                               │
│ A relationship defines a set of matching related records for│
│ each record in the current file.          ┌─────────────┐ │
│                                            │ Specify File...│ │
│ Match data from field in current file:    With data from field in related file:│
│ Personal Address Book                     Contacts        │
│ ┌──────────────────────────┐ ↑   ┌──────────────────────┐↑│
│ │ Last Name                 │     │ ::Address            │ │
│ │ First Name                │     │ ::Car Phone          │ │
│ │ Street                    │     │ ::City               │ │
│ │ City                      │     │ ::Comments           │ │
│ │ State                     │     │ ::Company Name       │ │
│ │ Zip Code                  │     │ ::Company Plus ZIP   │ │
│ │ Phone Number              │     │ ::Contact Code       │ │
│ │ Photo                     │     │ ::Contact First      │ │
│ │                           │ ↓   │ ::Contact Last       │ │
│ └──────────────────────────┘     │ ::Contact Title      │↓│
│                                   └──────────────────────┘ │
│ □ When deleting a record in this file, also  □ Allow creation of related records│
│    delete related records                                 │
│                              ┌────────┐ ┌──────────┐      │
│                              │ Cancel │ │    OK    │      │
│                              └────────┘ └──────────┘      │
└─────────────────────────────────────────────────────────┘
```

**5. Click the fields you want to match from your master file in the left
column and your related file in the right column.**

In this example, I've selected the Last Name field from the Personal
Address Book file and the Contact Last field — the field name for the
last names in this file — from the Contacts file.

In the Edit Relationship dialog box, you need to do four things, and
they're all important:

- Name the relationship you want. In this case, I've just called it
  Contacts, which is what FileMaker Pro defaults to. You can choose
  to name the relationship something different.

- Match the data from a field in your current, or master, file — here,
  it's the Personal Address Book — with the data from a field in a
  related file, which in this example is the Contacts file.

- Click to select the When Deleting a Record in This File, Also Delete
  Related Records check box at the bottom left of the dialog box.

- Click to select the Allow Creation of Related Records check box at
  the bottom right of the dialog box.

6. After you've selected the matching fields you want, click OK.

The Define Relationships dialog box reappears, as Figure 5-5 shows.
The dialog box shows what you've defined by highlighting the Relationship Name, the Relationship, and the Related File. This boogie step
brings you almost back to where you started. Remember that this
dialog box was once virtually empty.

So now you have the Relationship Name and Relationship correspondence (that is, the Last Name field in the Personal Address Book is
matched with the Contact Last field in the Contacts file), and the

Related File (Contacts) is set up and defined. You can edit the relationship by clicking the Edit button, or you can create a new relationship, duplicate an existing one, or delete one as you see fit. Now if only real-life relationships were that simple. . . .

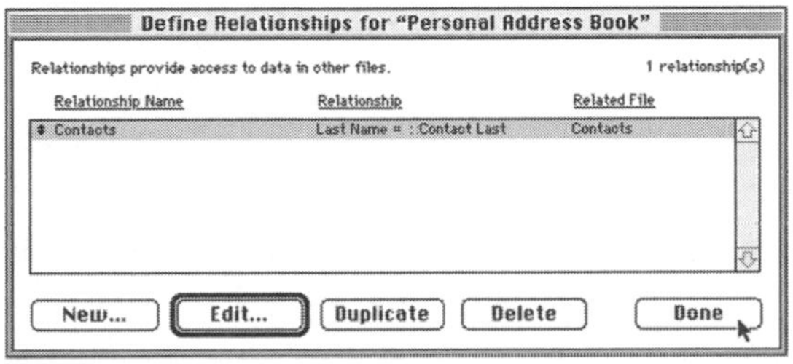

Figure 5-5:
The Define
Relationship
dialog
box now
shows a
relationship
defined.

7. **If all the relationships are defined the way you want in the Define Relationships dialog box, click OK.**

There you go! You've established a relationship between the two fields in two separate databases — in this example, two Last Name fields. You get to view and make changes to the master file, which in this case is the Personal Address file, and automatically match the last names from one file to the other. The match-up is logical, when you think about it, because you keep track of last names from your Contacts file in your Personal Address Book file. You don't have to duplicate the fields and records, so things are a bit more efficient in the way you've organized your data.

But you're not finished yet with the relational boogie. This is only Part I of the dance. Stick with me and stay light on your feet.

The Relational Boogie, Part II

After doing the hard work of choosing, defining, and editing the relationships you want with your matching fields in different files, you have a few easy steps ahead of you in the relational boogie. In the second part of this dance number, you experience the ultimate thrill of the relational boogie. When I first saw FileMaker Pro 3 in action, performing its relational magic, it practically knocked me out. I mean, are we talking ultra cool, or what?

In these steps, you open your master file (the familiar Personal Address Book, in this example) and type the last name of somebody you remember from your related file in the Last Name field (or whatever field in which you defined a relationship). You then suddenly find that person's name, along with his or her address and phone number, pop up in your master file. What's so cool about that? Well, for one thing, the related file (which is the Contacts file in this example) doesn't even have to be open! Anyway, here's how you want to proceed for the second part of the relational boogie:

1. **With your master file open, go to Layout mode by either choosing Mode⇨Layout or clicking Layout on the mode selector at the bottom of your screen.**

2. **In Layout mode, click the Field tool to the left of your screen, just below the Tool panel.**

   On Macs, the outline of a hand appears over the Field tool. In Windows, you see a crosshair with arrows.

3. **Drag the Field tool to your layout and place it down next to the Last Name field at the top of your layout.**

   The Specify Field dialog box shown in Figure 5-6 appears. Now keep in mind what you're doing here: You're specifying the field for the related file in your current, or master, file — the Personal Address Book, in this example.

Figure 5-6: Select your related file in the Specify Field dialog box.

4. **In the Specify Field dialog box, click your related file (in this case, Contacts) and click the Create Field Label check box.**

   The Specify Field dialog box adjusts to list the fields in your related file, similar to what Figure 5-7 shows for the Contacts file.

5. **Click the field you defined in the first part of this relational boogie and click OK.**

   In this example, I selected the Contact Last field. The layout screen from your master file reappears with the new field selected, as shown in Figure 5-8. Note that you can identify related fields by the double colon (::) inside the new field name box.

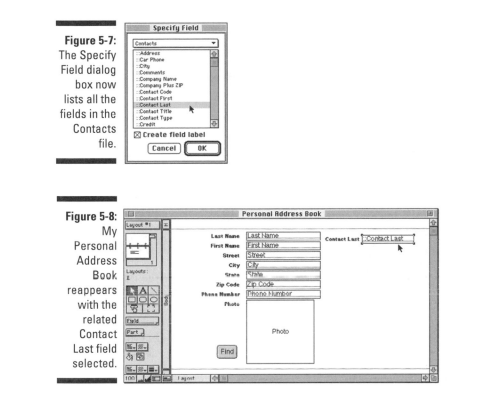

Figure 5-7:
The Specify
Field dialog
box now
lists all the
fields in the
Contacts
file.

Figure 5-8:
My
Personal
Address
Book
reappears
with the
related
Contact
Last field
selected.

6. Add new related fields by repeating Steps 2 through 5.

Figure 5-9 shows that I added three new related fields to my Personal
Address Book layout: Contact First, City, and Main Number.

What you're doing here is simply selecting the fields from the related
(Contacts) file that you want to appear in your master (Personal
Address Book) file, and then adding them to your layout by specifying
them in the Specify Fields dialog box. Are we on a roll? Yes.

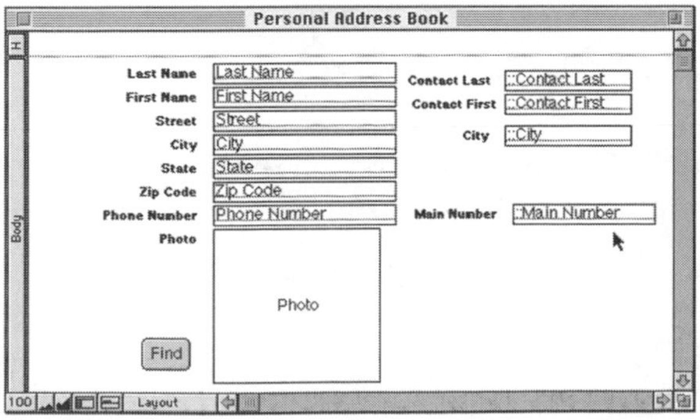

Figure 5-9:
You can add
many
related
fields to
your master
file.

7. **After you've finished adding related fields to your master file, switch to Browse mode.**

   The related records now appear in your master file, with a match from the related file to the master file. In this example, as Figure 5-10 shows, you can see *John Jones* appearing in both.

Figure 5-10:
Records
from both
master and
related files
appear in
your master
file.

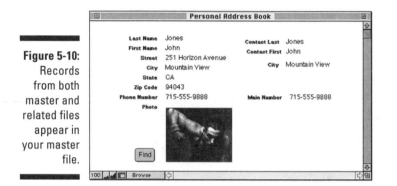

If you return to your related (Contacts) file, you can verify that all the fields you've defined as related still exist in the related file. Figure 5-11 shows that the data in this record matches the data related to my Personal Address Book.

Figure 5-11:
The
Contacts
file with the
record for
John Jones.

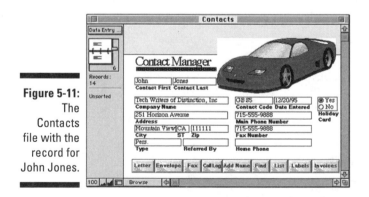

Now if you want to find, for example, the name of a person in your related file while browsing your master file, all you have to do is enter that person's name in the Last Name field. Figure 5-12 shows the name *Smith* entered in Browse mode in my Personal Address Book (note the placement of the pointer).

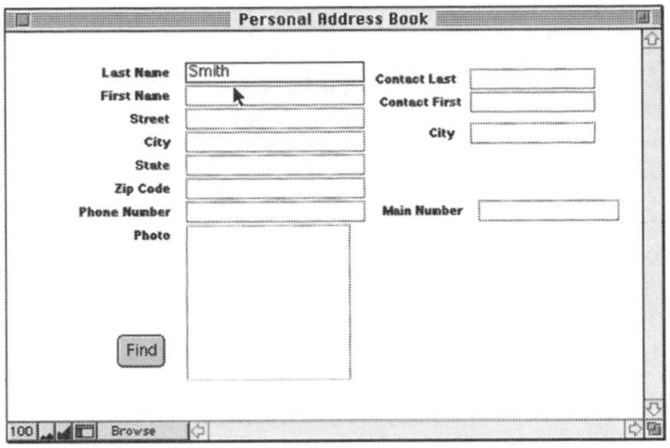

Personal Address Book

Last Name | Smith
First Name |
Street |
City |
State |
Zip Code |
Phone Number |
Photo |

Contact Last |
Contact First |
City |

Main Number |

Find

100 | Browse

Figure 5-12:
Calling all
Smiths in
my
Contacts
file.

After entering whatever data you're searching for, move the pointer away from the field, and — presto! — the matched data appears, including the other related fields you defined. Figure 5-13 shows a found Smith.

So there! You've done the relational boogie, at least for starters. Think, for a moment, of the possibilities. You could set up and define relationships with fields from many different files, couldn't you? Yes. And FileMaker Pro provides you with a very special, one-to-many tool called the Portal tool for doing just that. Chapter 23 explains more about relational stuff and some of its most useful applications. That chapter also introduces you to the coolest tool in FileMaker Pro 4: this Portal tool that really lets you boogie big-time. Hey, who said relationships couldn't be fun, particularly in the database world?

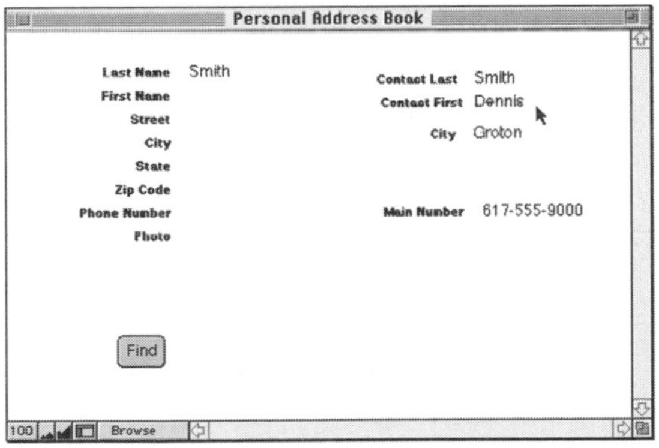

Personal Address Book

Last Name | Smith
First Name |
Street |
City |
State |
Zip Code |
Phone Number |
Photo |

Contact Last | Smith
Contact First | Dennis
City | Groton

Main Number | 617-555-9000

Find

100 | Browse

Figure 5-13:
A Dennis
Smith
record from
my Contacts
file appears
in my
Personal
Address
Book file.

The relational bug

If you're like me, you probably can't go through the day without making at least a half dozen lists of things that are going on. I'm talking about a Things to Do List, a People to Call List, a List of Projects to Work On, a List of Bills to Pay, and so on. I write these down in blue pen on yellow legal pads, or on stick-on notes. Then I stuff them into my pockets or briefcase. I call it my List-Mania.

For a while, I would gather up these lists and try to sort through them, much like you'd sort through a collection of business cards you've accumulated from a trade show. Until I got the bright idea that I ought to do something with my lists. I could at least input the bits and pieces in my list into a couple of nifty FileMaker Pro databases. Which I did.

Then FileMaker Pro went relational, and I got bitten by the relational bug. I started to look at my Personal Address database and my Family Album database and my Contacts database and my Diary database to see whether data in my files were related. Guess what? They were. In fact, I had a lot of duplicate information in my files. Which, if I had started out making them relational, I would have avoided.

The relational bug can be pretty virulent because it makes you want to rethink how you've set up your old databases, as well as how you ought to design new ones.

Chapter 6

Zen and the Art of Organizing Your Files

- -

In This Chapter

▶ Mastering FileMaker Pro in three steps: organize, organize, organize

▶ Finding files on a Mac

▶ Finding files in Windows 95

▶ Finding your files 'cause you know where you put them

- -

*T*hese days, you can't step inside a bookstore without getting hit by a ton of books on the subject of how to get better organized. When you add up all this organizational self-help literature, it seems to amount almost to a national obsession. Everybody, we're told, needs to get better organized, and the how-to books are filled with techniques for doing so. I don't want to contribute to this obsession — I only want to explore a few things I know about how to organize your FileMaker Pro files.

Mastering FileMaker Pro and the topics in this book will go a long way toward getting you well organized in your business, school, or home. A tool such as FileMaker Pro is effective because it allows you to get your life in order by helping you keep track of life's essentials, all those lists of people, places, and phone numbers we routinely make.

But what happens when your hard disk starts to fill up with FileMaker Pro files and databases? What happens when that stuff gets loosely scattered about on your desktop? And, lo and behold, you can't find things? I want to address some of those problems in this chapter. As I see it, you can take two approaches to organizing your FileMaker Pro files: the Zen approach or the Other approach.

The Zen Way of Organizing

The Zen approach is the one where you simply let your files be — that is, be wherever they happen to be on your hard drive. You create a FileMaker Pro file, add records, add new layouts, define new fields, add buttons, and even use scripts to tell the buttons what to do. And then when saving your work, you don't think twice about where the files or databases will live on your hard drive — you just save them. Period. The files may be in oddly named folders, or buried deep within other folders on both the Mac and under Windows.

The Zen approach, which everyone may fall into at one time or another, appears on the surface to be rather chaotic and certainly not well organized. I think you know what I'm talking about when you check out the files on your own hard drive and — surprise, surprise — find files that you'd completely forgotten about or weren't even aware existed. They're in some folder that was misnamed or gobbled up in another folder when you accidentally dragged the file icons into a different location.

Strangely enough, nothing may be intrinsically wrong with the Zen approach, as long as you've got a means of searching for your files. A good, fast Find File utility, in fact, does the trick. And you've got that utility both in the Macintosh System 7.5 and on Windows 95.

Zen and the art of finding a file on a Mac

Like the Windows utility, the Mac OS Find File utility can be a real lifesaver. You can find it in the Mac OS File menu under Find and when it opens for you, it looks like the screen in Figure 6-1.

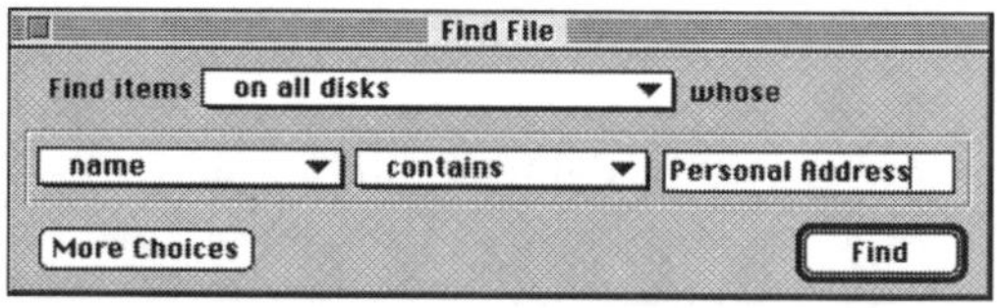

Figure 6-1:
The Find File utility in Mac OS.

I can't begin to tell you how many times the Find utility has saved my life. Even with careful attention to detail and saving your files in properly named folders, you lose track of your work from time to time. It happens, particularly now when large hard drives — capable of storing gigabytes — are appearing on the market, and people are trading in their old 200MB drives for multi-gigabyte drives with all that extra storage space that, of course, they must fill.

If you're going to use the Zen approach to organizing your files, or perhaps a partial-Zen approach, you ought to be up-to-speed on using this Find utility. For example, as you see in Figure 6-2, you have many choices about what parameters you can base your search on.

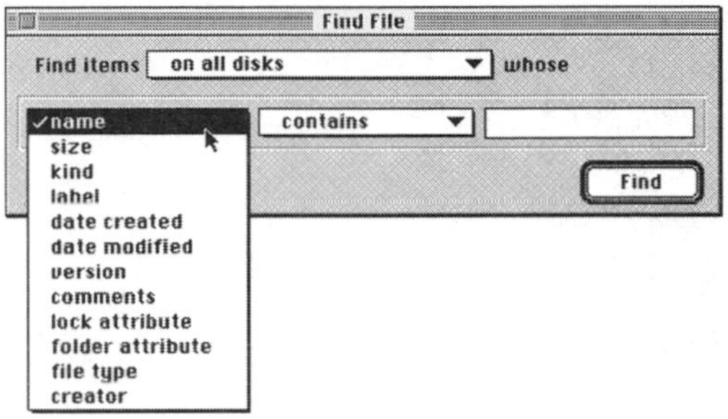

Figure 6-2:
The Find File utility listing your search choices.

I won't try to explain all these choices, which really define the ways in which the Macintosh operating system identifies the files on your disk. From one perspective, the Find File utility is a thing of magic because if you forget the name of the file you're searching for, but have an idea when it was created or how big it is, the chances improve that you'll find it.

I want to pass along a cool little technique here that will really help you, I think, in keeping track of your files. It involves an extra step after saving a file, but that step can make all the difference in the world.

After you save a file, click its icon (in the Macintosh Finder) and choose File⇨Get Info, which opens the Get Info dialog box, shown in Figure 6-3.

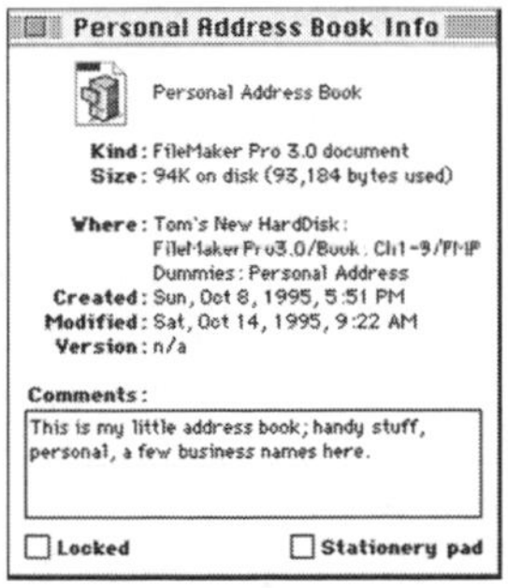

Figure 6-3:
The Get Info dialog box that you access from the Mac OS Finder.

In that dialog box, you see an item called Comments. That's where you can say anything you want about your file. Just type in the text. Whatever comes into your head — no rules restrict what you do or don't say about the file. It can be your way of personalizing the file, your way of characterizing or identifying it. I typed in the word handy, as you can see in Figure 6-3. I tend to think of this database as handy, so that was in my comments.

Guess what? If that file gets scattered about on the vast and well-populated landscape of my hard drive and if it somehow gets "lost" in a distant folder or location, all I have to do (if I've forgotten its name but remember it as "handy") is set up the Find File to search on comments for the word *handy*. That's the search criterion I set up in Figure 6-4.

Figure 6-4:
The search criterion in the Find File utility.

Find File
Find items   on all disks ▾   whose
comments ▾   contain ▾   handy
More Choices   Find

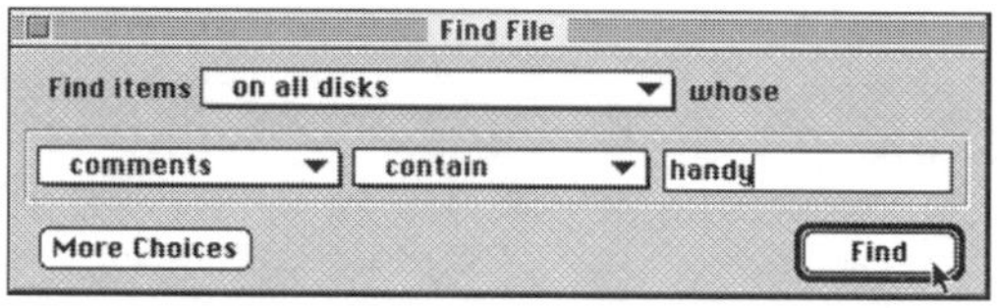

And presto! There it is. The utility has found my file, shown in Figure 6-5, just by searching the comments and looking for the word handy. Neat, huh?

Figure 6-5:
Items found in the Find File utility.

Items Found
Name   Size Kind   Last Modified
Personal Address Book   93K FileMaker Pro 3.0 docum... 10/14/95   9:22 AM
Tom's New HardDisk
Desktop Folder
FileMakerPro3.0/Book
Found 1 Item

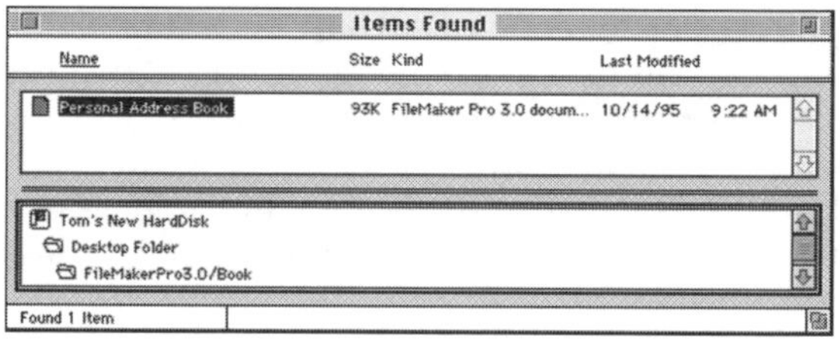

If you work with a version of the Mac OS before System 7.5.3, then be careful. If you rebuild your desktop, which is something you ought to do every couple of months or if you're troubleshooting a problem, you lose all the information in that little Comments box. Don't ask me why, but you do. So you want to be sure that you don't have truly valuable data in that Comments box. (Incidentally, to rebuild your desktop, you simply hold down the ⌘ and Option keys at startup. For the intricacies of rebuilding your desktop, check out David Pogue's witty masterpiece, *Macs For Dummies*, 5th Edition, published by IDG Books Worldwide, Inc.)

Using this utility, which comes with your Macintosh operating system, practically guarantees that you won't lose a file that's scattered somewhere on your hard drive. Of course, I'm not recommending the Zen approach for everybody (I don't use it myself), but I know how easily we can all fall into it. The Find File utility is your little Swiss Army knife. Use it wisely to get out of jams, but don't cut your fingers with it. Is that Zen, or what?

Zen and the art of finding a file in Windows 95

The Windows Find utility is similar in purpose to the Mac's Find File utility: to find that file that you know you created but, for all you know, may well be sipping a piña colada on a little island at the edge of your hard drive. The Windows 95 way of accomplishing this is different enough from the Mac method, however, to deserve special attention.

To find a wayward FileMaker Pro file on your Windows computer:

1. Choose Start⇨Find⇨Files or Folders.

The Start button is on the taskbar, which is at the bottom of your screen by default. When you have completed this step, you see the Find dialog box, as shown in Figure 6-6.

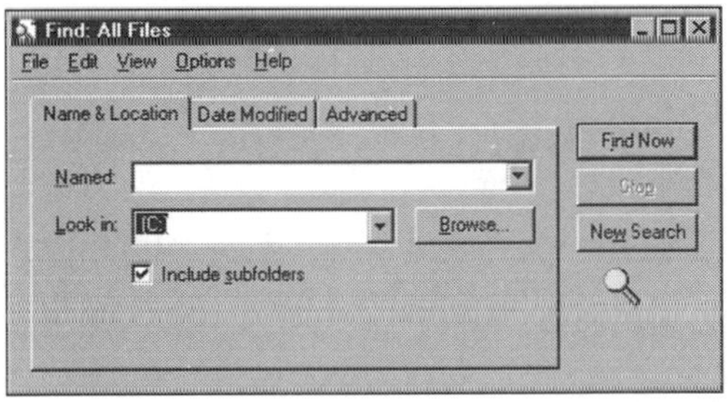

Figure 6-6:
The
Windows
Find
dialog box.

2. On the Name & Location tab, check to make sure that the Look In box contains (C:).

C: is what Windows 95 calls your hard drive by default; it's really one of the last reminders of the bad old days of DOS remaining since Windows 95 came out.

3. Ensure that the Include Subfolders check box is selected.

These settings check your entire hard drive for the file you want.

Of course, if you know the exact name of the file you are looking for, you can just enter it in the Named text box and click Find Now. But if you are like me, you have only the vaguest recollection of what you may have named that database file months ago, but you know it when you see it. I'm going on this assumption.

4. Click the Advanced tab.

5. Click the down arrow at the right side of the Of Type list box to reveal the list.

6. **Scroll down the list until you find the** FileMaker Pro 4.0 Database **item and select it.**

   The Find dialog box should now look like Figure 6-7.

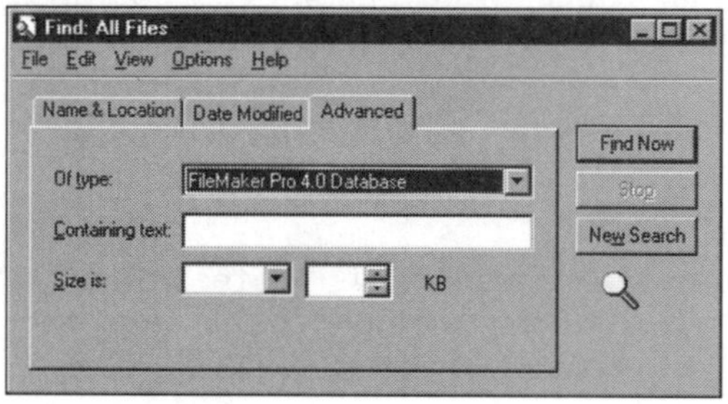

Figure 6-7:
The Advanced tab of the Find dialog box when you search for FileMaker Pro 4.0 database files.

7. **If you know some text that appears in the file, enter it in the Containing Text box.**

   Entering text in the Containing Text box is a way-cool option for limiting your search, especially now that there are so many templates that come with FileMaker Pro. The great thing about the Containing Text box is that Windows doesn't require you to do any extra work to make your files easy to find (like filling in summaries of your database with special keywords). If you can remember some text, like a name or address that appears in your database, the Find utility can find it, along with all the other FileMaker Pro 4.0 databases that contain that text. Neat, huh?

8. **Click the Find Now button.**

   The Find utility displays the results of the search in the window at the bottom of the Find dialog box, as shown in Figure 6-8. Of course, your results will look different from mine (unless you happen to be my long-lost twin who thinks and names databases just like I do).

   You can launch the file by double-clicking its icon in the results box.

If you are thrilled and delighted by the Windows Find utility, or if you want to find out why C: isn't just an item on a proctologist's To-Do list, pick up a copy of Andy Rathbone's fun and informative introduction to Windows 95, *Windows 95 For Dummies,* 2nd Edition, published by IDG Books Worldwide, Inc.

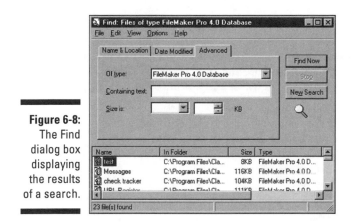

Figure 6-8:
The Find
dialog box
displaying
the results
of a search.

The Other Way of Organizing

The other way of organizing is, not surprisingly, the exact opposite of the Zen way. It's the more logical, systematic way of organizing your FileMaker Pro files. I don't think a specific methodology exists, however. Nobody, except perhaps a nerdy systems analyst with time on his hands, has really formulated any technique for taking 100 files, for example, and putting them together perfectly in one folder, or many folders, so that you always know where they are and so that they'll never be lost on your hard drive.

If you can figure out such a technique, better patent it quickly and make it into a commercial product. I'll be the first to buy it.

The fact of the matter remains that your files will be saved in one place or another on your hard drive. There's no getting around that. How you lay out those files on the Macintosh or Windows Desktop or in folders is still very much a matter of individual taste and preference. In other words, I doubt that two people ever organize their files in the same way.

Groupings and hierarchies of files

Every method of organizing your files involves, more than likely, two things:

✔ **Some form of grouping, either by type or by category.**

For example, doesn't grouping all your business files in one folder and your personal files in another make sense? Well, yes and no. The files may be related, and you may want access to them from the same folder. And yet, some form of grouping is necessary. Scattering them about randomly on your desktop makes no sense, does it?

Ideally, you want to organize your database by projects, departments, or perhaps categories (for example, art, products, contacts, and so on).

The bottom line is to organize your files in a way in which you can easily find and work with them.

✔ **A hierarchy of folders, with different levels,** similar to what you would find in an outline with different level headings using Roman numerals I, II, III, followed by A, B, C, and so on.

This organization sounds like the perfect solution, doesn't it? Yet the only way to visualize this method of organization is to see your files in folders within folders within folders. I'm sure you've come across stuff where you have to open five or six folders within folders to get to what you want.

A tree structure

If it helps, you may want to organize your files in some sort of tree structure, with folders of related files branching to other folders. This isn't really that hard to do, and makes sense as an organizing principle for your database. You can better visualize and retrieve information when you think of it this way — in other words, as a tree with appropriate branches that lead you to the files you want.

I prefer something that's a little like a tree, probably more like a pyramid, to organize my FileMaker Pro files. You can see it in Figure 6-9. The application icon is at the top of the folder (a departure for many folks I know who like to put all their Macintosh applications in a separate folder on the desktop, named, naturally, Apps). Anyway, working my way down from the FileMaker Pro icon, I get a sort of branching to Examples and Templates and then, further down, to my own databases: To Do, Home Inventory, Contacts, and Personal Address Book.

This structure seems to work for me and tends to reflect how I see myself navigating through the seas of my own FileMaker Pro files.

Figure 6-9:
The modified tree or pyramid structure for organizing your files.

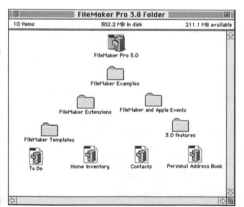

Part II
Doing It

The 5th Wave   By Rich Tennant

"I TOLD HIM WE WERE LOOKING FOR SOFTWARE THAT WOULD GIVE US GREATER PRODUCTIVITY, SO HE SOLD ME A DATABASE THAT CAME WITH THESE SIGNS."

In this part . . .

You've heard that Nike commercial where the message is to just do it. This is the part where you do it, that is, start *really* working with FileMaker Pro. You can get in the thick of things, designing and building the FileMaker Pro database of your dreams. You can start working with the tools that are available, and you can start to make things happen.

Chapter 7
Creating Your Dream Database

his chapter is the shortest one in the book. And for a simple reason: Rather than tell you how to design the database of your dreams, I assume that you've already started to do so and that you just need a little prodding to get your design to the next level.

Designing a database that works for you is like cooking a good meal. You need to have an idea of the ultimate taste you want, the ingredients you need to get that taste, the quantity of each ingredient, and the time needed to mix, match, and cook those ingredients. Notice that I'm working backward here — well, sort of.

The same technique ought to apply to database design. Start with the big picture and then work backward to see how you can achieve it.

The Magic Formula

No magic formula exists for designing the perfect database with FileMaker Pro. However, you may want to keep in mind a few general rules.

Rule #1: Simplicity

Keep it simple. If you're too ambitious with your design, you may end up with a cluttered beast, unwieldy and difficult to navigate.

Rule #2: The right metaphor

Find the metaphor that works for you. Then build on it. If you like Rolodexes and like to organize and retrieve your data that way, go with a Rolodex metaphor. But realize that you have more freedom and flexibility in the electronic world than you do with the old paper-based Rolodexes. Take a Rolodex and think about what you can add to it.

Where do you find good metaphors? Well, that depends on the kind of database you're building. If you need to catalog your CD collection, you can simulate the buttons on a CD player in your FileMaker Pro database and use them to navigate through the titles in your catalog. If your database is a collection of automotive parts, you can find a way to emulate a parts catalog. Be imaginative and ask yourself how you want to see the data in your database represented visually. There's really no formula here; whatever works for you is best.

If you look around, you'll notice immediately that you're living in a veritable sea of images and metaphors. That sea is called *advertising*. Copywriters get paid the big bucks to come up with cute phrases, visual puns, and metaphors. Remember that somewhere out there, you'll find a single metaphor that's appropriate for your database; you just have to be patient and keep fishing in that informational sea before you can reel it in.

Rule #3: Cool buttons to navigate

Think about how you're going to navigate your database. FileMaker Pro lets you drop buttons on your files, and each button can have a script that makes the button do what you want it to do. In any early design, on paper, try to think about the buttons that will take you to different locations in your database. You may want to check out Chapter 22 on the magic of scripting, which explains all the neat things you can make your buttons do.

Three Examples: The Good, The Bad, and The Ugly

No database is really bad if it works for you, so maybe I'm overstating the case here with a few of these examples.

The good

I like the first screen from the database example in Figure 7-1. This database is a catalog of FileMaker Pro resources. The three buttons in the lower portion of the screen that let you browse and get more information are good. The design here is straightforward; the typography is strong and visually exciting.

The main screen of your database really sets the stage for what's to come and establishes the look and feel you want, plus visual clues to whoever is going to use the database.

Defining your FileMaker Pro database metaphor early on is particularly important because the metaphor sends a set of visual clues to the user of that database. A good metaphor tells the user instantly if the database is friendly — easy to work with and navigate around in. We tend to think more visually than we realize. Information gets communicated much faster by visual symbols than by just text in fields.

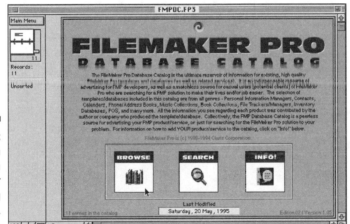

Figure 7-1:
The main screen of a FileMaker Pro catalog database.

The bad and the ugly

From the main screen in Figure 7-1, you go to the first screen with records in another database, which you can see in Figure 7-2. From my perspective, this screen is too cluttered. The records have so many fields that the information overwhelms you. The buttons at the bottom are out of alignment, and the screen has just too many buttons to take in all at once. This screen is a classic case of information overload.

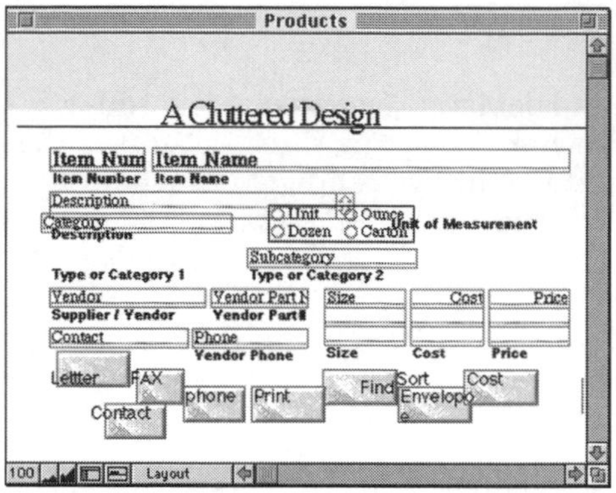

Figure 7-2:
The screen
from poorly
designed
database
with an
over-
whelming
number of
fields and
buttons.

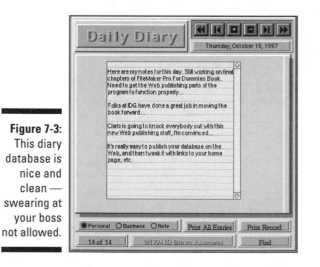

More of the good

Rather than concentrating on the bad, I thought it was better to show you more examples of good databases.

The screen you see in Figure 7-3 is from a Daily Diary FileMaker Pro database. It's cleanly designed and easy to navigate. The buttons are self-explanatory. Conceptually, the idea of using a diary as a database metaphor is novel: Normally, you wouldn't think of doing that. I like this design.

Figure 7-3:
This diary
database is
nice and
clean —
swearing at
your boss
not allowed.

A little bit of everything

Figure 7-4 is a screen from a FileMaker Pro database that uses a modified Rolodex as its central metaphor. Some of it I like, and some I don't. You can see that the Rolodex has tabs along the right side that take you to other files on People, Sales, and so on. This feature is cool. But it's not really a Rolodex, or at least the metaphor is confusing to me. I prefer something less cluttered and cleaner in design. I dislike getting bombarded with a lot of buttons — in this case, tabs — all at once.

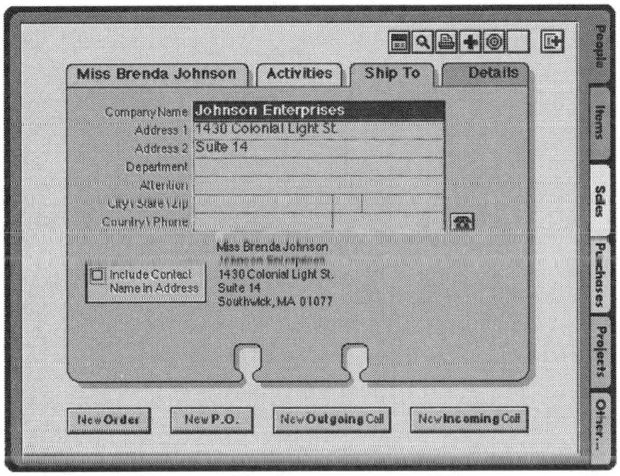

Figure 7-4: The database design has potential, but. . . .

A Few Questions to Ask When You're Dreaming Up Your Own Design

Here are a few questions you need to think about when creating your own design:

✔ Ask yourself how you want the database to look. How do you see it in your mind's eye? What's the visual metaphor you want?

✔ What information — important stuff — do you really need to store in your database? What are the essentials?

✔ How can you break up that information into smaller and smaller pieces? For example, last name, first name, street address, city, zip, phone number, and so on.

✔ Do you want to publish your database on the Web? The FileMaker Pro 4 Instant Web Publishing feature allows you to create a database that Web surfers using Netscape Navigator or Microsoft Internet Explorer can view, search, sort, or even edit.

Because many styles, backgrounds, and colors that you use ordinarily in a FileMaker Pro database don't appear when that database lands on the Web, you may want to go for a Standard layout. Using clean and simple layouts, with table and form views of your data, is better than getting too fancy. Find out more about plain vanilla layouts in Chapter 11.

Asking yourself questions about what you want to do with your database and sketching your design on paper with a couple of workable visual metaphors are steps that ready you to define your database. Getting your ideas together ahead of time saves you false starts and wasted time when you

✔ Define the fields that contain the data in your design (discussed in Chapter 8).

✔ Plan the layouts for your database (laid out in Chapters 9 through 14).

Chapter 8
Fields of Dreams

• •

• •

Farming is hard work, but straightforward. You plant the fields, irrigate them, and then let them grow as Mother Nature (and you) intended. Planting fields in your database with FileMaker Pro is a little harder, but not dissimilar. You have to figure out what types of fields you want and what exactly you want to put into them.

In Part II of this book, you're working the farm, as it were. "Doing It" is what I'm calling this section of the book. It's time. The planting must begin. And the first place to start is with those fields. What will the crop be this year? What fields do you want to plant in your database? Now, if you've done your homework (I'm hopeful that you have) and if you've already made an effort to conceptualize your database (see Chapter 7), those fields will indeed be your fields of dreams. Read on.

Before Defining Those Fields

You can think of fields as little storage bins for the various types of information your FileMaker Pro database holds. As a result, they need to be sturdy and well built. You're going to rely on them not only to store data but also to search for and sort the records that make up your database. That capability is the beauty of well-defined fields: You can find things quickly (search) and arrange them in a particular order (sort) that suits your needs. Fields in FileMaker Pro let you do both — and a whole lot more.

Now, if you haven't started conceptualizing the fields you want in your database, you may want to follow these steps:

1. **Plan out your fields on paper first.**

   Or if you prefer, use your favorite word processor or outline processor and start listing the types of information that you want to put in each field.

2. **Write down what you want to store (or "plant") in your fields.**

   For example, do you want to store the information that you have on business cards you've collected?

3. **Break down that information, such as the data you have on a business card, into specific fields — such as last name, first name, street address, city, state, zip, phone number, fax number, and so on.**

   Each of these data items requires a separate field. Trim and refine the list as much as possible to get to the essentials of what you really want to store and retrieve in your FileMaker Pro database. Remember that you're breaking down the information into smaller and smaller chunks, and each of your fields represents a chunk.

   Keep those fields small and as specific as possible. For example, make the first and last names of people separate fields in your FileMaker Pro database. That way, you can search and sort on those fields when you look up information. Likewise, make the fields for addresses — for example, street, city, state, zip code — separate rather than all lumped together. This advice is pretty obvious stuff.

4. **Determine how, what, and why you want to name each of those fields, and then . . . name that field!**

   No, this isn't a TV quiz show. You don't want to be guessing about what a field name really means. Names are very important, and you should consider them carefully because the field names you define appear in all your dialog boxes and in your layouts. Names need to be specific and to the point (you can always change the names later, but it can be a hassle, as well as confusing).

A technical term exists for what you're doing with fields; it's called *making field definitions.* A field definition comprises the name of the field, its type, and the options you have for entering data that is associated with the field.

Whether your database is large or small, loaded with records or not, the value of the information you have in it depends, in one way or another, on how clearly and intelligently you define its fields. So you may want to give yourself some extra time to think those field definitions through. You've moved up to the big time; everything counts.

Defining Those Fields

When you have a list of field definitions for your FileMaker Pro database, you're ready to rock 'n' roll. Remember that FileMaker Pro is going to hit you suddenly, unexpectedly — big-time — with this huge, empty dialog box that you find in Figure 8-1.

> ✔ To get to that dialog box, you can choose File⇨Fields⇨Define. If you're on a Mac, go for the keyboard shortcut, ⌘+Shift+D, which is a good one to remember. Under Windows, the keyboard shortcut is Ctrl+Shift+D. Use either ⌘+Shift+D or Ctrl+Shift+D to define fields for an existing file.
>
> ✔ To create fields for a new file, choose File⇨New. A dialog box appears with two choices: Click either the Create a New File Using a Template radio button or the Create a New Empty File radio button.

In this case, I decided to create a new empty file. After choosing between the two option buttons, you can name your new file and confront the big Define Fields dialog box.

What I've done, for starters, is create a new database by choosing File⇨New and entering the name Tom's New Address Book in the dialog box that opens next. You have to give your database a name before you can start defining fields and then save it. In Windows, you want to save it with the .fm extension, which makes life easier in keeping track of your FileMaker Pro databases and in sharing those databases. Now you're getting ready to plant those fields.

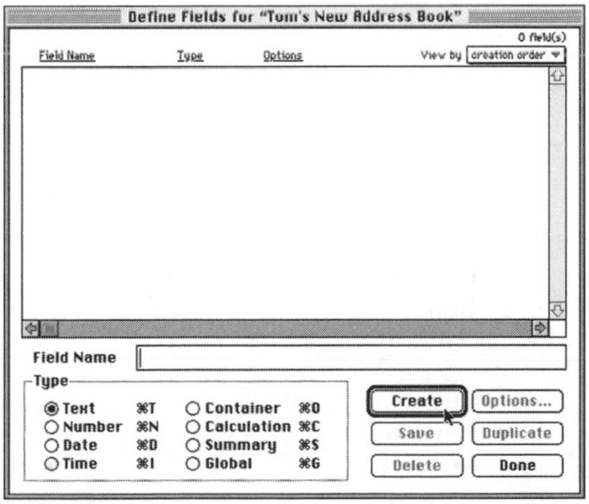

Figure 8-1:
The big, almost daunting Define Fields dialog box in FileMaker Pro.

Now's the time to swing into action and do your stuff:

1. **Type in the Field Name you want — for example,** Last Name.

   If you type in **Last Name**, you ought to leave the Text radio button highlighted because a Last Name field is going to be a Text field, not a Number or Calculation field.

2. **Click Create.**

   The dialog box changes to show you your new field, as in Figure 8-2.

As you continue to add more fields to your database, you eventually get a screen showing what your database looks like. For example, if you create an address book, your screen may look something like Figure 8-3.

You're really planting those fields now. When you're finished adding fields, just click the Done button at the lower right of the dialog box. FileMaker Pro now shows you the fruits of your labor by listing those new fields in long, rectangular boxes. FileMaker Pro puts you in Browse mode, ready to begin entering data into those fields. Don't worry if the field boxes aren't large enough or long enough to contain the data.

Each time you add a new field to your database, notice that the new field shows up on Layout #1, which is the standard default FileMaker Pro layout. You can find that Layout #1 in the upper-left corner of your screen. The thing to keep in mind is that Layout #1 isn't the only layout choice you have for your database; it's just what FileMaker Pro defaults to. It's there to get you started. (For more details, you may want to check out Chapter 14.)

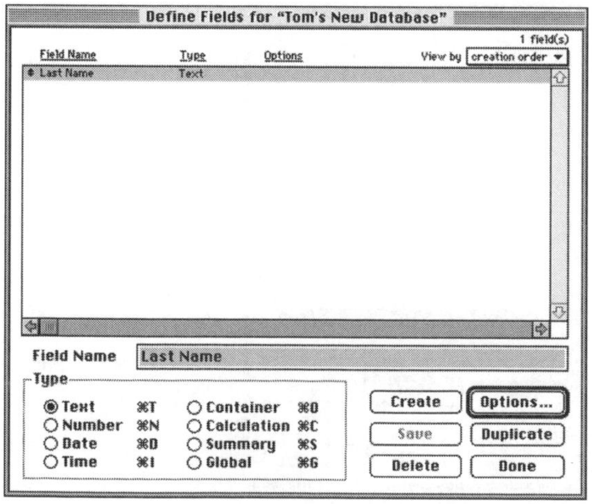

Figure 8-2:
Congratula-
tions!
You've
named that
first field!

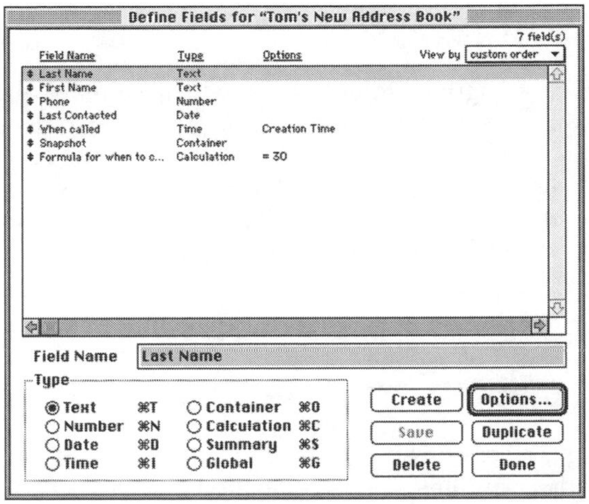

Figure 8-3:
Tom's New
Address
Book, now
filled up
with some
field names.

Okay, you're in Browse mode (check the mode selector at the bottom of the screen to be sure) and yet a Layout #1 designation is staring at you from the upper-left corner of the screen. Don't worry. FileMaker Pro is just helping you along by naming the layout for you. Later, you can always change the name of the layout.

You can also modify the layout — moving the fields around on-screen and stretching and rearranging them with FileMaker Pro's robust set of layout tools — which I talk about in Chapter 9. For the moment, keep your focus on defining those fields.

FileMaker Pro offers you as many as eight different field types to choose from (unless you're still using FileMaker Pro 2.1, which offers seven. This ought to be enough to meet all your needs. The hard part is figuring out which field type is appropriate to the database you've designed. You can find out more in the section "Field Types for Every Occasion," coming up later in this chapter.

The Field-Naming Game

FileMaker Pro has some rules you must follow, too. Listen up, class. I didn't make up any of these rules myself.

Limits on field length

FileMaker Pro limits the length of a field name to 60 characters. In the Define Fields dialog box, you see that long, rectangular name box to the right of the name. Well, it only takes 60 characters. I can't think of when you would name a field in your database longer than 60 characters, except, wait a minute. . . . How about this for a field name: **The names of all the people I have known over the past 20 years** (oops — 63 characters). You get the idea.

Other restrictions

You can't search or sort on records if those records are made up entirely of Container fields. Those Container fields typically have QuickTime movies, pictures, or sound files that you've imported into your database. Obviously, sorting on a picture or sound can be a bit difficult. But if you're cool about it, you can work around the restriction by adding a Text or Number field right next to the Container field. That way, you can search or sort on those pictures or sounds.

When you enter a date in the Date field, you have to enter both month and day. If you don't enter the year, FileMaker Pro makes the assumption that you want the current year in the Date field. If you want just the week or year, pick another field type instead, such as Text or Number.

In the Time field, the times can include any slice of time you want — for example, seconds, minutes, or hours.

Field Types for Every Occasion

Here's a list of the eight field types in FileMaker Pro and what you can do with each one of them.

Text fields

Text fields store, not surprisingly, text — anything from a single character up to 64,000 characters (just to give you an idea of scale, 64,000 characters make up about 45 pages of text at about 250 words per page). Text fields can be big — you can use them to store form letters, product descriptions, and reviews of books, records, and documents. Think of this field as a huge storage bin for text documents and information you want to store, search, and retrieve.

In an office, you can use the Text field to keep a record of the employment history of each person working at your company. At home, you can use this field to store text about your family history or to use as a personal diary. At school, you can store classroom papers you've written or other projects.

The beauty of FileMaker Pro is that you can search text entered into a Text field really fast, and I mean almost instantaneously. To get this fast-searching engine going, however, you must first specify that you want to index that particular text field.

To index a field (for fast searching and retrieval of your text), follow these steps:

1. **In the Define Fields dialog box, after naming your field and clicking the Text radio button, click Create, and then click Options.**

   A dialog box opens up with the Entry Options for the field you've named.

2. **At the bottom of the Entry Options dialog box, click Storage Options.**

   Another dialog box opens, with two radio buttons that let you specify whether you want FileMaker Pro to turn indexing *on* or *off* in the field you've named.

3. **Click On and then click OK.**

Number fields

Number fields let you store up to 255 characters. The characters, however, have to be on one line only. You can't press the Return key and add another line as you can with Text fields. You can insert dollar signs, decimal points, or percent symbols in this type of field.

Date fields

Date fields are neat. You store one date at a time, and you can modify the format of the date. This field has to include at least the day and month portion (*dd* and *mm*) of a date. FileMaker Pro indexes the dates in this field, so you can search for a particular date or a range of dates. With FileMaker Pro, you can sort your records based on a Date field and use Date fields in formulas specified in Calculation and Summary fields. You can sort Date fields chronologically from earliest to latest or latest to earliest dates, depending on the sort order that you specify.

Time fields

A Time field stores one specific time and contains the hours, minutes, and seconds portion *(hh, mm,* and *ss)* of a particular time. As with Date fields, you can sort your records based on a Time field and use Time fields in formulas for Calculation and for Summary fields. Again like Date fields, you can sort Time fields chronologically from earliest to latest or latest to earliest dates, depending on the sort order that you specify. If you want to modify or customize the format of the Time field, you can choose Format⇨ Time Format.

FileMaker Pro indexes each Time field so you can search or sort on a specific time or a range of times.

Container fields

Container fields are definitely way cool. You can use them to store graphics, sounds, or QuickTime movies in your database. With Windows, you can also store an OLE (object linking and embedding) object, if you choose. Think Container fields when you want to store those types of data.

QuickTime movies are not stored within the database. Instead, FileMaker Pro uses a special *pointer,* which is like an arrow that is pointing to the folder where the movies reside, to locate and play the movies.

Because the movies aren't actually *in* the database, however, you have a potential pitfall to avoid. If, for example, you want to pass along to a friend a database of your favorite QuickTime movie clips, you need to make sure that the actual QuickTime movies are also included. Otherwise, the movies won't make the trip.

Another gotcha: If you're thinking about publishing your database on the Web with Version 4's Web Companion Instant Publishing features, you can't include QuickTime or QuickTime for Windows movies. Web Companion for Version 4 doesn't support publishing QuickTime movies, which is too bad. But you never know: Things may change in the future.

FileMaker Pro doesn't let you search or sort records if those records are based on Container fields. So that restriction may be something you want to keep in mind if you're using them. The trick is to define Text fields to describe or identify the Container fields. Then you can search and sort your records based on the text describing the contents of the Container field, or better yet, by specifying a number in the field's value.

Calculation fields

The Calculation field is a bit tricky. It stores the result of a calculation made by FileMaker Pro. You can create a formula in a Calculation field by using functions, constants, or the information in other fields in the same record. You can get values for your formulas from any of the following types of fields: Text, Number, Date, Time, or other Calculation fields. After you click the Calculation Field radio button and the Create button in the Define Fields dialog box, you see a new dialog box. Figure 8-4 shows you what happens if you click the Create button in the Define Fields dialog box; the Specify Calculation dialog box opens to let you set up a formula for calculating the information in your field.

You can use a Calculation field if you want to calculate a result from values in other fields in the current record (or from other related records).

Summary fields

You use Summary fields when you want to compute a value for a field over a group of records (to compute a value for fields within the same record, use a Calculation field). You can use a list of predefined formulas for a Summary field, including Total, Average, Count, Minimum, Maximum, Standard Deviation, and Fraction of Total.

The result in a Summary field is the result of the records you're browsing. Using a Summary field produces a result that uses values in more than one record in your database.

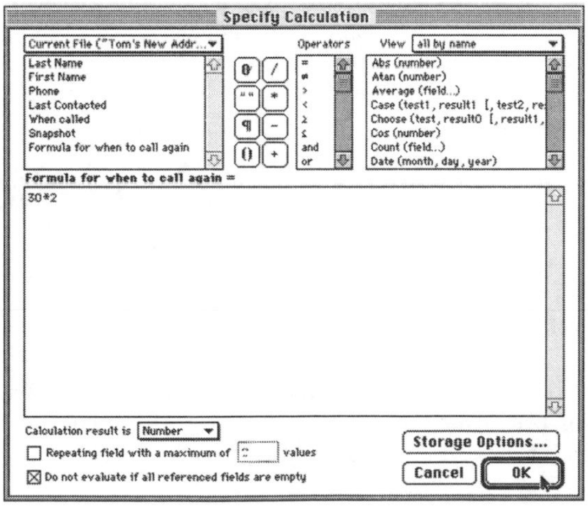

Figure 8-4:
The Specify
Calculation
dialog box
that you
access by
clicking the
Options
button
in the
Calculation
Field dialog
box.

The world according to functions

I'm assuming that you don't aim to be a mathematician or computer scientist, so this definition of *function* relates only to FileMaker Pro. A *function* is a predefined formula that performs a certain calculation for you and results in (or *returns*, to use the technical term) a specific value. Functions are incredibly useful because you can just type the function and let FileMaker Pro calculate the result of the function. You can also combine functions with other functions or expressions to do even fancier calculations.

Functions in FileMaker Pro use the following syntax: *Function name(parameter)*. Some functions need two or more parameters, as, for example, in Position(LastName,"Tm",1,1). The other thing you can do with a function is called *nesting*. That means you can embed one function within another function to perform even more complex calculations on your data. Take a look at this nested function in FileMaker Pro: Left(Name,Position(Name, ","1,1)). A *Position* function is nested in a *Left* function.

In defining Summary fields, you have to keep in mind that the value in the field depends on the layout part in which you place the Summary field. For more on this aspect of Summary fields, check out Chapter 9.

Global fields

Each Global field contains one value that's used for all the records in your database. A Global field can be text, number, date, time, or container. For example, you might want this one value to represent the mortgage rate on a home loan, so you specify this as 7.55 percent and use this value as a fixed value in your calculations in all your records.

Oh, Those Many Defining Field Options

Options and more options are what you get when you define each field type. But hey, what's life in the database world without a few choices? Better some than none at all, right?

After you enter a field name, select a field type (from one of the eight radio buttons on the lower portion of the Define Fields dialog box), and click Create, you see the Options button highlighted (refer to Figure 8-2). Follow these steps:

1. Click Options.

The dialog box you see in Figure 8-5 appears.

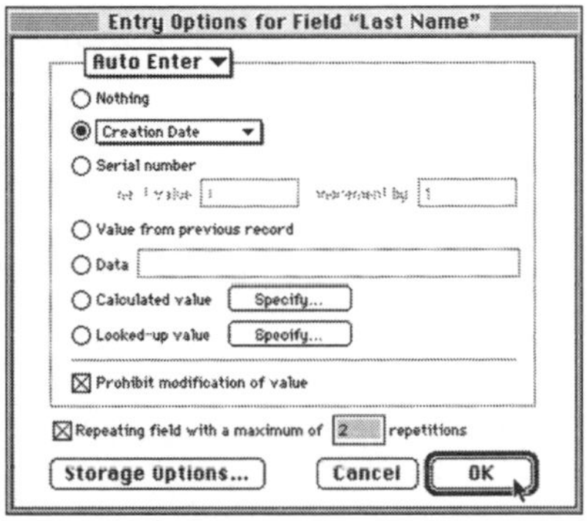

Figure 8-5:
The Entry
Options
dialog box
for a
particular
field.

2. In the Entry Options dialog box, choose the type of entry options you want to set from the pop-up menu at the top of the dialog box.

You have two choices: Auto Enter and Validation.

- **Auto Enter:** FileMaker Pro automatically enters a default value in the selected field (with a range of 0 up to 255 characters) for each record in your file. I won't try to explain all the options here, except to say that you ought to click the Creation Date box for the field you've defined, to help keep track of when you've created a particular field in your file.

- **Validation:** You can have the data in your field checked against the validation requirements that you've set for that field in each record. Figure 8-6 shows you a dialog box with the Validation selections. Don't let these options confuse you. Some options are for security purposes and are very useful if you're working with FileMaker Pro in an office where your database is networked. See Chapter 18 for more details about working in a networked office.

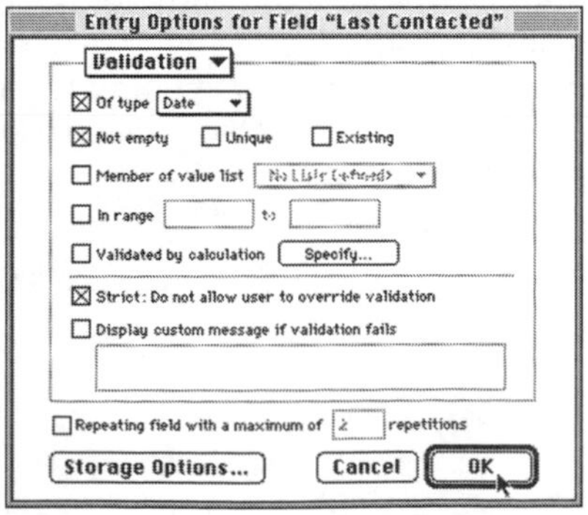

Figure 8-6:
The
Validation
Options
dialog box.

3. Click Storage Options at the bottom of the Entry Options dialog box.

The dialog box in Figure 8-7 appears.

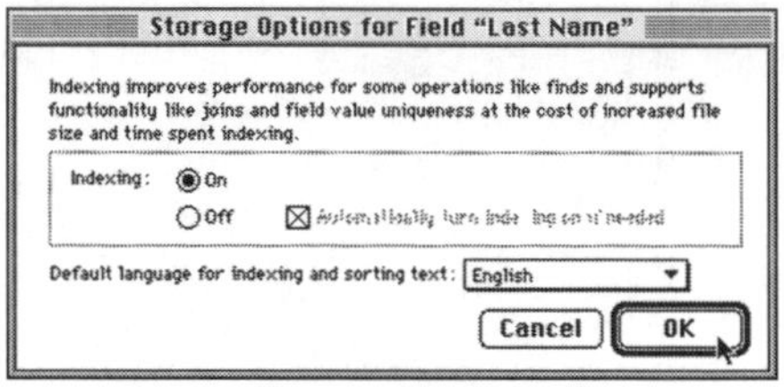

Figure 8-7:
The Storage
Options
dialog box.

> **Storage Options for Field "Last Name"**
>
> Indexing improves performance for some operations like finds and supports
> functionality like joins and field value uniqueness at the cost of increased file
> size and time spent indexing.
>
> Indexing: ● On
>   ○ Off   ☒ Automatically turn index ing on if needed
>
> Default language for indexing and sorting text: English
>
>   Cancel   OK

Now you have yet another option: namely, whether to index the information in the field that you've defined. Indexing is essential if you're going to work with related files, or set up a relational database (which is explained in Chapters 5 and 23). FileMaker Pro warns you that this may make performance sluggish, especially if you have a large file with many records. Still, indexing speeds up your searches.

The beauty of indexing is that you can index each value in a field (that is, each value in all the field types except Container, Summary, and Global fields). This way, FileMaker Pro can perform its magic of finding, matching, validating, and sorting data a great deal faster than if you don't index. However, what's called a *performance hit* may occur when FileMaker Pro performs this magic on large files. Because of indexing, sorting through your records just may take a bit longer.

4. Click the Yes radio button if you want indexing turned on for a particular field; then click OK.

This action takes you back to the Entry Options dialog box for the field that you've chosen.

5. Click OK, and you return to the large Define Fields dialog box.

6. When you're satisfied that you've defined the fields you want, click Done.

Where this dialog box was once empty, it's now full with fields that you've defined and options you've exercised, as you see in Figure 8-8. You now have a well-planted set of fields. At the very least, it's a beginning to the long season. Before you can harvest the crop, however, you need to know more about the FileMaker Pro tools at your disposal.

Figure 8-8:
The well-
planted
fields of
Tom's New
Address
Book, with
a variety of
fields and
options
defined.

```
Define Fields for "Tom's New Address Book"
                                              7 field(s)
Field Name        Type         Options          View by custom order ▼
◆ Last Name       Text         Indexed, Creation Date, Can't Modify Auto, Repeating
◆ First Name      Text
◆ Phone           Number
◆ Last Contacted  Date
◆ When called     Time         Creation Time
◆ Snapshot        Container
◆ Formula for when to c...  Calculation    = 30

Field Name   [Last Name]
Type
  ● Text      ⌘T   ○ Container   ⌘O      [ Create ]  [ Options... ]
  ○ Number    ⌘N   ○ Calculation ⌘C      [ Save ]    [ Duplicate ]
  ○ Date      ⌘D   ○ Summary     ⌘S
  ○ Time      ⌘I   ○ Global      ⌘G      [ Delete ]  [ Done ]
```

Deleting Those Fields of Dreams

Here's where you have to be careful. You've added and defined a bunch of fields, but then decide you don't need them. They already have bits and pieces of data in them, but so what? You go ahead and delete them. What happens?

Deleting a field from your file means that you permanently delete the field definition and all the data in that field in all your records. You won't be able to retrieve it again. What's gone is gone. So before you get carried away with deleting fields from your files, step back for a moment and think things through. Are you certain that you don't need any of the information contained in that field?

I mention this consideration because as you get proficient at working with FileMaker Pro layouts (which come up Chapter 9), you discover how easily you can delete a field without thinking of the consequences. I know: been there, done that. So watch your step!

The other thing to keep in mind is that if you change the definition of a field that contains data, you probably end up losing all or most of the data in that field. The same thing occurs if you change the field type from, for example, Text to Calculation, Summary, or Global. If you do, you lose all the data permanently and forever.

Chapter 9

Laying Out All the Cool Stuff in Your Database

In This Chapter

▶ Meeting the layout screen

▶ Getting personal with the layout tools

▶ Digging out the dirt on text formatting

All right, now's the time to put on your graphic designer cap. Here's where you lay out the fields in your FileMaker Pro database and make them look visually pleasing, as well as functionally useful, for viewing, reporting, or just finding your data. Form follows function — or is it the other way around?

I don't mean that you have to be a graphic designer to get the job done. I've seen databases that are badly laid out — visual dogs — and yet are still useful to their owners. Nonetheless, putting some thought into how you want your FileMaker Pro database to look is helpful. With any look, of course, comes a feel. And that look and feel is important, especially if somebody else will have to use your database and navigate through it on a day-to-day basis.

Design is a subjective thing; everyone can agree on that. In this chapter, I don't try to transform you into a world-class industrial designer with million-dollar accounts. All I want to do here is walk you through the toolset that FileMaker Pro provides for you to do layouts. Stick around.

Getting to Know Layouts

Before getting into FileMaker Pro's handy set of layout tools, I want to mention some things that layouts can let you do.

- ✔ **Add** lots of neat buttons, graphic images, and, of course, text.

- ✔ **Change** one layout without messing up the data in your records or any other layouts in your files.

- ✔ **Create** different views of your FileMaker Pro database — for example, one layout for entering a new record, another for creating a summary report, and still another for printing the records in your database. You're never stuck with just one layout.

- ✔ **Define** how you see data and the way it's organized.

- ✔ **Design** exactly how you want your records to print and what you want them to look like in terms of fonts and formats.

- ✔ **Display** the information or data you've put into fields.

- ✔ **Establish** relationships to other files and databases using the Portal tool in FileMaker Pro (no, this relationship stuff isn't a dating game; the relationships I'm talking about here are strictly platonic, just data in fields). For more information on establishing relationships between files and databases, make sure you check out Chapters 5 and 23.

- ✔ **Lay out** your database on either the Mac or Windows platform and have the layout look the same on the other platform.

- ✔ **Make** a separate layout for publishing your database on the World Wide Web by using the FileMaker Pro Web Companion, which is available in FileMaker Pro 4.

If you're thinking about publishing your FileMaker Pro database on the Web — a neat idea — keep in mind that you may have to tweak your layouts a bit, using the options available to you with the FileMaker Pro Web Companion. You may have to do some custom HTML work with Web Companion to make sure that Web browsers properly display your graphics and text. The FileMaker Pro Web Companion has Instant Web Publishing options that make publishing your FileMaker Pro database on the Web as easy and seamless as possible, but layouts — especially when you have to convert your graphics to GIFs and JPEG images — may require special attention. (For a complete explanation of FileMaker Pro's Web publishing capabilities, look at Chapters 20 and 21.)

- ✔ **Move** your fields around on-screen.

- ✔ **Show** all the fields you define.

- ✔ **Summarize** the data in your database so that you can print out a nifty summary report for yourself or your boss.

Using the Big Layout Screen

When you define the fields in your database and see the fruits of your labor in Browse mode, how does FileMaker Pro know where to lay out all that stuff? Well, it uses what's called a *predefined layout.* Your fields automatically fall into the places FileMaker Pro already designated for you. (It has to put them somewhere, doesn't it?)

But guess what? That predefined layout isn't set in stone. You can modify it once you shift gears and move into Layout mode.

To get to Layout mode, you have a couple of navigational choices, as you see in Figures 9-1 and 9-2:

  ✔ Choose Mode⇨Layout from the menu bar.

  ✔ Click the mode selector at the bottom of your screen and click the Layout menu item.

Note: You don't need to have a particular screen open to get to Layout mode. You can switch to Layout mode from Browse, Find, or Preview mode.

Figure 9-1:
The Mode menu selected from the menu bar in your FileMaker Pro database.

Mode	Show	Arrang
Browse		⌘B
Find		⌘F
✓Layout		⌘L
Preview		⌘U
New Layout...		⌘N
Duplicate Layout		
Delete Layout		⌘F
Layout Setup...		
Part Setup...		
Set Layout Order...		
Set Tab Order...		
Set Rulers...		

Figure 9-2:
The mode selector at the bottom of your screen.

Once you're in Layout mode, you can find the big layout screen with all those nifty tools I was hinting at. Figure 9-3 shows you the big screen for a simple address book database that I build in Chapter 1. Table 9-1 explains the different items that make up any database screen.

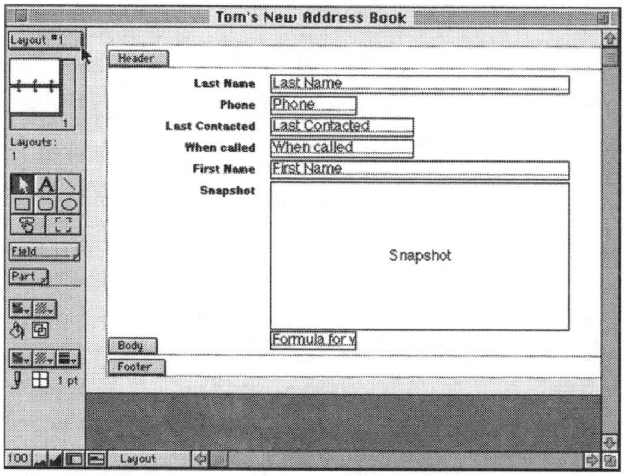

Figure 9-3: The big screen with all the FileMaker Pro layout tools in full view.

Table 9-1	FileMaker Pro Screen Items
Screen Item	**Description**
Text	Obviously, words you use for your titles, column headings, labels, instructions, and any form letters you want to produce
Fields	Those rectangular slots you use for entering and viewing your data
Parts	The elements of a layout, including headers, body, footers, and summaries
Graphic objects	Lines, rectangles, rounded rectangles, ovals, and other graphics that you use in your layout
Page	The current page setup, the printer you choose, and the layout type, which help you define how your data will look when printed

Here are the key points you want to keep in mind about what to do with all these elements on the big screen in Layout mode:

✔ Text elements let you create column headings, titles, labels, and so on.

✔ Fields let you enter and display your data.

✔ Parts let you define headers, footers, the layout body, and summaries. Every layout must include at least one part; it doesn't matter which part.

✔ Graphic objects let you add lines, rectangles, rounded rectangles, ovals, and pictures to your layout.

✔ The layout page, which every layout includes, lets you define your printer, page setup, and layout type. Just as in word processing, the page determines how your data will appear on a printed page.

If you need to print the data in your layout and you're using a Mac, open the Chooser (which you can find on the Apple menu) and click the icon that represents your printer. Once you've selected your printer, you'll want to click Page Setup from the File menu and then select from the options in the Page Setup dialog box. If you're using Windows, choose File➪Print Setup; in the dialog box that pops up, select from the set of options specific to your printer. FileMaker Pro uses this information — your printer and your page setup — when determining the boundaries and measurements of your layout. Check out Chapter 17, which talks about printing issues, if you plan to print out copies of your database.

FileMaker Pro limits the size of your layout: 110 inches x 110 inches. That's a layout of almost 9 feet x 9 feet. I've yet to see anything that enormous. To test layouts of that size, the folks at Claris probably use the screen at a football stadium between instant replays.

Layout Tools Up Close

Zoom in for a moment on the tools in your FileMaker Pro layout. Figure 9-4 shows you the Tool panel on the left side of your screen.

Figure 9-4:
The
FileMaker
Pro Tool
panel.

At the very top of your screen is a button labeled `Layout #1` — the default layout name for your file, which is what FileMaker Pro does if you decide to give your layout a specific name. You can change that name as you add more layouts to your database, or you can choose from other predefined FileMaker Pro layouts. (Check out Chapter 11 for a lot more information on using "predefined" layouts.)

Just below the Layout button is the FileMaker Pro Book icon, which is also a button. You can see it in Figure 9-5. If you have multiple records or layouts, clicking the Book icon lets you flip through your records or layouts while a number in the icon's right corner identifies the record or layout you've landed on.

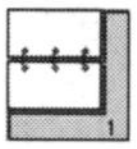

Figure 9-5:
The
FileMaker
Pro Book
icon.

I find this FileMaker Pro Book icon (or button) very handy, indeed. Because I like the feel of flipping pages, I guess, I use it often to cruise through my records, browsing and viewing them as I go along. The Book icon is like a cross between a mini-Rolodex and a spiral notebook. It's there with you no matter which of the four FileMaker Pro modes you're in — Browse, Find, Layout, or Preview. And it's always telling you which record or layout you've landed on.

The Two Most Frequently Used Tools

Below the FileMaker Pro Book icon are eight FileMaker Pro tools in a little Tool panel that you should become familiar with. Two of them — the Pointer and the Text tools — are among the most frequently used, and these two are the ones I want to talk about in this chapter. You can see them in Figure 9-6.

The next chapter gets into the other tools so that you're not overwhelmed with all these tools at once. Chapter 13 also explains more about how to use these tools.

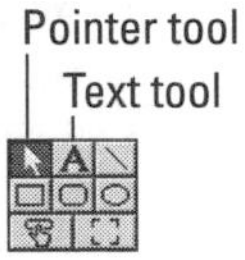

Figure 9-6:
The Pointer and Text tools in the Tool panel.

Pointer tool

Text tool

The Pointer tool

The tool in the upper left that appears pressed in or *activated* in Figure 9-6 is the Pointer tool. You use this tool frequently because it lets you point to and click all the graphic objects in your layout and move them around. It's also the FileMaker Pro *default* tool, the one that is automatically highlighted when you move into Layout mode.

The Text tool

Next to the Pointer tool, just to the right of it, is the Text tool, the one with the big A on it. (No, it's not a bad letter, like the one worn by the heroine in Hawthorne's *The Scarlet Letter*. This letter does nothing but good.)

Click the Text tool, and you can add a text object to your layout. It's one of the most powerful — and most frequently used — tools in FileMaker Pro because it gives you tremendous control over the size, style, line spacing, color, and alignment of any text you place into layouts.

The Text tool serves a double purpose. You can use it to enter text into a Text field, and you can use it to add text to your existing layout where you think text may be appropriate.

After you click the Text tool, you can select the font, size, style, alignment, line spacing, and even color of the text from the Format menu before you begin typing. That way, you're assured of getting just the right look for your text in your layouts. Pretty nifty, wouldn't you say? Give it a try.

I like the Text tool because you can use it to edit the text in your fields while you're in Layout mode. You can change the font, size, or color of the text. Just click the big A and move your cursor into the field you want to modify. You can drag your mouse to select the text, and edit the text on your keyboard to your heart's content.

After you add text to the body of your layout, you can see that text on every record. What really appears is a *text object*. Think of a text object as capable of containing a variety of styles, fonts, colors, spacing, and so on. Those things are the *attributes* of the text object. You drop text into your layouts just as you would drop a circle, an oval, or another graphic object.

You see a *bounding box* — a rectangle with dotted borders — appear when you add a text object to your layout, as Figure 9-7 shows. The box is automatically sized according to the point size of the text you enter. This box doesn't appear, however, when you print your records. The bounding box also doesn't appear in Browse or Preview mode. It's there to guide you and indicate the size of the text object you're working with.

Figure 9-7:
The bounding box for the text objects.

This is the Text|

If you want to add text to your layout, follow these steps:

1. **Click the Text tool in the Tool panel.**

   The pointer changes to a cursor with an insertion point.

2. **Click the place in your layout where you want to add text.**

3. **Type the text.**

   Your cursor moves from left to right as you type. If you want to move down a line, just press Enter.

Oh, the Things You Can Do with Text

The fun doesn't stop after you click the Text tool and click the place in your layout where you want to insert that text. You can do a variety of things with that text to enhance the readability and visual impact of your FileMaker Pro layouts. Here are just a few of your options.

Changing fonts

If you want to change the font of the text that you enter, follow these steps:

1. **In Layout mode, choose Format⇨Fonts.**

2. **Click the font you want from the submenu, as shown in Figure 9-8.**

   The fonts displayed are the ones you have installed on your system. Select any one that you prefer for your layout (though unless you have a budding career as a code breaker, the Symbols font may not prove very useful).

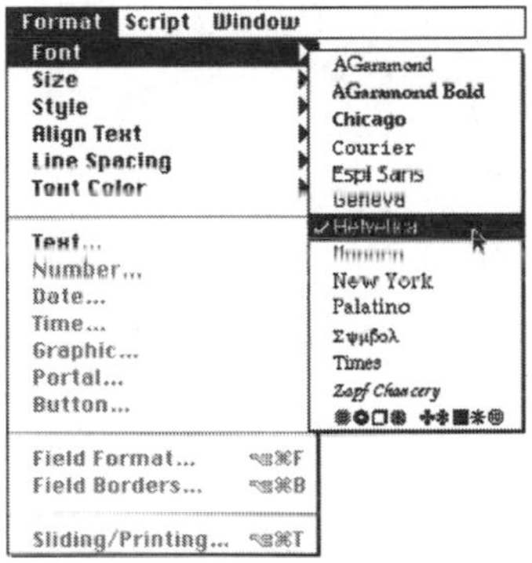

Figure 9-8:
The Fonts
submenu.

Format Script Window
Font ▸
Size ▸
Style ▸
Align Text ▸
Line Spacing ▸
Text Color ▸
Text...
Number...
Date...
Time...
Graphic...
Portal...
Button...
Field Format... ⌘F
Field Borders... ⌘B
Sliding/Printing... ⌘T

Font submenu: AGaramond, AGaramond Bold, Chicago, Courier, Espi Sans, Geneva, Helvetica, Ηππππ, New York, Palatino, Σψμβολ, Times, Zapf Chancery, ✴☯▢✦ ✦✚■✱☯

In Windows, you can choose Format⇨Fonts⇨Configure/More Fonts to select the specific fonts that you want to use in your FileMaker Pro layouts. This saves you from having to deal with a long list of all the fonts available to you. Use this feature to simplify the number of fonts you want to use in your layout design.

Changing the size of fonts

If you want to change the size of the text in your layout, follow these steps:

1. **In Layout mode on the Mac, choose Format⇨Size.**

2. **Click the size you want from the submenu, as shown in Figure 9-9.**

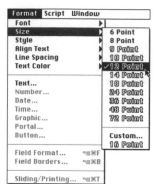

Changing the style of fonts

If you want to change the style of the text in your layout, follow these steps:

1. **In Layout mode, choose Format⇨Style.**

2. **Click the style you want from the submenu, as shown in Figure 9-10.**

   The folks at Claris are kind enough to show you what to expect when you select a Style submenu item. If you choose Style⇨Condense or Style⇨Extend, you either compress or expand the letter spacing in your text. Extend is useful if you want to stretch out a word for better readability or as a special graphic effect. I've often thought that the Extend feature would have been nice to have in college, when I was trying to stretch two pages into a five-page essay.

Changing text alignment

If you want to change the text alignment in your layout follow these steps:

1. **In Layout mode, choose Format⇨Align Text.**
2. **Click the text alignment you want from the submenu, which is shown in Figure 9-11.**

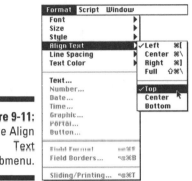

Figure 9-11:
The Align
Text
submenu.

Changing the line spacing of text

If you want to change the line spacing of the text in your layout, follow these steps:

1. **In Layout mode, choose Format⇨Line Spacing.**
2. **Click the line spacing you want from the submenu, which you can find right here in Figure 9-12.**

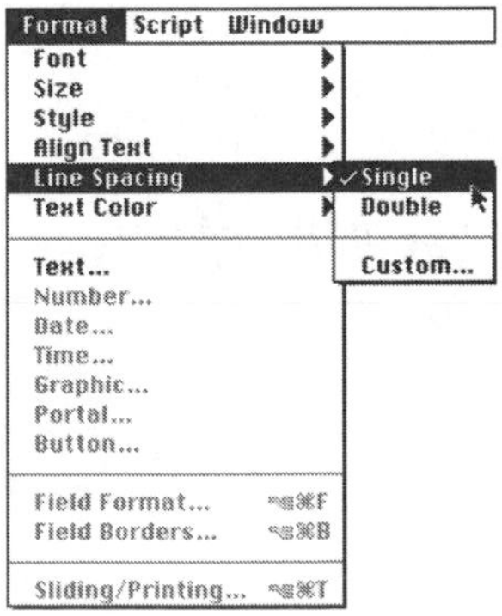

Figure 9-12:
The Line
Spacing
submenu.

Changing the text color

If you want to change the color of the text in your layout, follow these steps:

1. **In Layout mode, choose Format⇨Text Color.**

2. **Click the text color you want from the submenu, as shown in Figure 9-13.**

   Take my word for it, you have a few more colors to choose from than gray, gray, and gray.

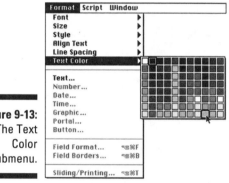

Figure 9-13: The Text Color submenu.

Changing text all at once

Doing all this stuff at once — changing the font, size, style, text alignment, line spacing, and text color of your layout — isn't difficult. What you can do is set the *default text format* that you want. That way, every time you type in a text box in your layout, the text has the font, size, style, alignment, and color you want.

You can't change the actual, existing text (the characters and words) in your fields all at once, but you can change all the default formatting of your text (the *appearance* of the characters and words).

To set or change all the layout text attributes of the fields you select, follow these steps:

1. **Start with no text selected.**

2. **Select the text object that you want to change, or create a new text object with the Text tool.**

3. In Layout mode, choose Format⇨Text.

The Default Text Format dialog box on the Mac, shown in Figure 9-14, appears. You see all the options you have to choose from there. Check out the Sample box in the lower-left portion of the dialog box to find out how your choices will display on your layout.

After you make your selections in the Default Text Format dialog box, your selections determine the way text will appear in the fields you define and add later on.

Figure 9-14:
The Default
Text Format
dialog box
on the Mac.

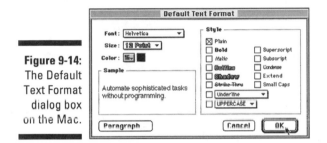

Pasting in the hot stuff

After you've made the text in your FileMaker Pro layout look cool in the font, size, style, and color you want, you can do another thing or two to enhance your layout. I'm not talking about its visual look and feel right now, but rather about its content — that is, the information you want to display on each record. And it's really simple: You can paste in the date, time, and user name, or symbols, that is, (//) for the date, two colons (::) for the time, or two vertical lines (| |) for the user name for each.

To paste in the date, time, or user name, follow these steps:

1. Choose Edit⇨Paste Special.

2. Click the option you want on the submenu shown in Figure 9-15.

FileMaker Pro inserts two slashes (//) for the date, two colons (::) for the time, or two vertical lines (| |) for the user name. When you browse, preview, or print the records, these symbols are replaced with the actual updated date, time, and user name, which your computer stores internally.

You can also paste in the actual page number by following these steps:

1. Choose Edit⇨Paste Special.

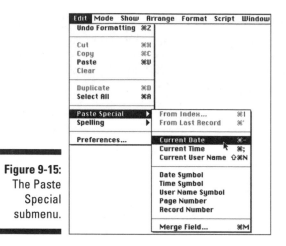

Figure 9-15:
The Paste
Special
submenu.

2. Click the Page Number option on the submenu.

What happens is that FileMaker Pro puts two number symbols (##) in your layout. And when you print or preview the records in your database, it replaces the number symbols with the actual page numbers.

You can do the same thing — that is, follow the same procedure — to insert a record number into your layout. Numbering is useful to keep track of your records, particularly if you have 50 to 100 records or more. It helps a lot.

Chapter 10

More Cool Tools for Laying Out Your Stuff

In This Chapter

▶ Meeting the layout tools: ovals, rounded rectangles, lines and all that

▶ Actually drawing in a database program, what a concept!

▶ Adding pictures for impact

▶ Importing your very own picture

I like tools and templates. That fact should be pretty obvious by now if you've checked out any of the other chapters in this book. I'm always looking for ways to make things simpler and better, and any tool that helps in the process wins my approval.

For a long time in the database world, layout tools were practically unheard of. You punched in your data, generated records, built a database, and that was that. With FileMaker Pro, the world has changed. You have tools that let you draw, move, position, and resize graphic objects and place those objects anywhere you want on your FileMaker Pro layout. Neat, don't you think?

In this chapter, I show you some of the cool things you can do with graphic objects in FileMaker Pro.

Working with Your Layout Toolset

To access the nifty tools in FileMaker Pro, you have to be in Layout mode:

1. Open a database in which you've defined some fields (see Chapter 9), or open a FileMaker Pro template, such as the one found in Figure 10-1.

2. Choose Mode⇨Layout from the menu bar, or click the mode selector at the bottom of your screen and click Layout from the menu that appears.

You're now in Layout mode, where you find all the layout tools. Figure 10-2 shows you a FileMaker Pro template in Layout mode.

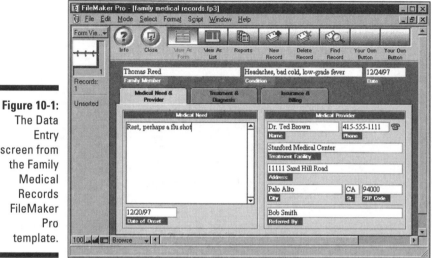

Figure 10-1: The Data Entry screen from the Family Medical Records FileMaker Pro template.

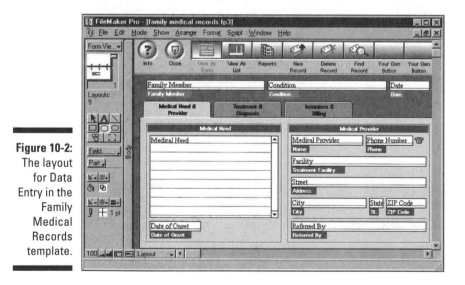

Figure 10-2: The layout for Data Entry in the Family Medical Records template.

You have eight tools to work with here. I discuss the two most frequently used tools, the Pointer and Text tools, in Chapter 10. Now I want to walk you through the other six layout tools to get you ready to create or modify your own layouts in FileMaker Pro.

Rules about tools

Before you get rolling with FileMaker Pro's layout tools, you ought to know a few things about them:

✔ If you want to use a tool, just click it to select it. After that, FileMaker Pro makes the tool gray and indented so that it looks like you've pushed a button to activate it — pretty standard operating procedure for most buttons in software programs. As soon as you start to draw an object with that tool, your mouse cursor changes back into a pointer.

✔ If you want to keep a particular tool selected, double-click it. The FileMaker Pro tool changes to a black color, showing you that it's going to stay selected until you change your mind and select another tool.

✔ To change from the tool you last used to the pointer, press Enter.

At times, you may want to keep the same tool selected each time you click. To do so, you can set your preferences in FileMaker Pro as they are set in the Layout Preferences dialog box shown in Figure 10-3.

To get to the Preferences dialog box, choose Edit➪Preferences. From the submenu, click Application. When the dialog box appears, click the General pop-up menu and click Layout. In the Layout dialog box, check the Always Lock Layout Tools box to activate this feature. FileMaker Pro retains that preference for you through all the layouts you work with on this file. For more about setting preferences, check out Chapter 3.

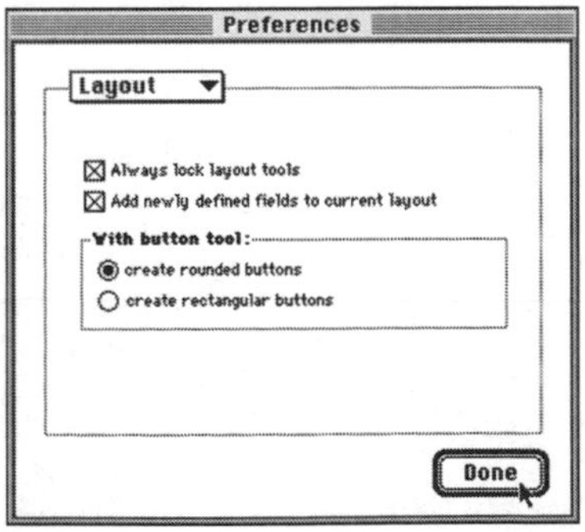

Figure 10-3:
The Layout Preferences dialog box lets you lock on the tools in your layout.

```
================= Preferences =================
┌─────────────────────────────────────────────┐
│  Layout      ▼                                │
│                                               │
│  ⊠ Always lock layout tools                   │
│  ⊠ Add newly defined fields to current layout │
│  ┌─With button tool:─────────────────────────┐│
│  │ ◉ create rounded buttons                   ││
│  │ ○ create rectangular buttons               ││
│  └────────────────────────────────────────────┘│
│                                               │
│                                   ( Done )    │
└─────────────────────────────────────────────┘
```

That cool Line tool

To the right of the big A — the Text tool — is simply a Line tool. I don't know why I say *simply,* because here's a tool that can do wonders for your layouts. Okay, adding a line to one of your layouts may not be a big deal. But wait a minute. If you go to the Pen icon at the bottom of your toolset, you can select the width of the lines you want to draw. The widths can be anywhere from hairline to 12 points in thickness. Figure 10-4 shows you the choices you have to work with.

Look closely at Figure 10-4, which is a screen from an example Contact Manager database, and notice that I selected a nice, fat 7-point width for my pen line and placed it under the title Contact Manager. These lines, fat or skinny, 12-point or hairline, can be useful for emphasis in your layouts. You use them like you underline the important words in a book. Just a quick underline here or there in your layout can make a big difference in how you emphasize the importance of the data and fields in your records.

Not only can you change the width of the lines, but you can also add color to the lines and change their patterns. Just click the icons to the left of the width icon, and you get the different pen palettes. Color, in particular, can make a big difference in the readability and visual impact of your layout. But if possible, go easy on the number of colors you use. Two or three should be your maximum; otherwise, your layouts may look clunky or out of whack. Use color sparingly.

Figure 10-4:
Line
thicknesses
you can use.

The Rectangle, Rounded Rectangle, and Oval tools

I call the next set of layout tools in your FileMaker Pro Tool panel — the Rectangle, Rounded Rectangle, and Oval tools — the "middle three." You can find them in Figure 10-5.

Figure 10-5:
The "middle three," or the Rectangle, Rounded Rectangle, and Oval tools.

Rectangle tool

Oval tool

Rounded Rectangle tool

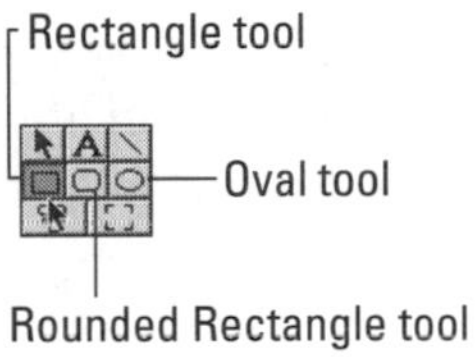

"Now what the heck can I do with these rectangles, rounded rectangles, and ovals in my layout?" you may be asking. It's a good question. My answer is that you should probably wait until you've gotten farther along in designing and laying out your database before dropping in ovals and rectangles. You may see the need for an oval in one of your records, for example, or in the main menu screen, where graphics are more important than in just your data entry screens and you want to jazz up the look of your database. As for rounded rectangles, they're perfect for creating graphic buttons to which you can attach a script that lets you perform a whole array of actions, such as sorting, finding, or moving from one record to another. Check out Chapter 22 for details about buttons and scripting their actions.

When you click these tools, your cursor changes to a crosshair, which you can then use to draw.

Drawing is pretty easy because, as in other Macintosh or Windows graphics programs, you can automatically create an oval or rectangle by clicking your mouse and dragging the crosshair across the layout. The crosshair becomes an oval or rectangle. This is all very intuitive stuff and pretty typical for any graphics or paint program. Give yourself time to get used to the feel of actually drawing in a database program (I know that may feel a bit odd) and keep in mind that whatever you draw isn't set in stone: It can be easily changed, modified or deleted if you're not happy with the results. My advice is just to place the cursor at the center of your layout and start drawing your ovals or rectangles from there.

You can use these ovals and rectangles to create separate sections for easy reference in your FileMaker Pro database. For example, in an invoice form, you can use the rectangles on your data entry screen to indicate sections for "bill to" and "send to."

Think of the middle three as your touch-up tools. You can use them to add the finishing touches to your FileMaker Pro database.

 Just as with the Line tool, you can use the Pen and Fill tools, located below the Tool panel at the very bottom of your screen, to enhance the image of a rectangle, rounded rectangle, or oval in your layout by adding color, patterns, or various thicknesses to your lines. Don't be afraid to experiment a little and try out these tools. Remember that these shapes are objects on your layout: If you don't like them or if you change your mind about using them, you can always delete them and start over.

Oh, in case you're wondering about the other tools in the Tool panel, I haven't forgotten about them; they're just not covered here. The following list tells you where I have deviously hidden them:

You use the *Field tool* to define fields in your layout. Look in Chapters 9 and 14 for the scoop.

You use the *Part tool* to add headers and footers to your layout. Check out Chapter 12.

You use the *Button tool* in script making. Find out about this stuff in Chapter 22.

You use the *Portal tool* when you design relational databases. Beam yourself to Chapter 23.

While You're at It, Why Not Add a Picture?

Scientists have been telling us for some time that we think visually as much, if not more, than we think verbally. A FileMaker Pro database without anything graphic or visual in its layout can be very dull indeed. No one expects you to be a graphic designer or superstar illustrator when building a database. But to ignore the visual element in your database is a big mistake, particularly if others are going to access, store, and retrieve information from your database.

You'll have no difficulty building up a visual library of images and pictures that can be useful in your database. FileMaker Pro lets you easily add a picture on your layout wherever you want. You just copy a picture onto the Macintosh or Windows Clipboard from another application or from your Mac Scrapbook and paste that picture into your layout. Figure 10-6 shows you an image dropped into a Contacts template.

Figure 10-6:
A picture of
a car
dropped
into your
layout, just
for fun.

After pasting the picture in, you can position the image anywhere you want, and resize it to fit the needs of your layout.

Copying and pasting a picture on your layout is pretty straightforward; just use the standard Copy and Paste options on the Edit menu or use the keyboard shortcuts, ⌘+C and ⌘+V on the Mac or Ctrl+C and Ctrl+V in Windows. Obviously, you want the picture to be appropriate to the design and structure of your FileMaker Pro database. I'm not suggesting that you copy and paste in pictures randomly or just for fun. Well, come to think of it, there's nothing wrong with a little fun now and then, is there?

Oh, don't forget one handy reason to add art to your database: You can always copy and paste your company logo onto your layouts.

You also have another option for putting pictures in your layouts — you can import them:

1. **Choose File⇨Import/Export.**

2. **Click Import Picture, as shown in Figure 10-7.**

3. **In the selection dialog box that appears (as shown in Figure 10-8), select the image that you want to import.**

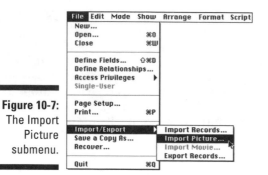

Figure 10-7:
The Import
Picture
submenu.

Notice that FileMaker Pro gives you a list of available types of graphic images you can import. This list is important because, as you can see in Figure 10-8, you have only a certain set of graphic file formats to choose from. So if the image or picture isn't one of those listed, you won't be able to bring it into your layout. Table 10-1 gives you the complete list of graphic file formats for both Mac and Windows platforms.

Table 10-1	FileMaker Pro Graphic Images You Can Import
Mac	*Windows*
GIF	Compuserve GIF [*.GIF]
JPEG	JPEG [*.JPG]
PICT	Macintosh PICT [*.PCT]
TIFF	Tagged Image File Format [*.TIF]
	Aldus/Windows Metafile [.WMF]
AutoCAD [DXF][MacLink]	
	AutocadSlide [*.SLD]
	Computer Graphics Metafile [*.CGM]
EPSF	Encapsulated PostScript [.EPS]
HarvardGraphics [CGM][MacLink]	
Lotus Freelance [CGM][MacLink]	
Lotus[PIC][MacLink]	Lotus Picture [*.PIC]
MacPaint	MacPaint [*.MAC]
PC PaintBrush[PCX][MacLink]	Zsoft Paintbrush [*.PCX]
Ventura Image [IMG] [MacLink]	

Mac	Windows
Ventura LineArt [GEM] [MacLink]	
Windows BitMap [BMP][MacLink]	Windows Bitmap [*.BMP]
WordPerfect Graphics [MacLink]	

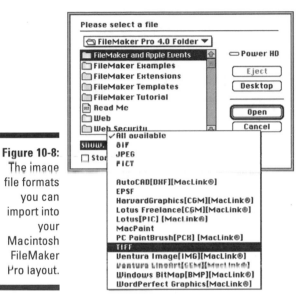

Figure 10-8:
The image
file formats
you can
import into
your
Macintosh
FileMaker
Pro layout.

FileMaker Pro 4 supports a much larger number of graphic file formats than FileMaker Pro 3, including GIF and JPEG, which represent the lion's share of graphics displayed on the Web. That's good news for those of you who are looking to publish your database on the Web by using FileMaker Pro's Web Companion. My hat is off to Claris for extending the number of supported file formats on both Mac and Windows computers. This extended support makes life much easier in a networked environment that has both Macs and Windows PCs, because you want to be sure that the graphics from one computer are displayed properly on another. Now if you're designing a FileMaker Pro database, you've also got the added advantage of importing lots of different pictures in different graphic file formats. That capability goes a long way, believe me, to making life easier in the computer world.

After you've imported a picture into your layout, you can do all the things with it that you can with any graphic object, that is, edit, crop, or resize the picture and position it by using the Pointer tool. As a graphic object, you can group it with other objects in your layout. You can also layer it, stacking objects on top of each other. Lots of cool things.

To find out how you can do more with graphic objects, check out Chapter 13.

Chapter 11

Plain Vanilla, or Predefined, Layouts You Can Choose

● ●

In This Chapter
▶ Using basic predefined layouts
▶ Going beyond basic predefined layouts

● ●

*Y*ou may be at a point in your work with FileMaker Pro where you can't afford to spend a great deal of time designing your own database from scratch. You have to start with the hard work of entering data in records. Save the fancy design for later. Just gimme the facts, Jack.

Well, you're in luck. FileMaker Pro comes with a set of what are called *predefined* layouts. No, you don't have to copy them from another floppy disk or go through some elaborate installation process to get them into your files. They're right there embedded in the program itself — and they're useful, though perhaps a bit plain vanilla in design.

Don't get me wrong. At times, I prefer plain vanilla myself — hold the toppings and rainbow sprinkles. Just the basics. The thing about these predefined layouts in FileMaker Pro is that you can build on them, modify them to your heart's content, and come out looking pretty darn good with your database.

Choosing Predefined Layouts

After you've defined the fields that you want in your file, FileMaker Pro automatically creates a layout for you. It's called a *standard layout,* with the fields appearing in the order in which you defined them.

A standard layout is fine, and it appears right there for you in Browse mode, ready when you are to take the data you want to enter.

But standard isn't the only predefined layout type available to you. Actually, you have six other layout types to choose from. If you want to use any of the other layout types, follow these steps:

1. **Open an existing FileMaker Pro template, or a database in which you've already defined your fields.**

2. **Choose Mode⇨Layout.**

   The mode changes to Layout.

3. **Choose Mode⇨New Layout.**

   The New Layout dialog box shown in Figure 11-1 appears.

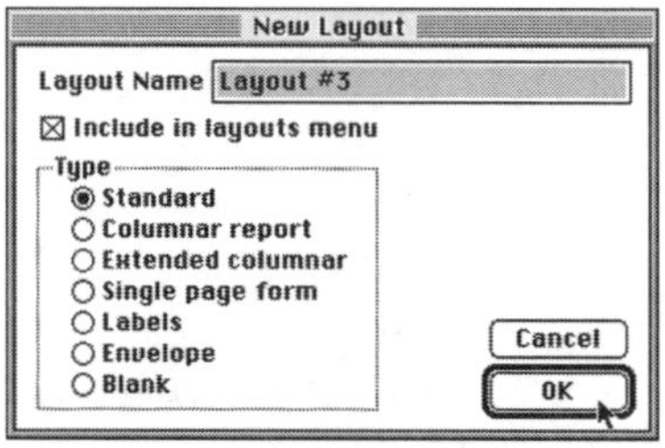

Figure 11-1:
The New
Layout
dialog box
with the
Standard
radio button
selected.

New Layout
Layout Name Layout #3
☒ Include in layouts menu
┌Type──────────────
⦿ Standard
○ Columnar report
○ Extended columnar
○ Single page form
○ Labels   Cancel
○ Envelope
○ Blank   OK

4. **If you want the standard predefined FileMaker Pro layout, click the Standard radio button and then click OK.**

What this dialog box lets you do, of course, is create a brand-new layout for your database. You have the predefined FileMaker Pro types to choose from, or you can simply click the Blank radio button as your type.

Note that you can also enter the name of that layout in the Layout Name box. If you don't enter a name, FileMaker Pro simply adds a number to each layout in your file. In effect, FileMaker Pro does the naming of your layout for you by number.

I recommend staying, at least when you're starting, with the numbering that FileMaker Pro supplies for you. You can always change that layout name later, if you want to. The name you choose has no effect on the layout template itself. You're just saving a layout version of your file.

The standard thing

The standard layout is pretty straightforward and obvious. All the fields in your database file are lined up in the exact order in which you defined them in the Define Fields dialog box, as rectangles in a hierarchy. What you see on-screen is one record. In that layout, you also have a body and a blank header and footer. Figure 11-2 gives you a good picture of the standard layout in a small Personal Address Book database.

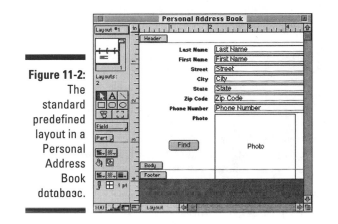

Figure 11-2:
The standard predefined layout in a Personal Address Book database.

Now just because this layout is called standard predefined doesn't mean you can't modify it. In fact, the beauty of a plain vanilla standard layout is that it's a good starting point for your layout; everything's neatly lined up and positioned. So, if and when you're ready, you can go into your layout and pick up those fields you've defined and move them around as you want.

How do you pick them up and move them around? Well, it's no magic trick. You just use the Pointer tool to click the rectangles and highlight them. Then with the Pointer tool, you can drag them by the lines to whatever location is appropriate on your layout. Clicking the corners of those fields resizes them. For more detail on using layout tools, take a look at Chapter 10.

If you're starting out with FileMaker Pro, nothing's wrong with just working with a standard layout. That's what I prefer to do. From there, you can get fancy and modify your layouts, moving all the fields around and adding borders and graphic objects.

The single page form

This predefined layout is a model of simplicity. To use the single page form as one of your predefined layouts, follow these steps:

1. **Choose Mode⇨Layout; then choose Mode⇨New Layout.**

   The New Layout dialog box appears; you can see it in Figure 11-3.

2. **Click the Single Page Form radio button and then click OK.**

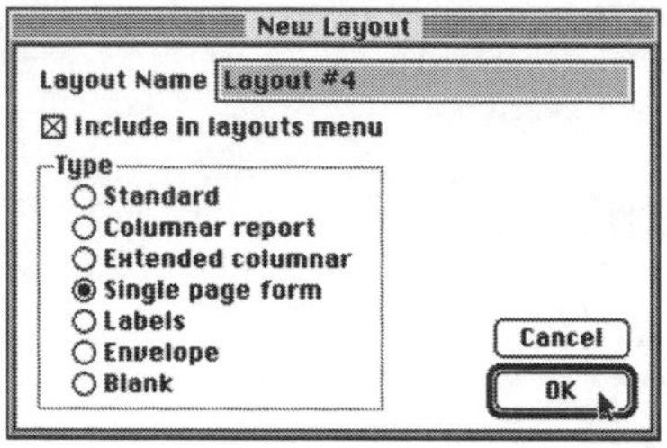

Figure 11-3:
The New
Layout
dialog box
with the
Single Page
Form radio
button
selected.

> **New Layout**
>
> **Layout Name** | Layout #4 |
>
> ☒ **Include in layouts menu**
>
> ┌─**Type**─────────────
> ○ **Standard**
> ○ **Columnar report**
> ○ **Extended columnar**
> ◉ **Single page form**
> ○ **Labels**
> ○ **Envelope**
> ○ **Blank**
>
> [Cancel]
> [**OK**]

The single page layout type provides you with exactly the same layout you get if you choose standard as your predefined layout type, but without the header and footer. This layout is fine because you don't need headers and footers if your form is only one page, right? All the fields that you've defined in the Define Fields dialog box are lined up in the order in which you originally created or later modified them. As with the standard layout, you get to see one record per page.

The single page form is pretty cool because, of course, it's the size of a single page. That's the way it prints, too.

Both standard and single page form layouts are ideal if you're doing a lot of browsing through your records, because you get to see the records one at a time. You also get to add records one at a time this way, which is, in my opinion, the most intuitive way of doing data entry.

Just because it's called a single page form doesn't mean, of course, that you're limited to just a single record in your database. (That would be a small database, indeed.) What it does mean is that all the records in your database are limited to just a single page each. That's nice if the information in your database fits neatly on single-page records. It also helps when you print the records, because each printed page corresponds to a single record.

There's a limitation here, of course, in that you can't display more than one record at a time. Also, if the information in a record doesn't fit neatly on a single page, you may not want to use this layout.

Staring at a blank layout

If you're really bold in your layouts, you can go the route of starting with a blank layout. I say *bold* because something is always formidable about staring at a blank layout. But wait a minute. This one isn't completely blank; you still have headers, body parts, and footers to work with. You just don't have the fields you defined in your Personal Address Book anywhere in view.

But you can do some things in that blank layout, and you definitely have some advantages in working with this predefined layout type because you've got more space to work with, more territory to populate with fields and buttons. (Kind of odd that a blank layout qualifies as predefined. The folks at Claris sure put a lot of effort into that. . . .) To use the blank layout, follow these steps:

1. **Choose Mode⇨Layout.**

2. **Once you're in Layout mode, choose Mode⇨New Layout.**

   The New Layout dialog box appears.

3. **Click the Blank radio button and then click OK.**

I probably shouldn't show you what that blank layout screen looks like, but I'm going to anyway. You can find it in Figure 11-4. (If you have trouble finding it, remember that it's blank!)

Figure 11-4:
A blank
layout
screen.

Now here's a blank layout you can build on. All you have to do is grab the Field tool on the Tool panel to start the ball rolling. Did I say *grab?* Yes, because on the Mac a little hand appears on-screen, and when you place the hand over the Field button and click the mouse, the hand "grabs" the field. It then lets you drag the field onto your layout and position it where you want.

Under Windows, you don't get a hand. Instead, you get an arrow with crosshairs, which is just as effective in grabbing a field and placing it where you want on your layout.

Note that the hand on the Mac appears only when you hover your cursor over the Field tool.

It all comes down to this: You grab a field with an animated hand or arrow with crosshairs, drag it to your layout, and plop it down to plant the seeds of your data. Fortunately, because all of this stuff is electronic, you don't have to wait til autumn for your harvest.

When you grab the field, the Specify Field dialog box shown in Figure 11-5 appears with a list of all the fields you've defined (in your Personal Address Book, for example). Even though you started with a blank layout, you still get to work with those fields you've defined, but selectively. This option is neat because you create a layout that contains only a certain number of your fields.

Figure 11-5:
The Specify Field dialog box listing the fields available in your current database.

Notice that I've selected Street in the Specify Field dialog box. When I select Street and click OK, my blank layout includes that field, just like the one in Figure 11-6.

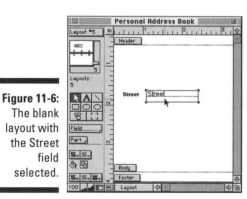

Figure 11-6:
The blank layout with the Street field selected.

If you want to see how your layout displays your data, just choose Mode⇨Browse and check it out. You can also pull down the Mode selector at the bottom of your screen and click Browse. In Browse mode, you see how that layout looks and works for your database. Personally, I like to toggle back and forth between Layout and Browse modes just to see how I'm progressing with my database and whether I need to make changes.

If you want to see how your layout is going to print, choose Mode⇨Preview or pull down the Mode selector and click Preview.

If you want to make a particular layout the one that opens every time you open your file, just choose Edit⇨Preferences⇨Document. The Document Preferences dialog box changes to let you set your document preferences, as in Figure 11-7. If you check the box Switch to Layout, you can set up your database so that it will automatically open to the layout you want. Pretty slick, I'd say. And useful.

Figure 11-7: The Document Preferences dialog box lets you specify which layout you want to open.

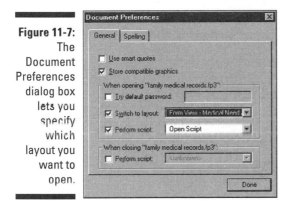

Columnar Report Layouts (Gasp!)

What do you do if you have many records in your database and you don't want to browse through them one at a time?

FileMaker Pro has an answer for you, and it's quite simple: the columnar and extended columnar predefined layouts. Don't be put off by the word *columnar*. I know it's a mouthful and a strain on anybody's jaw to pronounce. A tough word doesn't mean a tough layout to work with, however.

Columnar report layouts are easy to work with and perfect if you want to view and print more than one record at a time. You follow the same steps as you do for choosing the other layout types:

1. Once you're in Layout mode, choose Mode⇨New Layout.

The New Layout dialog box appears, yet again.

2. Click the Columnar report radio button and then click OK.

When you click that OK button, a new dialog box like the one in Figure 11-8 appears.

Now you can specify the order and the number of fields you want to display in your columnar report. But, and this is a big ol' *but,* the fields

Figure 11-8:
The Specify
Field Order
dialog
box for
columnar
reports.

you specify are now listed in columns. For example, all the first names
in your Personal Address Book are below the First Name field, which is
the heading of the column. Figure 11-9 shows an example of this layout.

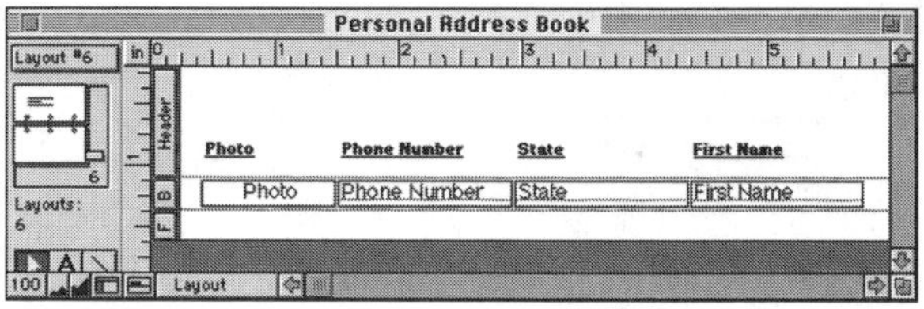

Figure 11-9:
The
columnar
report
layout.

Your fields are, in other words, displayed from left to right across the
body of your layout, in exactly the order in which you specified them. If
your field doesn't fit on a line, FileMaker Pro wraps it to the next line or
to multiple lines. Your field names are now column headings. Cool, eh?
This layout gives you another view of your data and is terrific for
printing out reports. You get to print the records in your database
much more easily than if you had to print one record at a time. Have I
made my case yet for using columnar report layouts? Hope you take
advantage of them.

Extended columnar layouts just take all the fields on a single line and stretch
them across the page. With extended columnar layouts, there are some
things you need to keep in mind:

 ✔ You don't have any wrapping of fields or stacked headings.

 ✔ Remember that any objects that go beyond the right edge of the page
   won't print.

 ✔ Extended columnar layouts are fine if the fields you've selected won't
   fit across the page and you want to modify those fields to make sure
   that the fields (and the data in them) fit on the page.

FileMaker Pro comes with two other predefined layouts that are important
for printing: the labels and envelope layouts. I talk about these layouts in
Chapter 17 on printing.

Chapter 12

Parts Is Parts (No More, No Less) in Your Layout

● ●

In This Chapter

▶ The parts scene: header, body, and footer parts

▶ Creating your own parts

▶ What you need to know about parts

● ●

*T*his chapter is the easiest one in the book to understand — well, almost the easiest. I mean, parts is (or is it *are*?) parts, right? And every layout has them. Lots of parts. When I talk about parts, I mean information that generally appears repeatedly in a word processing program: namely, headers and footers that include page numbers, titles, dates, and so on. FileMaker Pro lets you use parts when you want to repeat certain sections of your layout from one record or one layout to another. Useful stuff, indeed, I'd say.

You don't need to master all the things you can do with parts to do the work you have to do in your FileMaker Pro layouts. But you need to know what they are and how you can use them. Besides, every FileMaker Pro layout requires that you have at least one part.

The Parts Scene

Parts — where do they all come from and what do they mean? I'm glad you're asking philosophical questions. Actually, FileMaker Pro creates parts for you. Just follow these few steps, and you'll know what I'm talking about:

1. **Open a new or existing FileMaker Pro database by choosing File⇨New or File⇨Open.**

2. **Switch from Browse mode to Layout mode by choosing Mode⇨Layout.**

3. In Layout mode, choose Mode⇨New Layout.

4. When the New Layout dialog box appears, click the Blank radio button at the bottom of the box.

5. Click OK.

On your new blank layout, you find three parts automatically created for you, labeled Header, Body, and Footer. They appear as buttons at the far-left edge of your layout, positioned at the top, middle, and bottom of your layout.

Clicking the buttons for these parts highlights them; when they're highlighted, you can move them up and down on your layout to indicate how much space you want for each part. Note that you can only move them up and down, not left or right. A dotted line that extends the width of your layout appears below each Header, Body, and Footer part. This dotted line, which is like a slider, indicates the end of the amount of space for each part.

Every layout you work with in FileMaker Pro is divided into parts. Why? I thought you'd ask. Parts are how FileMaker Pro determines what to display in your layout and what to print. Depending on the parts you use, you specify what you want to print on each record and how frequently. That's pretty handy when you want to print only what's on the first page of a report or at the top of each page.

Essentially, parts break your layout into different sections. And into those different sections you can put a variety of FileMaker Pro objects, such as the following:

- Fields of any type
- Text in your layouts
- All kinds of objects that you can draw with FileMaker Pro tools, including lines, rectangles, and ovals
- Pictures, such as TIFF or EPS images (whatever you want to import or copy and paste into your layout)

You can pick and choose from these objects to make each part.

Now, these parts are great for putting your name, phone number, address, page number, or other fields that you want to repeat through all of your database files. The general rule is similar to what you encounter in a word-processing program: Headers and footers repeat information at the tops and bottoms of each page in your files.

Extending the definition of parts

If you've worked with any word-processing program, you'll find that working with parts in your FileMaker Pro database is similar to creating headers and footers in a text document on a Mac or Windows word processor. You use headers and footers in a word-processing program to repeat the same information, such as title, author, document number, or page number, on every page. There's no mystery about that.

The difference with FileMaker Pro, however, is that in addition to headers, body, and footers, you have other parts to choose from. These other parts include four different summary parts, which you can use to display information that's been calculated by a field. Summary parts are particularly handy if, for example, you want to display a summary at the beginning of a report. That summary will contain all the values for all records in a report. So what I'm saying is that parts aren't only headers, footers, and body — the ones you're familiar with from working with a word processor.

Header parts

If you look at the sample Expenses database shown in Figure 12-1, you can see some of the parts I'm talking about. To the left of the layout is the Header button. If you click this button, you see all the fields that are defined in the Header section of the layout. If you click the Body button just below the Header button, all the fields in the Body section of the layout are displayed. Same thing goes for the Footer button. That way, each part corresponding to the appropriate section of a layout is available for you to work with. The size of each part in your layout will vary according to the number of fields in that section.

Figure 12-1: Displaying your database's header limits how much of the rest of your layout FileMaker Pro shows.

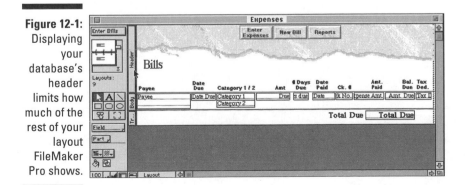

You use the header part for column headings, titles, and other pieces of data that will appear only at the top of each page in your FileMaker Pro layouts. That's pretty much the same thing that a header does in a word-processing program such as Microsoft Word.

You can even add a *title header part* to your layout, a part that prints only the first page, or title page, of your database. That can be very useful if you need to set off that first printed page from the other printed pages in your database. But what if the first page of your database changes for some reason? For example, what if your database is alphabetical and you add a record called Aardvark that now sits in front of Abnormal? Well, you can always change or delete the title header part from your layout. This means you've got a lot of flexibility when working with parts. You can modify those parts in your layouts when you need to make changes.

If you add any fields to a header part, keep in mind that those newly added fields are going to display or print on every page. You need to be careful and think through what repeating information you want to display or print in your database.

Double-clicking the Header part button in the Expenses database brings up the Part Definition dialog box, as shown in Figure 12-2. (Note that you have to double-click the *part button,* not just anywhere in the part section of the layout, to get the Part Definition dialog box to open for you.)

You find a lot of the fields *grayed out* in the Part Definition dialog box, which means that they're not accessible. You also find the Header radio button checked, which tells you that the part you are defining is a Header part. (Now, if you want to create other parts in your layout, you need to select the Part Setup menu item from the FileMaker Pro Mode menu. A dialog box pops open. When you click Create, you see the Part Definition dialog box without items grayed.)

When you click OK in the Part Definition dialog box, you define what the header does in your layout. I come back to this Part Definition dialog box throughout this chapter as I progressively define what each page in a layout does.

Figure 12-2:
The Part
Definition
dialog box.

Body parts

No, I'm not going to crack any jokes about an automobile repair shop in this chapter, nor any jokes that you'd find in a grade-B horror film or cop movie. Body parts are essential for anything you do with FileMaker Pro because the body is where you put the lion's share of your data in your layouts. If you want text, lines, or any graphics to appear in every record of your database, you put them in the body part. Anything that's in the body is printed for each record.

If you double-click the body part button, you see a Part Definition dialog box that tells you that you've defined Body as one of the parts in your layout.

Footer parts

From header to body to footer is a pretty straightforward shot, don't you think? You can use the footer in the same way that you'd use the header — that is, as a place for page numbers, dates, or other data that you want to appear at the bottom of each page. When you switch to Browse mode by selecting Browse in the Mode menu, the footer information is displayed, and FileMaker Pro prints it out as it appears. Keep in mind that footers, like headers, print on every page. If your database contains, for example, five or six different layouts, you may not want the same footer appearing in each layout. FileMaker Pro gives you the choice of deleting footers (or headers) from any of those five or six different layouts. Deleting footers may be necessary if you want to free up additional space at the bottom of your layout, or if you want to fit a whole record on one page and the footer makes the record come out at two pages.

Defining Your Own Parts

I can sense that you're itching to define your own parts now, after seeing, in Figure 12-1, somebody else's parts. (Shame, shame — we're still talking about databases!) That's easy. Just follow these steps:

1. **Move your cursor over the Part tool in the Tool panel on the left side of your screen and click the Part tool.**

   The cursor changes to a hand on the Mac, as shown in Figure 12-3, or a crosshair in Windows.

Figure 12-3:
The cursor
becomes a
hand on the
Mac and a
crosshair
on
Windows.

Figure 12-3:
The cursor
becomes a
hand on the
Mac and a
crosshair
on
Windows.

On the Mac a small hand grasping the Part tool appears, as shown in Figure 12-4. On Windows, a crosshair appears.

Figure 12-4:
The hand
on the Mac
grasps the
Part tool,
or on
Windows
the
crosshair
appears.

2. Drag the Part tool over to your layout and drop it on the section of your layout that you want to define.

You see a dotted outline of the part on your layout before the Part Definition dialog box shown in Figure 12-5 appears. Notice that the part in this figure is defined as a footer, with the radio button highlighted accordingly. That's because I dropped the part at the bottom of the layout, telling FileMaker Pro to make it a footer part. By moving the Part tool to the top of your layout, for example, right up there next to the header, you define the part as a title header. Pretty clever, I'd say.

FileMaker Pro saves you a lot of messing around this way. You just grab the Part tool from the Tool panel, drag it onto your layout adjacent to the panel, and place it down wherever you want. Then FileMaker Pro lets you define the part — that is, it lets you specify what the part does in your layout, whether it's a header, body, footer, or another part. Table 12-1 provides you with a complete explanation of all the different layout parts and what they do.

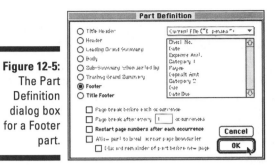

Figure 12-5:
The Part
Definition
dialog box
for a Footer
part.

Table 12-1   FileMaker Pro Layout Parts and What They Do

Layout part	What It Does
Header	Use this part for column headings, titles, graphics, and other information that you want to appear only at the top of every page in your database.
Body	Use this part to put everything you want to appear in each record of your database, including all the fields, text, lines, and graphics. The body is the only part used with FileMaker Pro Web Companion Instant Web Publishing.
Subsummary	Use this part to print a summary of information for each group of records that are sorted on a particular field. If you want to, you can add additional subsummaries either above or below the body part of your layout.
Leading grand summary	Use this part to summarize all records that are being browsed above the data in your records. FileMaker Pro only lets you use one leading grand summary part.
Trailing grand summary	Use this part to summarize all the records that are being browsed below the data in your records. Again, you can use only one trailing grand summary.
Footer	Use this part for page numbers, dates, graphics, or other information you want to appear only at the bottom of every page.
Title header	Use this part for printed reports. The title header replaces the regular header on the first page only.
Title footer	Use this part for printed reports. The title footer replaces the regular footer on the first page only.

Another way to define parts in FileMaker Pro is like this:

1. **While in Layout mode, choose Mode⇨Part Setup.**

   The Part Setup dialog box appears, as shown in Figure 12-6. Now if you click Create, you can't create a part from scratch. Note that if you click Create, the Part Definition dialog box opens, allowing you to choose from a set of part types rather than create a part from scratch.

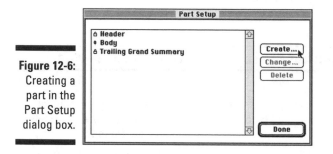

Figure 12-6:
Creating a part in the Part Setup dialog box.

2. **Click Body so that it's highlighted in the dialog box.**

3. **Click Change, and that same ol' Part Definition dialog box in Figure 12-7 pops up.**

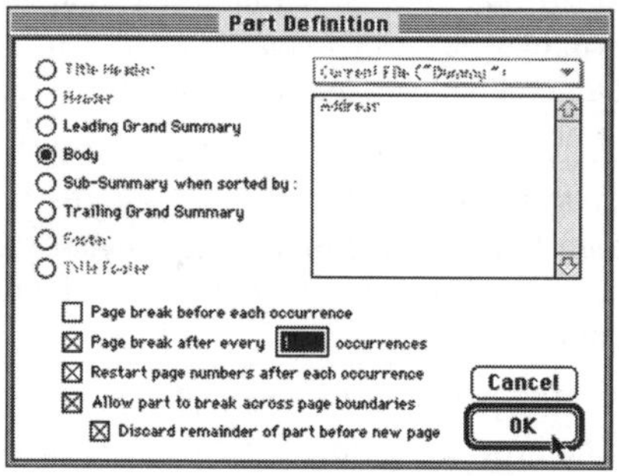

Figure 12-7:
The Part Definition dialog box, one more time.

Now you can change certain things about how you want that body part to appear in your layout. In the case of a header part, for example, you can click the Restart Page Numbers after Each Occurrence check box near the bottom of the Part Definition dialog box to restart the page numbers each time that header appears in your layout.

Some Things You Need to Know about Parts

Now that you've got a taste for FileMaker Pro parts, here's a final checklist of things you ought to keep in mind when working with parts. Using layout parts has limitations as well as advantages, including:

- Each layout is limited to just one header, one body, and one footer. Use these parts wisely because you have to use them sparingly.

- Layout parts are cool because you can put all kinds of text, graphic objects, and fields into them. And by magic (well, a kind of programming magic, really), those elements that you place into parts will appear in your records in repeating fashion. For example, if you have your name in the header and your address in the footer, your name and address appear on all of your records. It's as simple as that. All you have to do is copy and paste those name and address fields into the headers and footers.

- You have no problem adding, changing, or deleting parts (as long as one part remains). You can just delete them from your layouts as you want, but you have to remember that what you're doing isn't applicable to just a single record — it's for all of your records for a given layout.

Chapter 13

Positioning Those Lovely Objects

*P*ositioning is one of my favorite words in the English language, and I've used it in the title of this chapter knowing full well that it borders on cliché. These days, we seem to be positioning ourselves to death. We have "position" papers, market "positioning," books on how to better "position" ourselves, and so on. You get the idea.

Well, not to be outdone, here's a chapter on how to position objects in your FileMaker Pro layouts. By *position,* I mean the true sense of the word: to *place.* But placing objects in your layouts isn't quite enough to describe all the things you can do with those objects. Yes, you can place them, but you can also move them around, resize them, and control how they appear in your layouts — all the other senses of the word *position.* FileMaker Pro gives you the tools you need to do these things.

Of course, your goal in all this positioning work is to produce a better layout, one that looks and feels right to you.

Thinking of Objects

In working with FileMaker Pro, you quickly come to realize that what you're really doing is working with graphic objects. Text and even text fields, as well as imported graphics and QuickTime movies, become objects — a novel concept for a database program.

You may have difficulty thinking of text or a text field in your FileMaker Pro layout as, well, an *object*. Text is text, right? Wrong. A bit of rethinking, perhaps even a slight leap of the imagination, is in order here. I'll do my best to explain.

The idea is that objects are easy to move around in a layout because all you have to do is simply drag and drop them where you want. For example, you can build a layout for an invoice record or an address book record much faster by using FileMaker Pro's layout tools to move your text fields around than if you had to work without them. (Just for fun, try creating a layout without using your mouse and see what happens; you'll get bogged down before you know it trying to position your fields.)

The rule is to think of anything and everything in your FileMaker Pro database as an object, pure and simple. That includes things that you might not imagine as being objects, such as a calculation or summary field that contains a mathematical formula.

Objects can be text, yes, and graphics such as rectangles, ovals, and imported images. But objects can also be fields or even QuickTime movies that you import into your layouts.

Thinking of all these diverse elements in FileMaker Pro as objects is a little jump. But they are objects, and the reason they are is that you can do a variety of things with them that you would typically do with a graphics or drawing program. The following are just a few of the options you have when working with objects:

- ✔ Draw
- ✔ Move
- ✔ Resize
- ✔ Copy
- ✔ Delete
- ✔ Group and rearrange

In short, you can manipulate the objects in your FileMaker Pro layout by using the tools made available to you in the Tool panel. "Okay, that's fine," you may say. "But what's the point?"

The point is not only that you can manipulate the objects but also that you can position them — there's that word again — with a high degree of accuracy and precision. FileMaker Pro provides you with the means to do so.

Rules of the tools

Quickly, I want to go over some of the techniques you can use with the tools in the Tool panel:

✔ If you're going to use a tool only once, just click the tool to select it. The tool becomes gray.

✔ If you want to keep a tool selected, double-click it. The tool then becomes black, so you know it's selected until you change to another tool.

✔ If you want to change between the last tool you've used and the Pointer tool, just press Enter.

Working with Objects on a Grid

You've undoubtedly seen blueprints and, maybe, architectural drawings. And what's the one thing you remember about them? Yes, the drawings are all on a grid.

I bet you never thought you'd be using a grid in a database program. Well, FileMaker Pro isn't asking you to become an architect; it's just giving you the necessary tools to map out the positioning of the objects in your layouts. And it's doing that so you have better control of where those objects are, exactly, precisely, mathematically on the grid of your layout. Makes sense, doesn't it?

If you have your drafting hat on, the first step is to establish the units of measurement in which you want your layout displayed. You've got three choices here: inches, centimeters, or pixels. Most architects and graphic designers work with inches or centimeters. And if you're comfortable with those units of measurement, fine. But I suggest that you work with pixels in your FileMaker Pro layouts. Why?

The reason for working with pixels is simple enough: Pixels match your layouts to monitor size. Typically, you want your layout to fit into the screen size of a commonly used Macintosh or Windows display. I'm thinking here of the standard 15-inch or 17-inch display with a screen resolution of 640 x 480 pixels. If your monitor is that size, or the folks who use your FileMaker Pro database have monitors that size, well, you want your layout to be 640 x 480 pixels. Obviously, monitor sizes have grown dramatically in both the Mac and Windows worlds. You won't necessarily go wrong if you adjust your layout size to 768 x 1024. In any case, it's a good idea to think through what the monitor size of your database users may be.

The first step is to set your rulers to pixels:

1. **Open a new or existing FileMaker Pro database by choosing File⇨New or File⇨Open.**

2. **In Layout mode, select the Set Rulers menu item, as shown in Figure 13-1.**

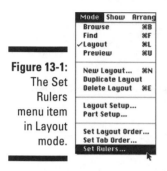

Figure 13-1:
The Set
Rulers
menu item
in Layout
mode.

3. **In the Set Rulers dialog box shown in Figure 13-2, click the Units pop-up menu, select Pixels, and then click OK.**

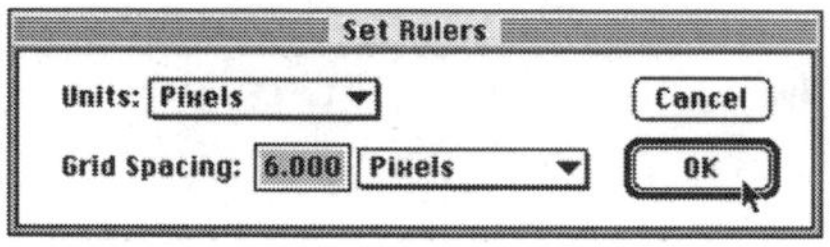

Figure 13-2:
The Set
Rulers
dialog box.

Now you've established pixels as the unit of measurement for the rulers in your FileMaker Pro layouts.

To work with positioning and sizing objects, here's what you do:

1. **Open up your database, by choosing File⇨Open.**
Figure 13-3 shows a sample Projects database, ready for object positioning.

2. **View the database in Layout mode by choosing Mode⇨Layout.**

3. **With your Pointer tool, click an object on your layout.**
You're now ready to determine the precise size in inches or fractions of an inch of that object. This information is useful in keeping track of how large or small the objects in your layout really are. Remember, you're working on a grid where precision counts for a lot.

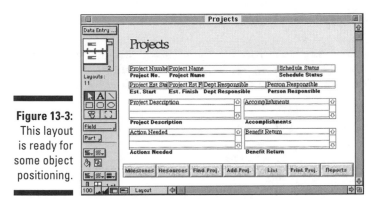

Figure 13-3:
This layout
is ready for
some object
positioning.

4. Choose Show⇨Size.

Clicking the Size menu item takes you to a neat little Size box, shown in Figure 13-4.

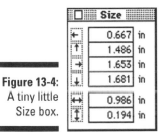

Figure 13-4:
A tiny little
Size box.

The Size box is one of the coolest little tools in your FileMaker Pro arsenal. What does it do? Well, it gives you the precise measurement in inches and fractions of an inch for every field and graphic object in your layout. The numbers in the box change, of course, as you resize the object you've selected.

Sometimes, working on a computer screen, depending on its dimensions, you don't get WYSIWYG (What You See Is What You Get). Things are off-kilter; documents or files don't print exactly the way they look on-screen. Anyway, this Size box is a handy feature to help you get an idea of how big or little your fields and graphic objects are in your layouts. Knowing the dimensions is particularly useful if you import a picture or graphic image into your layout and want to know how much space it's going to take up. It's all part of getting better control of the objects in your layouts.

Page margins

Before printing out the records in your files, you should find out what you're up against as far as page margins are concerned. Some printers may clip margins in printing, and as a consequence, you aren't be able to see the complete layout of your records.

To check your page margins, follow these steps:

1. Open your database in Layout mode.

2. Choose Show⇨Page Margins.

In the database screen shown in Figure 13-5, you can see that FileMaker Pro displays the page margins with a dotted line around your layout. FileMaker Pro also shows a grayed-out area next to the layout to indicate the space you have for the page margins.

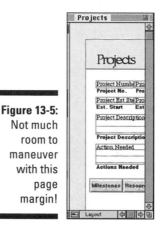

Figure 13-5:
Not much
room to
maneuver
with this
page
margin!

Actually, you can, as graphic designers say, *eyeball* it — just check out the way the page looks, without checking the exact margin measurements — and see that this page has a very tight margin. You may want to think about increasing the margins, especially if you want to print these records.

To change the margin size, here's what you do:

1. In Layout mode, choose Mode⇨Layout Setup.

Note that you must be in Layout mode. You don't get this Layout Setup option if you're in Browse, Find, or Preview mode.

2. In the Layout Setup dialog box (see Figure 13-6), check the box marked Fixed page margins, which is near the middle of the dialog box.

The numbers that appear in the corresponding boxes show you precisely the top, bottom, left, and right margins in your layout. In this case, they're marked either 0.43 or 0.42 inch. This margin may be tight for printing. Usually, any margin that's less than a half inch (0.5 inch) may present some problems for you when you go to print (depending, of course, on the type of printer you use). I recommend changing the numbers in your fixed page margins to a number greater than 0.5 inch and then doing a trial print run, just to verify how your printer handles the output.

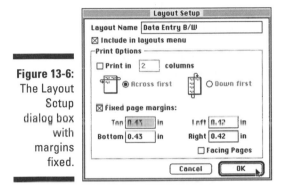

Figure 13-6:
The Layout
Setup
dialog box
with
margins
fixed.

3. **To change the page margins, click in any Fixed Page Margins box, enter the new margin, and click OK.**

Of course, if you're not printing the records in your database, you don't have to mess with page margins. But as I've learned from experience, printing out your records and storing the hard-copy version of your FileMaker Pro database is always a good idea. Printing out your records is also useful for seeing how your layouts really look on an $8^1/_2$-x-11-inch page rather than a computer screen.

The lovely text ruler

I don't remember earlier versions of FileMaker Pro having a text ruler that you could use in Layout mode. This feature is a nice addition to FileMaker Pro 3 and FileMaker Pro 4. For some reason, partly because we're conditioned to think in terms of $8^1/_2$-x-11-inch pages, having a text ruler is very useful for finding out how your text lines up across the page of your layout.

To access the text ruler, make sure that you're in Layout mode. Then choose Show⇨Text Ruler.

Your layout now has a neat ruler across the top of your screen, as you can see in Figure 13-7.

Figure 13-7:
The neat
FileMaker
Pro ruler
lets you
measure
your layout.

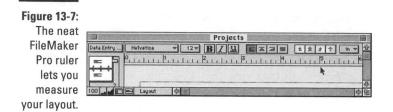

I can hear you asking, "What's so cool about that?" Well, there's more here than you might expect. For example, in Figure 13-7, the measurement is in inches. You can change that to other units of measure, such as picas, if you want by pulling down and selecting the menu in the far upper-right corner of the screen, as shown in Figure 13-8. I've got inches selected, but you can see the other options available to you.

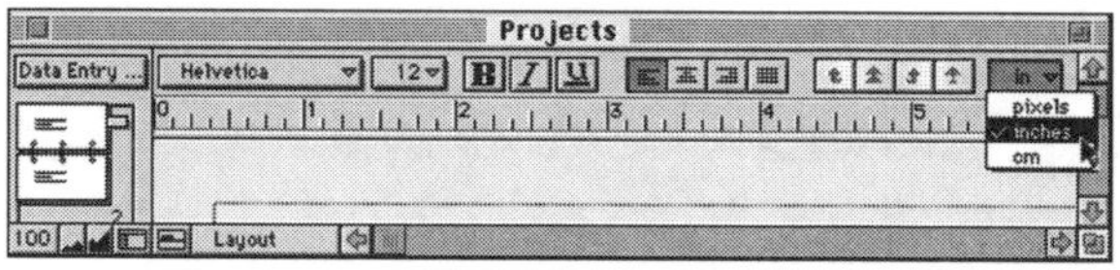

Figure 13-8:
Choosing
inches, not
picas or
centimeters.

But what I really like here is that you get not only a ruler across the top of your layout, but also access to your fonts, with the options of changing the font size, style, and alignment (whether you want the text centered or justified). It's like having your word processor available to you right there in your graphic layout. You get to choose the fonts you want when you enter text in your fields — for example, I chose Helvetica in Figure 13-9. You can also make that text bold, italicized, and underlined with the click of a button just above the ruler.

Now comes the totally cool part. Whoever thought of this next design feature ought to get high marks at Claris. Just follow the steps, and you'll see what I mean.

Figure 13-9:
Selecting a
font with
the Text
Ruler.

1. **In Layout mode, after choosing Show⇨Text Ruler, pick a spot on your layout where you want to drop some text or, as shown in Figure 13-10, select the text field with the Projects heading.**

2. **Click the Text tool in the Tool panel — you know, the button with the big A.**

   A little ruler pops up above your text, as shown in the Projects database in Figure 13-10. Within that little ruler, you can set tabs for the text that appears in the Projects title field. This option is way cool, from my point of view. Setting tabs in text fields? Sounds simple, but it's not. The wizards of FileMaker Pro figured out a way to do it and make it work for the text in your fields.

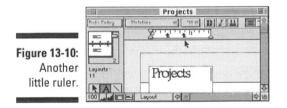

Figure 13-10:
Another
little ruler.

Again, because of these new measurement tools, you have much greater control over how your layout appears, for both browsing and printing.

Cool Positioning: Applying What You Know

In this section, I walk you step-by-step through the actual, physical work of positioning so that you get a feel for how to use some of these graphics tools. All the tools are designed to give you as much control as possible over your FileMaker Pro layouts.

Graphic ruler, ruler lines, and T-squares

While in Layout mode, the Show menu lets you choose a graphic ruler, ruler lines, and T-squares.

Graphic rulers help you measure and position objects in both horizontal and vertical directions. A ruler appears on the left of your layout if you select this option, and then a cross-bar pops up on-screen to guide you around. Needless to say, this ruler is really for graphic designers and desktop publishers who are probably using PageMaker or QuarkXPress or another high-powered desktop publishing tool in their arsenals. They'll also like the ruler lines and T-squares that are available on the Show menu.

You may not really need to use these measurement and positioning tools in your simple FileMaker Pro layouts (I don't use them). But if you step up in the world to graphics designer status, you can use these tools in, of all things, a database program — which is nice to know.

Take, for example, a database called My Address Book, which is pretty much the same address book that I use as an example in Chapter 1. Here, I want to add to the database a new layout called Tom's Positioning Layout. Follow these steps:

1. **Open the database you want by choosing File⇨Open and clicking your database from the list of files.**

2. **Go to Layout mode by choosing Mode⇨Layout (or you can click Layout in the mode selector at the bottom of your screen).**

3. **Click New Layout from the Layout mode menu, or use the keyboard shortcut, ⌘+N on the Mac or Ctrl+N on Windows.**

4. **In the New Layout dialog box that appears, enter a new name for your layout in the Layout Name box.**

5. **Click the Blank radio button near the bottom of the dialog box.**

   Figure 13-11 shows the New Layout dialog box, with a new layout name — Tom's Positioning Layout — and the Blank radio button selected.

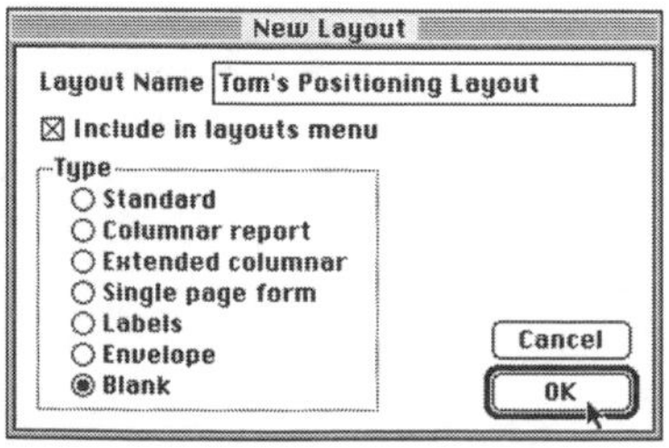

Figure 13-11:
The New
Layout
dialog box.

A new, blank layout appears on-screen. The Book icon on the left side of the layout lists the number of layouts in your file. My example (see Figure 13-12) has 22 layouts.

6. In your new layout, choose Show⇨Size.

The Size box appears on your layout.

7. From the pop-up menu in the upper right of your layout, select pixels, as shown in Figure 13-12.

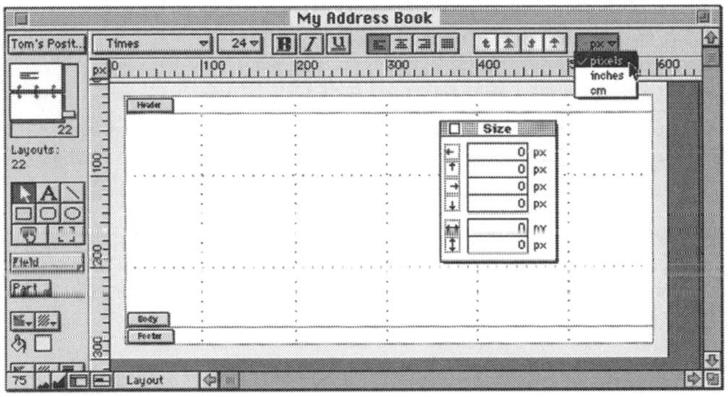

Figure 13-12:
A new
layout with
the Size box
ready for
action and
the pixels
measurement
selected.

Pixels, rather than inches, are now the unit of measurement for your layout.

Because you're working with a blank layout, you can position the text, number, and container fields wherever you want. The order in which they're positioned is not predefined, as is the case with other layouts, such as standard.

8. Choose File⇨Page Setup on the Mac or File⇨Print Setup in Windows.

Remember that the size of your layout is determined by the page size you've specified in the Page Setup dialog box.

9. In the Page Setup dialog box on the Mac (which varies depending on the printer you happen to work with), click Options.

Another dialog box appears, giving you options to choose from.

10. If you find a Custom option, click that. If not, go back to the Page Setup dialog box and click the US Letter radio button next to Print.

11. Click OK.

If you selected US Letter, FileMaker Pro displays your layout as a standard $8^1/_2$ x 11 inches. If you clicked Custom, you can set your layout to a different size of your choosing.

If you've established the size of your layout as $8^1/_2$ x 11 inches but want to adjust that size so that your layout corresponds more closely to the size of a 14-inch monitor with a screen resolution of 640 x 480 pixels, the following steps help you create a layout that matches, as nearly as possible, what the user, or viewer, of your database sees on a computer screen.

1. **With the Pointer tool in your layout, click the edge of the line that extends from the Body part button.**

   My example layout in Figure 13-13 shows header, footer, and body parts along the left edge of the layout. By checking the Size box (which you can access from the Show menu), you can find out how much space on your layout you've allocated for each part.

2. **Drag the body part to the size you want for your layout.**

3. **Pull down the dotted line adjacent to the body part until you have stretched it to a depth of exactly 480 pixels.**

   Figure 13-13 shows you the body part selected by the Pointer tool, stretching down on the layout.

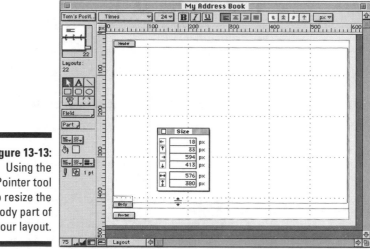

Figure 13-13:
Using the Pointer tool to resize the body part of your layout.

In the Size box, the bottom pixel amount shows the depth of your layout (380 pixels in Figure 13-13). The box just above the Size box displays the width of your layout.

After you've set the size of your layout's body part, you're ready to start populating your layout with the specific fields you've already defined in your database, such as Contact First, Contact Last Names, Company Name, Address, Phone Number, Date Entered, and so on. (See Chapter 1 for more on adding and defining fields.)

4. **Click the Field tool and, when the hand on the Mac appears grasping the tool, move and place the tool to the appropriate place on your layout.**

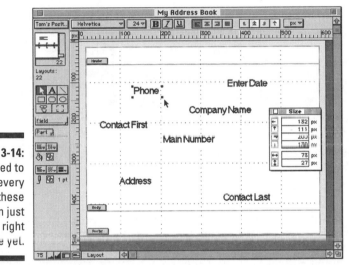

Figure 13-14: No need to place every one of these fields in just the right place yet.

When the dialog box appears for specifying which field you want, select the fields that you want for this particular layout.

5. **Continue with Step 4, placing the fields on your layout randomly, as shown in Figure 13-14.**

6. **Click the very bottom-left corner of your layout and set the zoom control number to 75.**

Your layout is shown at 75 percent of its actual size, creating a shrunken view of your layout so that you can see how all the objects line up. At this point, you may also want to check the Size box, when you have selected a field, to find out what size your text fields are. That way, you know which fields are taking up the most room in your layout.

7. **If you want to add art to your layout, import a picture by choosing File⇨Import/Export⇨Import Picture.**

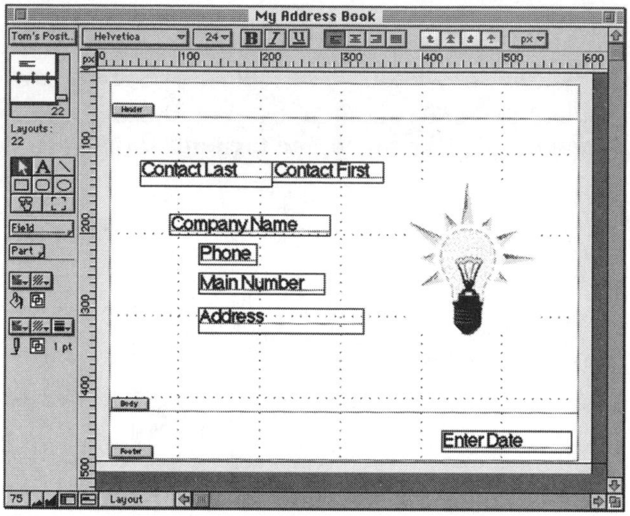

Figure 13-15:
The fields in
My Address
Book neatly
arranged,
with the best
stuff at the
top and the
least
important
stuff at the
bottom.

8. With the Pointer tool, you can rearrange the text fields until you have a layout you like and can live with.

Figure 13-15 shows one such layout.

The general rule here is to position your fields (which are really graphic objects, of course) from the top down, placing the most important at the top because the top is where the eye naturally goes in a layout. Fields of lesser importance should appear at the bottom of your layout. Use common sense in making your layout clean and uncluttered. And use those rulers and T-squares to make sure everything lines up right.

Well, there you have it! Positioning can be lots of fun as well as lots of hard work, particularly when you have to sweat the details and come up with a visually pleasing layout. In the end, though, good positioning of your FileMaker Pro objects can make the difference between a boring layout and one that is way cool.

Chapter 14

Fields in Layouts

● ●

In This Chapter

▶ Finding out how fields relate to layouts

▶ Adding new fields to your layout

▶ Working with the Specify Field dialog box

● ●

*F*ields in a FileMaker Pro database are glorious, from my point of view. Fields in your layouts are even better, because you get to do all kinds of neat things with them, as I point out in this chapter. Not to mention that your database is no good without them.

Get your thinking cap on and prepare to be dazzled by fields in layouts and by the Field tool, which lets you harvest the abundance in your layouts.

Fields of Glory in Your Layouts

If you haven't defined fields yet for your new database file, you'll want to be sure that you make the effort, as explained in Chapter 8. After you've defined the fields of information that you want to populate with data, you'll be ready to work with those fields in Layout mode. Just switch from Browse to Layout mode and you're ready to roll. You'll see right away that each field of your database in Layout mode has a field label attached to it.

After your fields are defined, you're ready for action in Layout mode. That's where you can modify, resize, and reposition fields.

Guess what? In Layout mode, you can also add fields to the current layout, delete them if you don't want them displayed or printed in your layout, and even select the formats you want for the data that's displayed in your fields. The whole idea behind this is that you can design different layouts for different purposes. For example, one layout can be just for entering new contact information while another layout can be for printing a directory. Nifty, don't you think?

In Layout mode, your fields become objects that you can move around and resize in the same way that you would other graphic objects in FileMaker Pro.

In those fields, you've got a field name, which is Item Description, as shown in the Invoices template in Figure 14-1 (the arrow cursor is pointing right to it). In the Item Description field, as in many of the other fields in the layout, the font (Times), its size (12 points), style (Plain), alignment (Left), and even line spacing have all been defined.

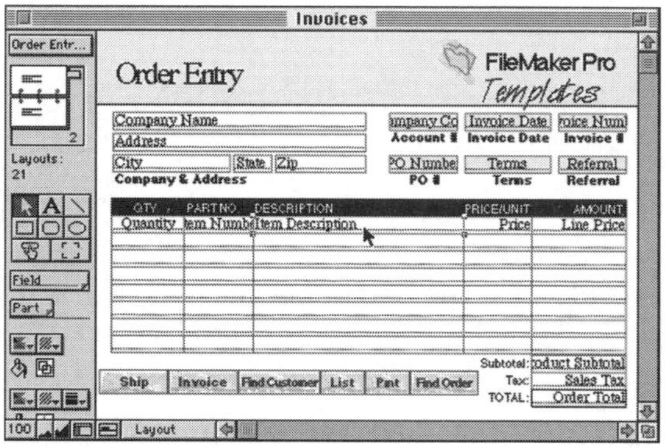

Figure 14-1: Fields placed in an Order Entry layout of a FileMaker Pro Invoices template.

At the corners of the Item Description field (shown in Figure 14-1), you find tiny boxes that, when you grab them with the Pointer tool, let you stretch and resize the field. You know that you're using the Pointer tool because that tool is highlighted in the layout's Tool panel to your left. With the Pointer tool, you can pick up and drag your field anywhere you want on your layout.

Now check out the dotted line just under the Item Description name. That dotted line is called a *baseline,* and that's where your data sits happily in your field.

If you choose Show⇨Text Boundaries and Show⇨Field Boundaries while you're in Layout mode, you see where the data is located, more precisely, in your layouts.

Adding New Fields to Your Layout

One cool thing I really like about FileMaker Pro is that you can add a new field to your layout while you're in Layout mode. You don't have to go back to defining fields and toggle back and forth from the fields you've defined and the layout in which you want the fields to appear. FileMaker Pro does all of that automatically, when you're in Layout mode.

Using the Field tool to add the field to the layout

Adding a field to your layout is a simple drag-and-drop operation. Here's what you do:

1. **In Layout mode, click the Field tool on the left of your screen, just below the Tool panel.**

   The pointer changes to a hand cursor on the Mac or an arrow with crosshairs in Windows when it hovers over the Field tool, as Figure 14-2 shows.

Figure 14-2:
The Pointer tool changes to a hand.

Field

2. **Drag the hand icon from the Field tool over your layout and drop it on the layout where you want the field to appear.**

   The Specify Field dialog box comes up for your current database, listing for you all the fields currently in your file. Figure 14-3 shows this for the Invoices database.

   The Specify Field dialog box also includes a Create Field Label check box. If you click the check box, FileMaker Pro places a label for the selected field in your layout — a good idea, so you can keep track of the names of your fields.

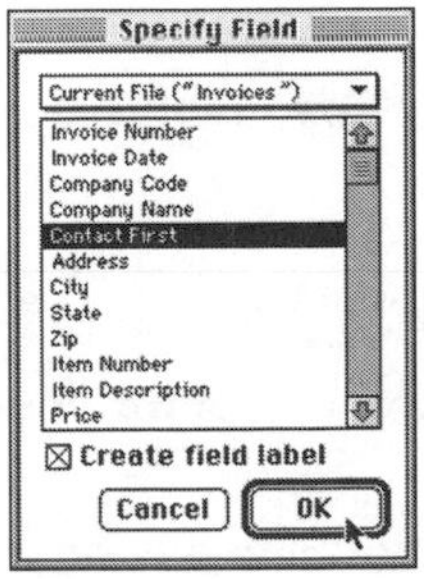

Specify Field

Current File (" Invoices ")

Invoice Number
Invoice Date
Company Code
Company Name
Contact First
Address
City
State
Zip
Item Number
Item Description
Price

☒ **Create field label**

Cancel | OK

Figure 14-3:
The Specify Field dialog box.

3. **Select the field you want to add — in Figure 14-3, it's the Contact First field — and then click OK.**

   The field you select now appears on your layout. You can move it around to another place on the layout or resize it by selecting the Pointer tool in your layout's Tool panel and then clicking in the field. You can also stretch and resize the field by grabbing one of its corners while the field is selected.

Remember that your field, in effect, becomes a graphic object at your disposal to move around on your layout, much like any graphic in a paint or drawing program, in that you can edit, crop or resize it. You can also add text in a new font or style and set the alignment, color, or line spacing of that text.

You don't want to place the field in the gray area below all the layout parts in your layout. If you try to go below the body or footer parts in the gray area, FileMaker Pro simply doesn't let you place the field there.

Specifying the field in the Specify Field dialog box

In Layout mode, the Specify Field dialog box has more options than when you are adding new fields to your database. Some of these options, for example, let you copy fields from other database files, such as Contacts and Products shown in Figure 14-4, to the one that you're currently working on. This is really handy because you don't have to duplicate your efforts in defining fields from one file to another. You'll also see a menu item in Figure 14-4 below the dotted line: Define Relationship, which I explain in a minute.

The neat thing here is that you really can choose fields from other files in your database and place them in your current layout. To copy an existing field from another database, just follow these steps.

1. **Open the pop-up menu at the top of the Specify Field dialog box, as Figure 14-4 shows.**

   FileMaker Pro displays a list of other files in your database, files in which you've defined a bunch of fields already.

2. **Select a file that has other fields that may be useful for your currently active file.**

   Figure 14-5 shows a list of the fields in the Products file that are now available to the currently active Invoices file.

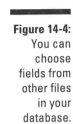

Figure 14-4:
You can
choose
fields from
other files
in your
database.

Figure 14-5:
The
Products
file offers
other
available
fields.

3. Select the field or fields that you want to add to your current file, and click OK.

What's really cool here is that when you click one of those fields from a different file, that field also appears in your current file — in this example, Invoices. Now that's the way to add a field, I think.

Taking Fields One Step Further to Defining Relationships

As I mentioned, the other option available to you in the Specify Field dialog box when you open the pop-up menu at the top is the last choice below the dotted line: Define Relationships.

No, this option isn't about going steady or placing a personal ad at the back of your hometown newspaper. It's about establishing and defining the relationships you want from one field in a file to another field in a different file. By defining a relationship between files, you save time and duplication of data from one file to another. Chapters 5 and 23 explain this relationship stuff in much greater detail. Check them out!

Part III
Off to Work We Go

The 5th Wave   By Rich Tennant

ON A BET, HOWIE LINDELMAN, THE OFFICE TINKERER, TRIES LINKING HIS CALCULATOR INTO THE WORKGROUPS NETWORK FILE SERVER.

HE'S GETTING FILES!
HE'S GETTING FILES!

In this part . . .

*A*rbeit macht das Leben süss. An old German proverb my mother passed on to me, which, roughly translated, means, work makes your life sweet. And I don't mean sweet as in candy.

I take a more philosophical, Kantian view of work; namely, you gotta do it, you gotta do it. So off to work we go, not always whistling like the seven dwarfs in that Disney movie.

Hopefully, FileMaker Pro will make your work easier. I know it's done that for me.

Chapter 15

Managing Your Records
and Doing Cool Stuff

The next step after creating your own FileMaker Pro database or modifying one of the existing templates that come bundled with the program is, simply, managing the information in that database. I don't know about you, but I like to manage my stuff and make it work for me. Managing, in this context, means browsing, sorting, finding, adding, deleting, duplicating, and moving through your records. Essentially, it's just keeping things in order. A house in order is a good house, indeed.

In this chapter, you find out how to manage the information in your FileMaker Pro database and get out of it what you worked so hard to put in.

Moving from Record to Record

Moving from record to record in your database is probably your number one activity in managing information. I don't have any hard-and-fast stats here, but it seems to be a process that repeats itself with some frequency.

The best way to move from record to record, at least from my point of view, is to use the Book icon in the status area to the left of your layout. If you're not familiar with this Book icon, now's the time to find out about it: You can see it in Figure 15-1.

In the example in Figure 15-1, you're getting a great deal of information in a small space. By the position of the slider on the right of the icon, and by the number 3 below it, you know you're on Record 3 in your file. The slider is there to move you through the records in your database, and obviously, the number identifies on which record you've currently landed.

Just below that, FileMaker Pro shows you the total number of records in your file — in this case, 11.

Figure 15-1:
The handy
Book icon.

—Slider

By clicking the Book icon, you can flip through the records one by one in your file, or, if you want to move quickly from, for example, Record 3 to Record 11, you can move that slider down (or up, to go in other direction).

TIP

If you're browsing your records, you can see the current record indicated by a solid bar to the left of the fields, as Figure 15-2 shows.

Figure 15-2:
A solid bar
to the left of
your fields
indicates
your
current
record.

Expenses

Date	Ck.#	Payee
4/3/95		Beginning Ba
4/15/95	101	SD Symphon
4/30/95	100	ABC Phone C
5/1/95	103	Smith Hard v

Records: 11
Found: 8
Semi-sorted

Solid bar

TIP

If you're a keyboard freak and like to move through your records one at a time with a couple of keystrokes, here's what you do on the Mac:

  ✔ To move to the next record in your file, press ⌘+Tab.

  ✔ To return to the previous record, press ⌘+Shift+Tab or ⌘+Option+Tab.

Note that Windows keyboard freaks can use similar commands:

  ✔ To move to the next record, press Ctrl+↑.

  ✔ To return to the previous record, press Ctrl+↓.

Check out Chapter 27 for a list of other cool keyboard shortcuts you can use with FileMaker Pro.

If you have a large number of records and you want to get to a particular record fast, you can click in the box at the bottom of the book icon and type in the number you want. Figure 15-3 shows what happens when you type in the number 7, (or any number): The box goes black. Then you just press Return on a Mac or Enter on a Windows computer, and FileMaker Pro takes you right away to that record.

Figure 15-3:
Finding a
record fast.

Another method is just to move the slider down or up until you get to the number of the record you want. As you move it, the record numbers change.

Browsing Your Records

Taking second place in the competition for ways to have fun with your FileMaker Pro database is . . . drumroll, please . . . browsing. (The first-place winner is defining your fields, which I explain in Chapter 8.)

In moving from record to record with the Book icon, you're browsing because you can see on-screen the information stored in each record.

But while you're in Browse mode, you can also get another view of your records: You can view all the records you have in your file in a list, rather than just one record at a time. This list is a handy way to see all your records from top to bottom. Let me show you how you can do that.

To view your records as a list:

1. **Open your database in Browse mode by selecting Mode⇨Browse.**

2. **Choose Select⇨View as List, as you see in Figure 15-4.**

   The list view of an Expenses file, as you see in Figure 15-5, shows you four records and the contents of each field. A little solid bar to the left of the fields shows you what the current record is — in this case, Record 4.

Figure 15-4:
Select a
viewing
option.

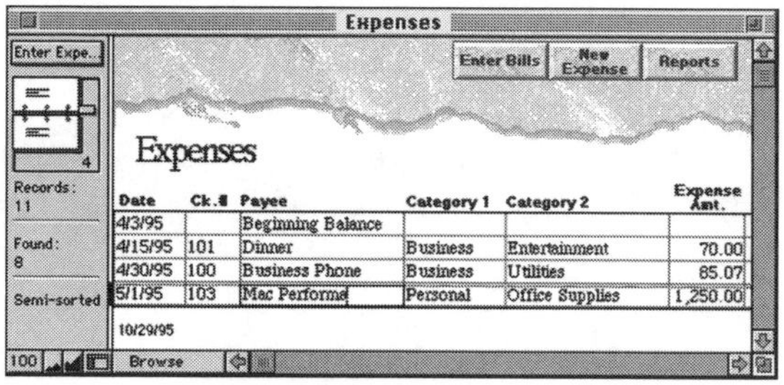

Select	Format	Script
Find All		⌘J
Find Omitted		
Modify Last Find		⌘R
Perform Find		
Omit		⌘M
Omit Multiple...		⇧⌘M
View as Form		
✓**View as List**		

Figure 15-5:
A list view of
an Expenses
file.

Expenses

Date	Ck.#	Payee	Category 1	Category 2	Expense Amt.
4/3/95		Beginning Balance			
4/15/95	101	Dinner	Business	Entertainment	70.00
4/30/95	100	Business Phone	Business	Utilities	85.07
5/1/95	103	Mac Performa	Personal	Office Supplies	1,250.00
10/29/95					

Records: 11
Found: 8
Semi-sorted

Enter Expe...   Enter Bills New Expense Reports

100   Browse

How many current records at a time can you have on-screen in FileMaker Pro? No, this isn't a trick question. The answer is pretty obvious: only one. But don't let me confuse you. That doesn't mean that you can look at only one record ever.

If you want to see all the records in your database at one time, you can do so by clicking the button above the Book icon and selecting List from the drop-down menu. That presents you with the List view of records in an Expenses file shown in Figure 15-5. Notice that the current record is marked by the solid bar to the left of the record. The number of the current record is right there for you to see, under the Book icon in the status area.

Keep in mind that although you can view all the records in your database in a list view, you can only edit them one at a time.

If you need a form view of your records, that's easy enough to get to.

To view your records as a form:

1. **Open your database in Browse mode by selecting Browse from the Mode menu.**

2. **Choose Select⇨View as Form.**

   What you get now is what you see in Figure 15-6, the current record viewed as a form.

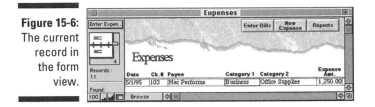

Figure 15-6:
The current
record in
the form
view.

Adding, Duplicating, and Deleting Records

The steps for adding, duplicating, and deleting records are a cinch most of the time, so you forget how easy FileMaker Pro really makes these tasks.

To add a new record:

1. **In Browse mode, choose Browse➪New Record or use the keyboard shortcut, which is probably faster: ⌘+N on the Mac or Ctrl+N in Windows.**

2. **When the blank record pops up on-screen, enter the values you want in the various fields in that record: for example, the names and addresses for a Personal Address database. Check out Chapter 8 for more information on populating the fields in a new record.**

While I'm on the subject of keyboard shortcuts, I want to pass on a few of my Mac favorites. I'm sure you'll come up with a few of your own as you work with FileMaker Pro and do more data entry. Each keyboard shortcut is designed to save you time. Here goes:

✔ ⌘+' (apostrophe) copies data from the previous record into the selected field. It's a real time-saver. Also, I should add that if you want to insert data and then tab to the next field, you can press ⌘+Shift+' (in other words, ⌘+" — quotation marks).

✔ ⌘+- (hyphen) inserts the current date into the field that you've selected.

✔ ⌘+; (semicolon) inserts the current time into a field. For some reason, I tend to use these last two shortcuts frequently. I guess I'm just a date and time freak.

To duplicate a record, choose Browse➪Duplicate.

Consider duplicating a record if much of the information is the same from one record to the next.

To delete a record, or all records in your file, choose Browse⇨Delete Record.

When the Delete Permanently dialog box in Figure 15-7 appears, be sure you've thought it through. You won't be able to recover or retrieve a record or group of records that you've permanently deleted. Make sure you have a backup copy of your files before you engage in any deleting action. I know the temptation of automatically deleting files that you think may be unnecessary or out of date. You might think you can undo that delete if you change your mind, but that isn't the case. What's gone is gone forever.

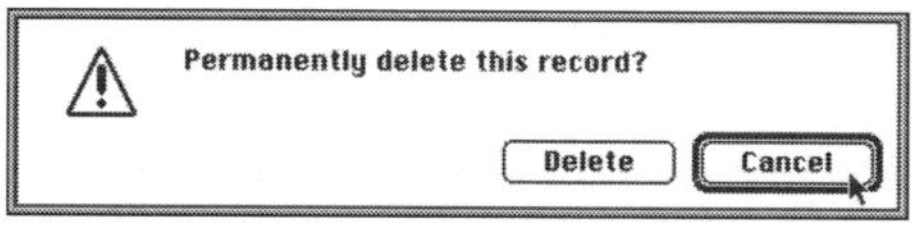

Figure 15-7:
Think
carefully!
There's no
undo here.

> ⚠ **Permanently delete this record?**
>
> [Delete] [Cancel]

Omitting Records

This option in FileMaker Pro may be a little confusing — at least it was to me when I first saw it and started working with it. But now I use it all the time.

Omitting a record is not the same thing as deleting one. By exercising this option, you're not removing records from your file. All you're really doing is making them unavailable on a temporary basis. They're still there, so you don't have to worry about losing them. You're just not including them in the group you've selected to browse, sort, print, or export to another file. Did you see *print* in that last list?

Omitting records, I find, is really useful when printing. You can specify Records #23, #42, and #55, for example, as records you don't want to print and just omit those records from printing.

To omit records, follow these steps:

1. **Open the record that you want to omit from your current print job.**

2. **To omit a single record: Choose Select⇨Omit or press ⌘+M on the Mac or Alt, S, M in Windows.**

To omit multiple records: Choose Select➪Omit Multiple.

For omitting multiple records, the dialog box in Figure 15-8 appears, letting you specify the number of records to omit, starting with the current record.

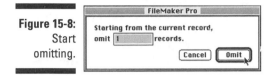

Figure 15-8:
Start
omitting.

3. **Just enter the number of records you want to omit, and click the Omit button.**

To bring back omitted records, choose Select➪Find All or Find Omitted. Instantaneously, FileMaker Pro searches through your files and comes up with the records you've omitted. Instantaneous is fast, all right.

Editing Existing Records

FileMaker Pro makes routine editing of your records easy. In the old database world, which was definitely prehistoric, editing your records could be a real pain because moving from field to field and changing your entries was a hard process. Now, with a simple point-and-click routine, you can copy and paste the values from any of your fields in your FileMaker Pro database to any other field. And here's where copy-and-paste gets really valuable: Those fields can include a variety of types — not just text, numbers, dates, and time, but also pictures, movies, calculations, and summary fields. In each case, you use the same procedure to edit your records.

To copy values from one field to another:

1. **Press and drag with your mouse to select the field contents you want to copy to another field, or choose Edit➪Select All if you want to select all the fields.**

2. **Choose Edit➪Cut (or press ⌘+X on the Mac or Ctrl+X in Windows) to cut the contents of your selected field and place them onto the Clipboard.**

   Choose Edit➪Copy (or press ⌘+C on the Mac or Ctrl+C in Windows) to copy the contents of your selection onto the Clipboard.

3. **Click the field where you want to paste the contents, or use the Tab key to move to the field you want.**

4. Choose Edit➪Paste (or press ⌘+V on the Mac or Ctrl+V in Windows) to paste the contents of the Clipboard into the current field.

There it is. You're done.

Now suppose you want to get ambitious with your editing. You want to replace a field's value in several records at once. Hey, no problem. You can replace the contents of your field in all the records in your database or in a group of records. You use the Replace command, which is available to you on the Edit menu. This is very useful, for example, if you find that the area code for part of a state has changed and you want to change the area code on three cities at once.

If you want to replace the contents of a field in more than one record, follow these steps:

1. Browse the records with fields you want to replace.

You may need to use Find, Find All, or Omit Records from those that you're browsing. This way, you can select the group of records with fields you want to replace. Those records become the *found set*.

2. Click the field in the record with the value — for example, the date or name — you want to replace in all the found records.

3. Choose Mode➪Replace or press ⌘+= on the Mac.

A dialog box opens, asking whether you want to replace the contents of the fields in all the records you're browsing.

4. Check that the radio button in the dialog box is highlighted and click the Replace button.

FileMaker Pro takes care of the rest, replacing the field in the records you've chosen.

The Big Sort

Sorting is another thing that makes working with FileMaker Pro fun, not to mention that it's a good method for managing your information.

Sorting is really at the heart of all database programs, including FileMaker Pro. It's like taking a deck of cards and electronically telling the deck how you want the cards to be dealt — that is, the order of the deck, by suit, by value, by whatever.

The thing to keep in mind is that FileMaker Pro stores your records in your files exactly in the order that you add them. Which is pretty logical, right? Now, that order may not be the order in which you want to view them or retrieve information from them later on.

When you sort, you temporarily change the order of either a group of records or all of your records. As a consequence, after you sort, you can browse, modify, or print your records differently.

To sort the records in your file:

1. **Choose Mode⇨Browse.**

2. **Click Mode⇨Sort, as you see in Figure 15-9.**

   Note: You can sort only while you're in Browse mode.

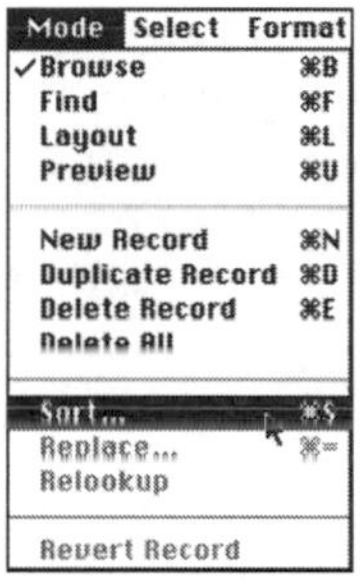

Figure 15-9:
Getting ready to Sort.

3. **The Sort Records dialog box appears, as you see in the example Expenses file in Figure 15-10.**

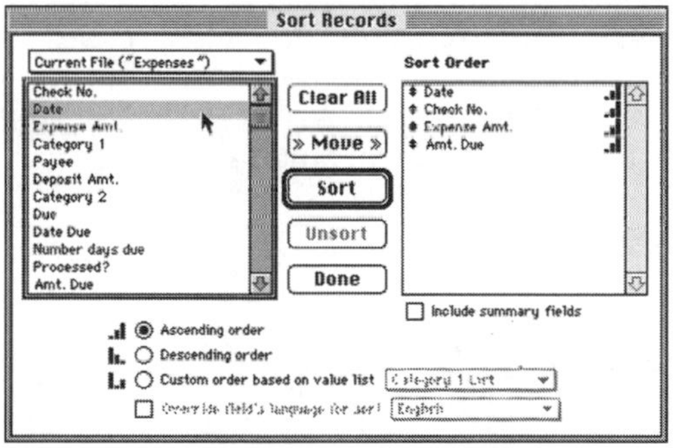

Figure 15-10:
The Sort Records dialog box.

4. **Click the fields in the Current Expenses file that you want to sort; then click the Move button to place them in the Sort Order box to the right.**

   What you're doing here is setting up the sort order for your records. You also use the three radio buttons at the bottom of the dialog box:

   • **Ascending order:** Sorts records by alphabetical order (A to Z) for words, the lowest-to-highest order for numbers, and chronological order (earliest to latest) for dates or times.

- **Descending order:** Sorts records just the opposite of ascending order: Z to A for words, highest to lowest for numbers, and latest to earliest for dates.

- **Custom order:** Matches the order of a field's value list. You can define the value list by pulling down the menu on the far right of the radio button.

5. **Click Done when you've completed moving the fields to the Sort Order list. This closes the dialog box on both Mac and Windows. As soon as a field is in the Sort Order box, the Sort button is enabled.**

6. **Click Sort.**

   FileMaker Pro now sorts the records in your file according to the sort order you defined and displays for you the first record in the new sorted order.

Sorting has its peculiarities, so here are some things you ought to know:

✔ **Container fields.** If you're going to sort any records that have container fields in them, you need to create a text or number field first. In that text or number field, you need to identify what you have in the container field. Then you can sort by that field without a problem. For more information on Container fields, check out Chapter 8.

✔ **Unsort.** You have an Unsort option if you want to restore your records to the order in which they were first added to your file. Choose Mode⇨Sort and click Unsort in the Sort Records dialog box that appears.

✔ **The Sort order.** Keep in mind that when you add a record to sorted records, FileMaker Pro attempts to maintain the sort order. The message in the status area changes to `Semi-sorted` to indicate the approximate order of the sort. When you finish adding records, you can re-sort them.

Dragging and Dropping for Fun and Profit

FileMaker Pro 4 — as well as its predecessor, FileMaker Pro 3 — has some cool stuff that you ought to know about for managing your records more easily.

Among other cool things, FileMaker Pro supports drag-and-drop as an effective way to move your information around faster, particularly from one application to another. This feature is very handy and very intuitive when you're transferring data in your files to or from FileMaker Pro and other applications. It's cool because you don't have to use the Macintosh or Windows Clipboard.

What you have to do, if you want to drag and drop text in your database fields, is enable this feature when you set your Application Preferences.

To enable drag-and-drop:

1. Choose Edit⇨Preferences⇨Application.

The dialog box in Figure 15-11 appears.

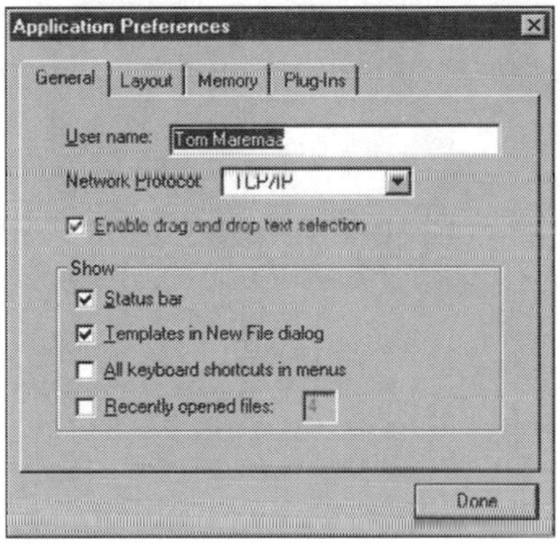

Figure 15-11:
The
Application
Preferences
dialog box
with drag-
and-drop on
text fields
enabled.

2. Check the Enable Drag and Drop Text selection.

However, in order to use drag-and-drop, you need to have System 7.5 or later installed on your Macintosh. That's the version of the Macintosh operating system (the Mac OS) that implements the drag-and-drop feature. (Incidentally, if you haven't considered upgrading to Mac OS 8, the latest version of the operating system, now may be the time, not just because you can take full advantage of drag-and-drop capabilities, but for a slew of other reasons. Suffice to say that FileMaker Pro 4 runs very happily on Mac OS 8.)

Here are a few key points about this cool feature in FileMaker Pro:

✔ You can use drag-and-drop in Browse, Layout, and Find modes.

✔ In Layout mode, you can use drag-and-drop to move and transfer objects, graphics, or text. If you're working with Windows, you can also use this feature to transfer OLE objects.

✔ In Browse mode, you can use drag-and-drop to transfer text or the contents of a particular container field to another field.

✔ You can use drag-and-drop between FileMaker Pro and other applications.

If you're using drag-and-drop between FileMaker Pro and another application, you need to make sure that the other application supports the type of data you're transferring. Another limitation exists, too: Graphics cannot be dragged and dropped into certain fields, namely text or calculation fields. This makes pretty good sense, when you think about it. You wouldn't expect FileMaker Pro to be able to handle a picture or graphic image in a field that is designed to perform a mathematical function.

You ought to be sure that both applications you're working with are open and that you can see them while you're in Browse mode or Layout mode.

Follow the appropriate step:

✔ **To move an object from one application to another:** Select the object, drag it, and then drop it into the other application. Which is pretty easy, no?

✔ **To move an object to an area that's not visible in the other application:** Continue dragging the object in the other application's window in the direction in which you want the window to scroll.

✔ **To copy an object from one application to another:** Hold down the Ctrl key, drag the object, and then drop it into the other application, in the auto-scroll region, which is near the scroll bars.

✔ **To copy an object to an area that's not visible in the other application:** Hold down the Ctrl key, select the object, drag it, and continue dragging it in the other application's window in the direction in which you want the window to scroll.

You can't drop an object into a locked record or a noneditable field. FileMaker Pro won't let you and makes your pointer change shape.

Chapter 16

Finding the Stuff You Want

· ·

· ·

I don't know about you, but I have a tendency to lose things, and not just car keys. When storing my data in a FileMaker Pro database, I breathe a sigh of relief because I know I can't really lose anything. What's there is there, stored electronically. The problem is that sometimes I can't find what I'm looking for.

This chapter is all about finding information in your FileMaker Pro database. Interestingly, many people I know never think that's why you build your database in the first place; not only to store your data but also to find it fast.

Inevitably, as your database grows and you continue to add more records to it, finding becomes more important. You spend more time just hunting down a particular record, name, or address than you do entering data or defining fields.

Finding Out about Find: The Fourth Mode

If you've worked on building your database in FileMaker Pro, you've undoubtedly moved from Browse to Layout to Preview modes. Those modes are certainly the Big Three. Browse enables you to move through your files one record at a time. Layout challenges your designing skills and offers you a robust toolset to modify your fields and make your information presentable. Even Preview is extremely useful if you need to print your records, because you get to see what you're going to print.

Now comes Find mode. You may be thinking, Well, heck, I have Browse —
what do I need Find for? You have a point there, and it's probably valid until
your database suddenly grows large — for example, 100 or 200 records —
and takes longer than expected to browse through. Then you need to
sharpen your finding skills.

To find information in your FileMaker Pro database, what you do is create a
find request. No, you don't have to be Mr. or Ms. Polite and ask your program to find something for you. Just fill out the request form and let the
FileMaker Pro search engine do the rest.

If you want to know what's under the hood of the FileMaker Pro search
engine and a little bit about how it works, here goes:

✔ **The search engine in operation.** For any search to work effectively,
you need to have a powerful engine to do the job. FileMaker Pro's
engine is really good because it takes all the information you've entered
into your database and creates an index from it. Bet you didn't know
that was happening behind the scenes. Well, it was. While you were
busy doing other things, FileMaker Pro was busy, too, generating an
index so that you can search your records and find any records containing specific text, numbers, dates, or time.

✔ **The found set.** After you search your records, FileMaker Pro performs
another neat trick that's really helpful. It displays the records that it
found during its search, typically either in Form View or List View,
depending on the layouts in your database. These newly found records
are called the *found set*. They're actually a subset of the total number of
records in your database, and the cool thing is that you work on them
as you would any other database — that is, edit, delete, sort, print,
view, export, or copy to another file.

Don't worry. The rest of the records are still accessible to you. All you
have to do is choose Select➪Find All and that returns you to your
complete record set in your database.

You really appreciate this found set feature when your database gets
large, filled with many records, and difficult to navigate. At that point,
you welcome the opportunity to work with a subset of the information
in that large database.

✔ **Finding records with mistakes.** We all make mistakes, don't we? That's
how we learn, right? Well, if you're like me, you may make mistakes
while entering data into your FileMaker Pro records. The beauty of
using the Find command is that you can find and correct these mistakes
in your records. I'm talking about records that may have empty fields or
duplicate values, or records that have invalid dates and times and
other erroneous information.

> ✔ **The criteria.** What values or criteria you set up for your search through your FileMaker Pro records are very important. Criteria are what you type in the blank record that you use to make your request — the values that you want to find in a particular field.

Doing a Find

To find records, you have to fill out a request form so that FileMaker Pro knows what you're looking for and what the criteria are for your request.

Here's how:

1. **Select the layout that you want to use to find records.**

   The layout has to include every field in which you want to enter your search criteria.

2. **Choose Mode➪Find, as Figure 16-1 shows.**

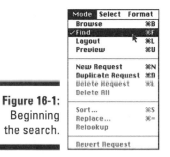

Figure 16-1:
Beginning
the search.

A blank request record pops up. In Figure 16-2, you see a blank record from my contact database, Tom's Cool List of Contacts, which I made by modifying a FileMaker Pro contacts template. Notice that just below the book icon is the number 1. That's the number of the current request. And below is another number 1, which is the number of requests currently made. If you make additional requests, FileMaker Pro keeps track of those as well.

3. **Click the Symbols button to get the list of operators, such as greater than (>) or less than (<), that you can use to paste into your request, as you see in Figure 16-3.**

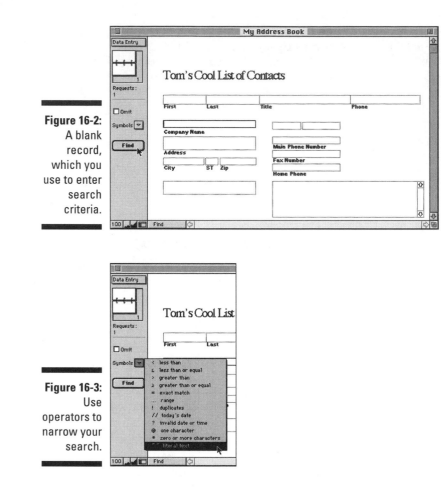

Figure 16-2:
A blank record, which you use to enter search criteria.

Figure 16-3:
Use operators to narrow your search.

4. **On your blank record, click in the field where you want to enter a search criterion.**

5. **Type in the values or combine the values that you type with the operators from the Symbols pop-up list. For example, you can enter the operator equal (=) followed by another operator duplicate (!) and then click the Find button.**

   Enter the criteria in as many fields as you want, and FileMaker Pro finds the records that match all the criteria in your request. This capacity is cool because FileMaker Pro matches those criteria, field by field, in your database. What this means is that your search results will be pretty thorough. For example, in a Names and Addresses database you can find all the people who live in a certain city, work for a certain company, and have the same first names.

FileMaker Pro puts some limitations on your search criteria. For example, you can't enter search criteria in container fields, summary fields, or global fields that you've stored.

Here's a list of the symbols you can use for your search criteria:

<	Less than what you type next	!	Duplicate values
<=	Less than or equal to what you type next. On the Mac, this is ≤.	//	Today's date
>	Greater than what you type next	?	Invalid dates, times, or calculated results
=>	Greater than or equal to what you type next. On the Mac, this is ≥.	@	One unknown or variable text character
=	An exact match	*	Zero or more unknown or variable text characters
...	Within the range you specify	""	Literal text
		= =	Field content match.

The field content match symbol is new to FileMaker Pro 4 and comes in pretty handy if you need to find an exact match in the *order* that you specify. For example, if you need to find *Tom Jones* in your address database, you can use this operator to return only *Tom Jones* and not *Jones Tom.*

Finding the Text You Want

If you want to find words that start with specific characters, you just type the characters in the text field. For example, if you enter **John Jones**, your request finds *John Jones, John Jonestown,* and *Jones John.*

To find an exact word, just use an equal sign (=) before the word. For example, **=Bill** finds *Bill* (but not *Billington*).

To find an exact sequence of words in a particular order, use the double equal sign (= =). In this case, **= = Ted Brown** finds *Ted Brown* (but not *Brown Ted*).

To find exact matches on several words in the same text field, you just use an equal sign (=) before each word in the search criterion in that field. For example, **=Ted =Turner** finds *Ted Turner* or *Turner Ted,* but it doesn't find *Ted Turnball.*

If you want to find words that change by one or more characters, you can use the wildcard character @ for each of those unknown characters. For example, **T@m** finds *Tom* and *Tim.*

To find words that change by more than one character, you can use the wildcard character * for all those unknown characters. For example, **D*n** finds *Davidson* and *Dickson.*

Chapter 17

Printing What You've Got

· ·

· ·

I don't know about you, but printing my files tends to be something of a challenge for me. I guess something about printers — their unpredictability — scares me. You know, print gremlins, gotchas, and unexplained encounters of the messy kind.

Although printers — especially laser printers — are among the most reliable machines in the computer world, I'm a klutz regarding how to feed and stack the right amount of paper in the sheet feeder or change a toner cartridge.

Now, with something as important as the files in my database, I get doubly apprehensive around printers. I have this irrational fear that not only is my printer going to screw up my print job, but it's also, somehow, going to screw up my precious data files. I know it's irrational, but. . . .

Actually, printing with FileMaker Pro is a snap. There's not much to it, really, once you get things set up. I've formulated a ten-step plan of attack that should keep the print gremlins away from your FileMaker Pro database.

Up front, I ought to mention that if you're using the new FileMaker Pro 4 Web Companion, which lets you print your database from the Web, you're at the mercy of your browser, usually Netscape Navigator or Microsoft Internet Explorer, as far as printing is concerned. Your browser controls the printing of records that you've published on the Web — it's as simple as that.

Know Thy Printer

It's the first rule of order — well, maybe the First Commandment in the Gospel According to Print: *Know thy printer.* Every printer is bound to have its quirks and idiosyncrasies. Printers are only human, like the rest of us, I guess. If you have a printer of your own at home, or work with one in your office or school, you probably know what I'm talking about.

Getting to know your printer doesn't involve any formal rules. All I can say is that if you don't take the time to figure out what your printer is doing, it's going to *make* you take the time.

Start on your Windows computer by checking your Windows default printer, which is selected in the Control Panel. That's the printer, you'll be working with the behavior of which you must know. Keep in mind that if you designate a different printer in your Print Setup dialog box, well, that printer becomes your default printer for FileMaker Pro.

Start on the Mac by checking the Chooser (choose ⇨Chooser) and seeing what printers you have access to. Then make sure that you have the latest version of the printer driver installed in your system. If you don't, make every effort to get the latest version. Why? Because each version of a printer driver invariably fixes bugs that customers reported when they tried to print with earlier versions. Keeping up with the times is just the name of the game.

So call your printer manufacturer to find out the latest versions of their printer drivers. That call could be one of the most important you make, as far as the quality of your print job is concerned.

Take care to make sure that you've followed all the right procedures for loading paper, cleaning ribbons and laser wires, loading ink cartridges — taking care of whatever physical elements are critical for your print job. Proper maintenance is absolutely necessary to avoid getting a print job all messed up. You've put a lot of time into building your FileMaker Pro database; you don't want the job all blotched when you print, do you?

Ten Steps to Print

Actually, more than ten steps may be involved in printing, but bear with me for the sake of argument (you may actually experience fewer than ten steps, too). In any case, this section shows how to print by the numbers, just to keep things straight.

Follow these steps:

1. **Go to the layout in your database that you want to print by choosing Mode⇨Layout, and then choosing the layout you've named in New Layout dialog box.**

   For example, you may want to print the invoices in your Order Entry FileMaker Pro template, as you see in Figure 17-1.

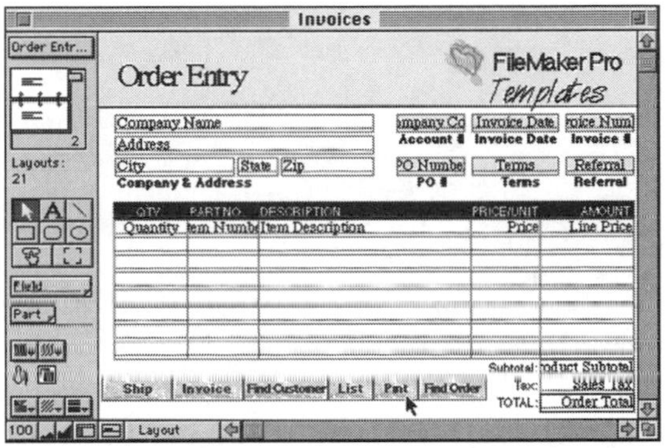

Figure 17-1:
Opening a
layout to
print.

[Invoices window — Order Entry template showing Company Name, Address, City/State/Zip fields, and buttons: Ship, Invoice, Find Customer, List, Print, Find Order]

If you look closely at the layout of the template shown in Figure 18-1, you see at the bottom of the screen a button labeled Print. Cool, huh? The template comes ready made with that button, which has script attached to it that lets you print the layout by just clicking the button.

You can add a button like that in your own layouts, too — it's not hard to do: You just click the button tool in the FileMaker Pro Tool panel on the left of your screen. After your cursor becomes a button, you drop it on your layout. From there, you define a script that, essentially, tells the button what to do — that is, print. I explain all this business about using scripts and scripting in Chapter 22. Just thought you might be curious about it now.

2. **Check over your layout to make sure it has what you want to print.**

3. **Choose File⇨Page Setup on the Mac (see Figure 17-2) or choose File⇨Print Setup in Windows.**

4. **When the dialog box appears for your printer — Figure 17-3 shows my Personal LaserWriter LS — select the options that you want. Click OK.**

   These options, you need to remember, apply to your current layout only.

Figure 17-2:
The Page
Setup menu
item.

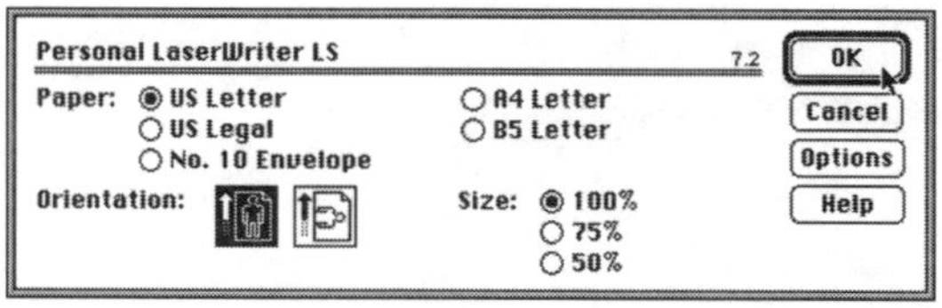

Figure 17-3:
Preparing
your page
for printing.

5. Once again in your file, select the records that you want to print by choosing Mode⇨Browse.

In the Invoices Order Entry template, for example, I want to print three records, as you see in Figure 17-4.

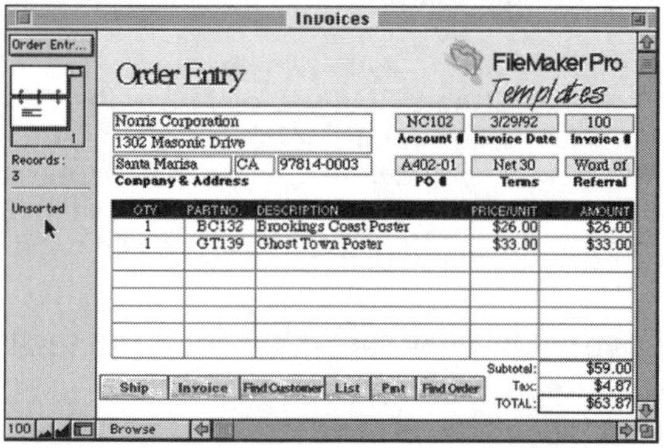

Figure 17-4:
Three
records to
print in this
database.

Note that these records are unsorted, meaning that they're not arranged in a particular order. Well, we can't have that for printing purposes, can we? It's time to sort, baby, sort.

6. In Browse mode, choose Mode⇨Sort, as you see in Figure 17-5.

Figure 17-5:
Sort before
you print.

7. **In the Sort Records dialog box that you see in Figure 17-6, select the items that you want to sort by highlighting them, and then click the Move button to move them over to the right portion of the box.**

What sorting does is specify the order in which your records will be arranged by the fields you specify.

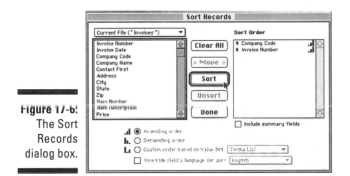

Figure 17-6:
The Sort
Records
dialog box.

8. **Click the Sort button and return to your records in, for example, the Invoices Order Entry template.**

You see to the left, below the Book icon, the number of records in your file and the designation Sorted just below that, like the one in Figure 17-7.

Now you're just about ready to print because you've told FileMaker Pro the order in which you want your records printed. One last thing before you finally print. . . .

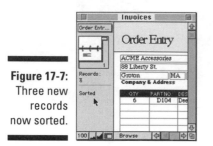

Figure 17-7:
Three new
records
now sorted.

9. **Change to Preview mode by choosing Mode⇨Preview for a look at how your records are going to appear when they print.**

Using Preview is always a good idea. If you need to, you can make any changes or adjustments in your layouts after you've previewed them. In Preview mode, you can see the margins for your printed pages and, if necessary, adjust them, but remember, you can't adjust them in Preview mode. You have to switch to Layout mode to make any changes.

What you see in Preview mode is what you get when you print.

In the Order Entry example you see in Figure 17-8, you have two order entries on one page. Remember that I sorted three records, so that's how many I'm going to print.

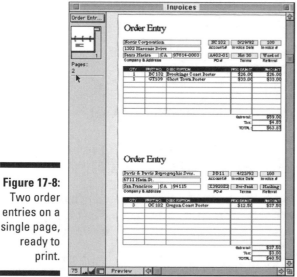

Figure 17-8:
Two order
entries on a
single page,
ready to
print.

10. If everything looks okay, choose File⇨Print.

The Print dialog box shown in Figure 17-9 appears. You have a few more options to choose from. The Mac and Windows dialog boxes do all the same things, but they are laid out just a little bit differently.

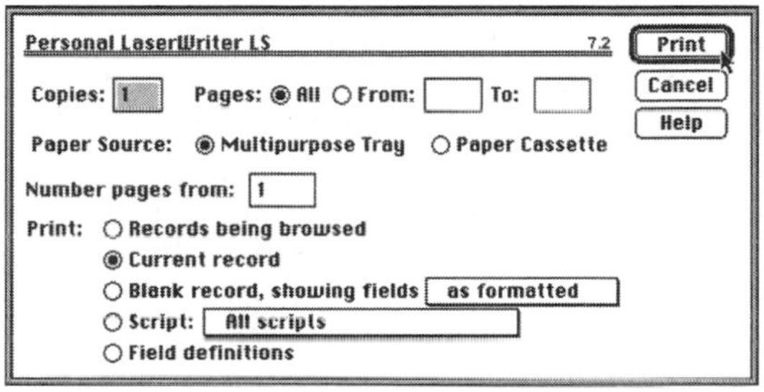

Figure 17-9:
The Mac
Print
dialog box
(pictured)
has the
same
options
as the
Windows
dialog box,
but they
look a little
different.

Printing What You've Previewed

In the top boxes of the Print dialog box, you can enter the number of copies you want to print, followed by the range of pages you're going to print, either all or a specific range. Below that, you click a radio button to identify your paper source. And below that, you enter the number from which to start numbering the pages in your file.

Now things get a bit more complicated as to the additional choices you have. Stay cool.

The first choice is whether to print the records you've browsed; you see in Figure 17-10 that the Records Being Browsed button is selected. If you click that button, FileMaker Pro prints a report of your records — that is, all records in the found set — rather than print the records themselves.

The second choice, to print the Current record, means that you want FileMaker Pro to print only the currently selected record in Browse mode.

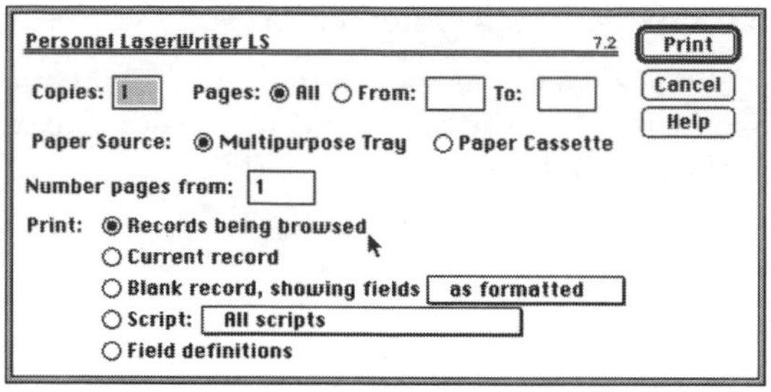

Figure 17-10:
Telling
FileMaker
Pro to print
the records
you're
browsing.

> Personal LaserWriter LS   7.2   [Print]
>
> Copies: [1]   Pages: ◉ All ○ From: [   ] To: [   ]   [Cancel]
>   [Help]
> Paper Source: ◉ Multipurpose Tray   ○ Paper Cassette
>
> Number pages from: [1]
>
> Print: ◉ Records being browsed
>   ○ Current record
>   ○ Blank record, showing fields [as formatted]
>   ○ Script: [All scripts   ]
>   ○ Field definitions

The third option is to print a Blank record. Here, you also have some
additional choices, as you see in Figure 17-11: As Formatted, With Boxes, or
With Underlines. If you select As Formatted, FileMaker Pro prints your fields
just the way that you formatted them in the Field Borders dialog box. If you
select With Boxes, you get a box around each field when you print. Selecting
the With Underlines option makes FileMaker Pro print a line under each of
your fields.

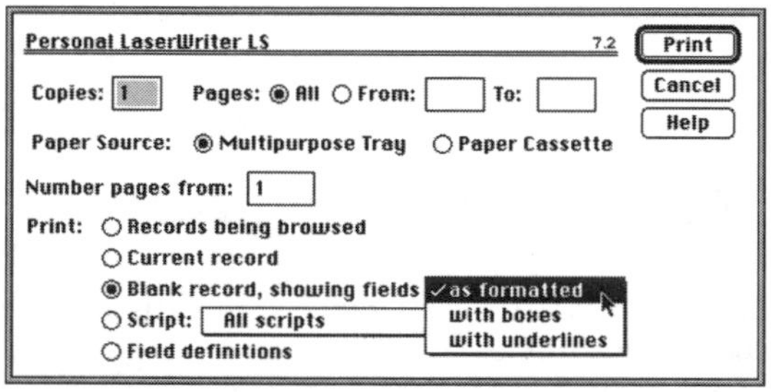

> Personal LaserWriter LS   7.2   [Print]
>
> Copies: [1]   Pages: ◉ All ○ From: [   ] To: [   ]   [Cancel]
>   [Help]
> Paper Source: ◉ Multipurpose Tray   ○ Paper Cassette
>
> Number pages from: [1]
>
> Print: ○ Records being browsed
>   ○ Current record
>   ◉ Blank record, showing fields [✓ as formatted]
>   [with boxes   ]
>   ○ Script: [All scripts   ] [with underlines]
>   ○ Field definitions

Figure 17-11:
You can
even print a
blank
record.

Printing a blank record can be really handy to get an idea of how your
database looks, in case you want to modify it at some point.

The fourth option is to print a script. If you're using templates or modifying
somebody else's database that includes lots of scripts defining the actions
of various buttons, you may want to print out the scripts. What FileMaker
Pro does, in this case, is print a list of all the steps and options that have
been defined for the scripts that you select. For more information about
scripting, check out Chapter 22.

Factors affecting how you print

All kinds of factors can affect how your printed output appears on paper, as opposed to how it displays on-screen. Obviously, with a laser printer, you get a better-quality output than if you print with a dot-matrix printer. A PostScript printer is the way to go for high-quality output, especially if your database contains a number of graphic images.

Some things to keep in mind:

✔ You get faster printing if you turn off the color or gray scale printing options.

✔ PostScript fonts print better — sharper and clearer — than bitmapped fonts, such as New York, Geneva, or Monaco.

✔ Avoid mixing a bunch of different fonts in your layout; try to keep your font selection to a maximum of three. Your printing looks much better as a consequence.

The last option is the Field Definitions option, which is a good option to exercise because you get to see on paper how you've defined all those fields, something that you may lose track of in your database. Because how you define fields is at the heart of working with FileMaker Pro and getting the most out of the program, anything that helps you see what you're doing in those fields is useful. Nothing wrong with printing them out from time to time.

When you've selected all of your options, click Print to start that printer churning.

Chapter 18

Networking with Files and Friends

· ·

In This Chapter

▶ Understanding file sharing and networking

▶ Making your file network-accessible

▶ Defining who can access your files

▶ Sharing files between Mac and Windows computers

· ·

1 f you're a single user of FileMaker Pro (or even if you're married but don't use FileMaker Pro on a network), you might want to skip this chapter. Actually *single user* is a technical jargon word for someone running on a *stand-alone* (that is, not hooked into a network) computer. What's someone running on a network with a lot of other computers called? A user. Not double user, network user, or multiuser. Just a user. Hey, you figure it out. Professional nerds just naturally understand this kind of logic.

This chapter is for you if you're working with FileMaker Pro on a network or thinking of joining in a network marriage. It's also for you if you need to define certain *access privileges* (who can and can't get access to the data and even the layouts in your files to your FileMaker Pro database) and passwords to enforce the access privileges you set. This chapter is especially geared toward those people who find themselves in an office that has both Macs and Windows PCs running on a network, sharing FileMaker Pro files between them. After you're comfortable sharing your files in an office, you'll be ready to share files in the biggest network of all — the Web. With the new FileMaker Pro 4, you can share the files in your database on the Web with FileMaker Pro's Web Companion, as Chapter 20 explains.

Welcome to the Brave New World of file sharing!

The Brave New World of File Sharing

All right. Here's a scenario for you to imagine. You've just started working for a small software company, maybe a dozen hardy souls in cyberspace. The company is progressive and hardworking. The boss hired you with the expectation that you could "work with FileMaker Pro on the net."

"Whoa, what net?" you may well ask. The computer network in the office, that's what.

At first, when you step in the door, you may be in for a shock. You may see five, ten, or more Macintosh computers all running FileMaker Pro. Or you may see five, ten, or more Macs and Windows PCs all running FileMaker Pro in a *mixed environment,* which is just a fancy way of saying that, despite the differences between the Macintosh and Windows operating systems, the computers can still "talk to each other" and share information across the net.

Don't let this scenario intimidate you. Working with FileMaker Pro on a network is fundamentally no different than working with FileMaker Pro on a single-user machine. You just have more computers to deal with, meaning "network traffic" and little inconveniences such as access privileges (who gets to view what FileMaker Pro files and who gets to modify them). In addition, you have to deal with issues of password protection, which you find out more about later in this chapter.

Remember that FileMaker Pro on a network sounds more complicated only because the program is running on more machines.

You must understand two key words if you're going to live happily ever after in the world of networking: *host* and *guest* (no, this is not a Christmas party). Here's the distinction: The first person who opens a file and shares it is the *host;* any user after the host is the *guest.* For example, in sharing files between a Macintosh and a Windows PC, you can have the host file on the Mac and the guest on the PC (it can be the reverse, too).

The cross-platform boogie

Sharing files cross-platform between Macintosh and Windows FileMaker Pro users is pretty smooth sailing when you get right down to it. The wizards at Claris had this idea in mind when they made a big thing about FileMaker Pro being able to work across a network in a cross-platform office or company. It's not that much different from sharing files on a Macintosh-only or a Windows-only network. If you're a host, you can open your FileMaker Pro database on your Macintosh as a multiuser file so that guests on the PC running Windows can open the same file you're using. A guest on the PC sees the same things on his or her screen as a guest on the Macintosh. Pretty cool when you think about it.

All that's required to share files is Farallon Computing's PhoneNet Talk software (or similar software from another vendor), which lets you connect Macs and Windows PCs to each other via an AppleTalk network. You can reach Farallon Computing at 510-814-5000 or at info@farallon.com on e-mail.

Of course, things aren't perfectly seamless when Macs and PCs hook up: All your FileMaker Pro Macintosh files must have the .FM suffix so that Windows PCs can read and recognize the files. Check out Chapter 19 for details on differences between Mac and Windows file formats.

Beating the Cold Network Sweat

Stepping into an office is no picnic when, all of sudden, you're working on a network with other people, opening and closing files, entering data into new records, and printing out the results of your efforts. Things can get tense, particularly if you encounter network traffic or confusion, or if, on a bad day, you have a system crash or your hard drive fails right in the middle of your work. I call this experience the Cold Network Sweat. It can be pervasive, but you can do some things about it. To avoid the cold network sweat on the first day, just try this:

- ✔ Take a deep breath.

- ✔ Accept that you can't master FileMaker Pro on a network overnight. Nobody can be an instant network guru.

- ✔ Be patient and give yourself time to find your way around the network.

- ✔ Realize that the main thing you'll be doing in the beginning is adding new records to the existing company or office FileMaker Pro database. That's pretty straightforward after you see how the database is set up and what information you have to enter in each record's fields.

Nobody expects you to redesign the company's existing FileMaker Pro database. But if you master the ideas in this book and know your way around the world of FileMaker Pro databases, there's no good reason why you shouldn't think of ways to improve your company's database. For one thing, you have a fresh perspective on what works and what doesn't.

- ✔ Find out who the System Administrator is in your office. And make friends with that person. Offer some treats, if necessary (M&M's, chocolate chip cookies, a double mocha, whatever), in exchange for tips on how to work with FileMaker Pro on your network.

System Administrator is just an important-sounding word for the guardian of the net, the person who's in charge of maintaining the records and files in your company's FileMaker Pro database. That person is known as a Sys Admin (which sounds like a bad flavor of computer candy). But that person can save your life — at least that part of your life that lives on the company net in virtual space.

It's a tough job, but somebody's got to do it, right? That somebody in the office must take responsibility for maintaining and upgrading the system, deleting duplicate records, and performing other routine database housekeeping chores. That's a person you want to get to know.

All of these things ought to help you get over the Cold Network Sweat. As you find out more about working with FileMaker Pro on the net, you gain more confidence. Remember that the better you get at working with FileMaker Pro, the more quickly you'll advance in your company or business, and the more people will come to rely on you for ideas on how to maintain and improve your database — or even come to you for in-house technical support! Be prepared for a career change. Be prepared to be pestered to death.

Going from Single to Multiuser in One Mouse Click

To make a file available to the other users on your network, select File⇨Sharing⇨Multi-User. You're there.

Note that if a Network Protocol (in Edit⇨Preferences⇨Application⇨General) is not selected, the Multi-User choice is disabled.

The first person who opens up a multiuser file in a database is designated as the host. Other people in your office then can open up the same multiuser file as guests. To open that file, they need to choose File⇨Open and click the Network button. Naturally, when you're on the network and you click the Network button, you see a much longer list of files displayed, which you can then access, depending on how your System Administrator has defined your privileges to access network files.

You live on the network that way — as either host or guest. Remember that you may have to play both roles, at times host and at other times guest, depending on whether you're the first person to share your files.

Sharing Good Information

The beauty of having a host and guest (or many guests) on the network is quite simple: You can share the same information (life gets easier when you do what you were taught way back in third grade — namely, *share*). Of course, having one updated database is better than several copies, each reflecting a different user's changes. Having several copies of the same database means that someone has to consolidate them, which can be a very big chore, indeed.

After a guest opens a file, both host and guest can sort through different records, toggle between database layouts, and even use FileMaker Pro scripts without disrupting or changing the other person's work.

However — and here's the catch — only one person on the network can *edit* a FileMaker Pro record, layout, or script at any given time. In other words, you can't have two people pounding away on the same record at the same time, making changes simultaneously. FileMaker Pro just doesn't allow that, because the users end up clobbering each other's work to death.

Other people on your network can read your record, layout, or script while you're working on it, but nobody (whatever the person's rank in the food chain) can modify your work before you've finished it and pressed Enter to confirm a record entry. In effect, you have to move on to the next record, layout, or script before anybody can touch your work.

Because FileMaker Pro protects your work until you're finished with the record, layout, or script, you have no need to fear some faceless being matched against you in a network tug-of-war over the same record. (In the early days of the database world, networks didn't always work that way. But these days, you have programs like FileMaker Pro with a great deal of built-in smarts.)

Now, the last thing to keep in mind is that any changes you've made to your file appear in the window in which you're working. The changes are saved to the hard drive where the host opened up the file.

All this file sharing across a network is, of course, just the sharing of the information you have in those files with other people. Once you've shared information like that, FileMaker Pro lets you know what's going on by giving you a couple of odd symbols to watch:

- **Network arrows pointing in opposite directions:** This symbol looks like something from outer space just breaking through Earth's atmosphere and shows you that FileMaker Pro is sharing the information in your file with the information in somebody else's file.

- **Little coffee cup:** This symbol — which doesn't *necessarily* mean you should go out and get a cup of coffee — is FileMaker Pro's way of indicating that your host is processing a request from another person on the network. Of course, if the network is running slowly, please enjoy the coffee.

Obviously, things move faster on a single-user system running FileMaker Pro than they do in a multiuser environment. The net almost inevitably operates with a certain sluggishness when you're sharing files with other people. The smart thing to do, if you want to get optimum performance, is to turn on the single-user control. Then when you've completed your work, switch back to multiuser status, and you're once again happily sharing the information in your files.

Defining Access Privileges

Your System Administrator is the person who controls the flow of information in your FileMaker Pro database and, as a consequence, protects the security and confidentiality of the data on the net. That's the person who can help you define the access privileges and passwords for the groups of people in your office or company on the network. Your System Administrator can explain what your role is and what you need to do.

By definition, privileges and passwords limit access to important data. Here are some points that you should keep in mind about privileges and passwords:

- The job of the System Administrator is to establish the levels of access to the company's records and files. When setting up, one group or person — usually the first one defined — *must* have complete privileges. This point is crucial.

- Chances are that you belong to a particular group in the company — Sales or Marketing, for example — and your group's access is limited in one way or another.

- A password specifies exactly the level of access you can have to a particular file. Certain passwords may also limit your activities within a file. You may only be able to browse records with one password, and edit records or design your own layouts with another. The System Administrator is in charge of these limits — essentially defining your access privileges.

Be sure to get your access privileges clarified early on. If you're not sure of something, don't hesitate to ask. If you find that you need greater access to files, present your case to the System Administrator.

Defining access privileges is something you need to know, too, because it's your way of specifying whom you allow to gain access to your files. You can define those groups and assign passwords to them. For example, when you choose File⇨Access Privileges, a submenu with three options appears:

- Define Groups
- Define Passwords
- Overview

Follow these steps to define the access privileges for a group:

1. **Choose File⇨Access Privileges⇨Define Groups.**

2. **Type each group's name in the Group Name text box.**

   Figure 18-1 shows you a sample screen where three groups are defined: Dummies Group, Template Makers, and Tech Editors.

Figure 18-1:
Enter the
names of
groups
whose
access
privileges
you want to
define in
the Define
Groups
dialog box.

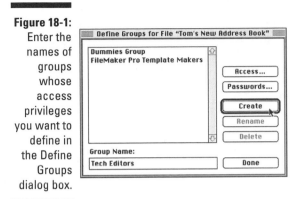

Figure 18-1:
Enter the
names of
groups
whose
access
privileges
you want to
define in
the Define
Groups
dialog box.

3. **Click Create to enter the names of the groups.**

4. **Click the Access button.**

   The screen in Figure 18-2 appears, showing you in various columns the access privileges for groups, along with their passwords and their rights to modify layouts.

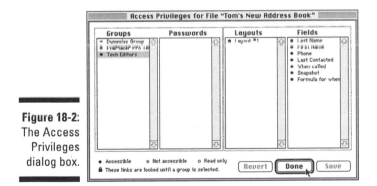

Figure 18-2:
The Access
Privileges
dialog box.

5. **Click Done.**

6. **Choose File⇨Access Privileges⇨Define Passwords, as shown in Figure 18-3.**

   The dialog box you see in Figure 18-4 opens. Here, you can enter the passwords you want for particular groups of users.

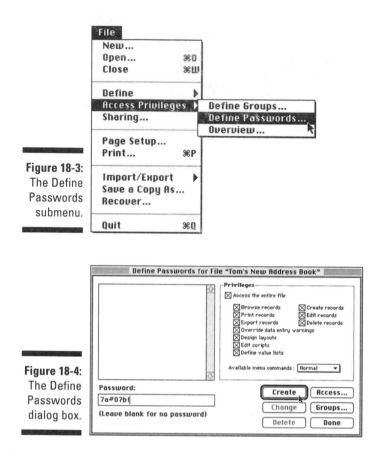

Figure 18-3:
The Define
Passwords
submenu.

Figure 18-4:
The Define
Passwords
dialog box.

7. Click Create.

8. Choose File⇨Access Privileges⇨Overview.

The screen in Figure 18-5 appears, showing you which groups have
which privileges and passwords.

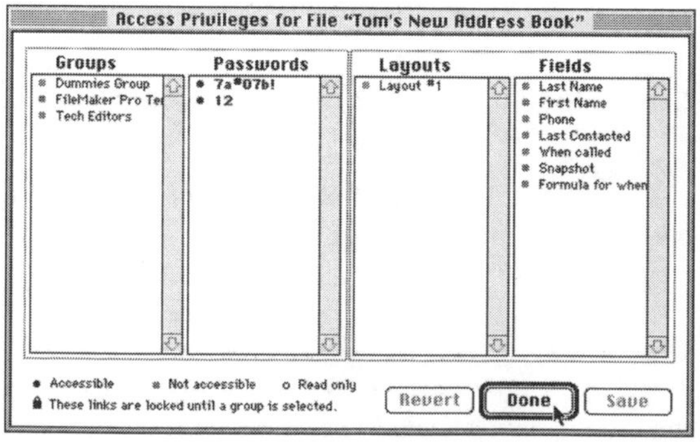

Figure 18-5:
An
overview of
access
privileges.

Cross-Platform File Sharing —
Almost Seamless

If you're sharing files on an all-Mac network, you don't have to worry about too many things. Each Macintosh computer ought to have a copy of FileMaker Pro running on it. And each Macintosh ought to have the FileMaker Network file installed in the Claris Folder, which is in the System Folder. You need to be on an AppleTalk network with other Mac people.

On an all-Mac network, you don't have to worry about different fonts in your FileMaker Pro database. Nor do you have to deal with different file-naming conventions as you do in the Windows world.

However, if you're working in that mixed-office environment, with Macs and Windows computers living and breathing side by side, hooked up by network cables and software, things may get a bit more complicated. Problems may crop up with different fonts and certainly with different naming conventions. For example, Mac users have to take into account that files created with FileMaker Pro for Windows have an .FM3 extension (although when you're opening a file, you can see only .FM).

But not to worry. FileMaker Pro was designed for seamless (well, almost) sharing of FileMaker Pro files from Macs to PCs across the network. The idea here is that if you're a host and you designate a file as multiuser on your PC, you can have guests who are using Macs and PCs able to open and work with the same file. The guests on both computers can even see the same files at the same time and do what they have to do with those files — browsing, sorting, and so on — on the net, though they can't edit or modify the same record at the same time.

What does a file server serve
when it's not serving files?

If ten or more people are on your all-Mac network, you probably have a dedicated file server that stores all the FileMaker Pro files and records in your office.

Don't be puzzled or confused by the phrase *file server*. Typically, a file server is nothing but a big Macintosh or Windows computer with a huge hard drive — enough storage capacity to keep all the data from your office in one happy place. Think of it as a humongous beast

of storage that's there for only one reason — to serve you.

If you think about it, FileMaker Pro actually "lives" on the network among a group of people, and your database has its home on the file server, where it ought to be safe and secure.

As for what a file server serves when it's not serving files, well, from the user's point of view, not a whole heck of a lot.

In order to bridge these two worlds and make Macs "talk to" PCs, you need the right network hardware and software. I won't bore you with the details of this software or the necessary network cards that you have to install in your PCs to make this bridging all happen. This is pure geek stuff.

If you know the Mac but not Windows, keep in mind that Windows has its own set of file-naming conventions that differ from the Mac's. All the files you create with FileMaker Pro for Windows, for example, have an .FM extension. If you work with the Mac, you may want to use DOS-naming conventions so you can move files back and forth from one world to the other without a lot of hassle.

Fonts may look different from one platform to the other, or may be just plain unavailable. For example, if you're moving a file from the PC to the Mac, FileMaker Pro does a font substitution. Table 18-1 shows you how this font-substitution game works.

Table 18-1	FileMaker Pro Font Substitutions
This PC Font	*Is Substituted for This Macintosh Font*
MS Serif	Times
Times New Roman	Times
Times	New York
Times Roman	Times
Courier New	Courier
Courier	Monaco

This substitution is no big deal. Your Network Honcho is probably aware of this problem already and is working to match the font sets on both platforms as closely as possible. Still, you may have to do some tweaking when you align text in your layouts because there are size differences between the fonts in each set.

Other differences between platforms that you ought to be aware of:

✔ Windows PCs and Macs use different file formats for pictures and graphic images. To see those pictures or graphic images on your Mac, you have to turn the Store Macintosh Picture Format option in the document preference file in FileMaker Pro for Windows. That way, you get the image stored as a PICT file, so you can see it on both the Mac and the PC.

✔ Printing may vary from Mac to PC. For example, a file that you create on the Mac but then open and print on the PC may look different when it comes out of the printer. Mac printers and PC printers print differently — it's as simple as that. A good idea is to create layouts that are specific to one or the other computer, and then print what you have on the printer that gives you the best results.

AppleScript is not supported on the PC, and PC batch commands don't work on the Mac.

If you want to get more detail on some of the cross-platform issues between Mac and Windows PCs, I'd suggest that you check out the Claris Web site: www.claris.com. The Web site has many articles, FAQs (frequently asked questions), and technical notes on cross-platform issues. You'll get a pretty up-to-date analysis of things that differ and what you need to be aware of if you're working in a mixed network environment. The more you know, the better, right?

Chapter 19

Playing the Import and Export Game

. . . .

. . . .

There's no doubt in my mind that FileMaker Pro is a powerful tool for exchanging information. But why exchange information in the first place? What's the point? Why not keep it all to yourself?

Well, if you've worked with FileMaker Pro on a network, as explained in Chapter 18, you know that you're in the business of transferring data from one file that's accessible to one user to another file that's accessible to many users. I guess you could call this a one-to-many approach to exchanging information. The information gets updated faster as more people on the network share in the process of entering, storing, and sharing the information.

But exchanging information has another, equally important facet — importing and exporting data — and that's what this chapter is all about.

Getting the Hang of Import and Export

You have times when you need to import data from another application into your FileMaker Pro database. You also have times when the reverse may be true: You need to export data in your database to another application. That application may be a word processor, a spreadsheet, a database, or a completely different application. How do you handle importing and exporting? Well, I'll start with some terminology.

There's a simple distinction you need to be familiar with when you're sharing or exchanging information with import/export:

- **Source file:** The file where your data comes from
- **Destination file:** The file where your data goes

Why is importing and exporting necessary at all? Well, it's because programs use different *file formats,* or methods of storing information. A spreadsheet, which needs to keep track of formulas and the positions of data, saves different information than a word processor, which has no need to save such data. Beyond that, file formats are like opinions: Every program's got one, and they all seem to be different. Even the same types of programs (word processors, spreadsheets, databases, and so on) made by different companies save information in very different (and usually incompatible) formats. If not for the ability to import and export, all these different formats would mean that you could never use any data in FileMaker Pro that was created in another program. Luckily, that's not the case. FileMaker Pro can import and export a large number of file formats.

You do face some limitations to what you can import and export. Here are two that may trip you up:

- You can't import or export data if you're working with your records on the Web and using the FileMaker Pro Web Companion. (Refer to Chapters 20 and 21 for the story on this hot new feature.)
- You can't import or export your layouts from one file to another, although you can copy and paste the objects you've created from one layout to another.

In addition, if you're exchanging files between your Mac and Windows computers, you may also encounter some problems. For example, you may see different filenames which may throw you for a loop at first, but these differences are nothing too serious. Mac and Windows 95 are very similiar: Both support a 32-character limit for file names and it's not necessary to end the name with a three character extension, as you need to do in Windows 3.1. On the Mac, you can enter the name of a file using punctuation marks (everything except a colon). The only punctuation Windows 95 supports is the underscore character (_).

Aside from these limitations, importing and exporting data from and to your FileMaker Pro database is pretty straightforward. It's useful, too. I work in software development, and I've seen engineers easily export bug-list databases from FileMaker Pro to Microsoft Excel, where they can then manipulate the information and generate lots of neat charts and diagrams (mostly to explain why many software bugs aren't getting fixed as rapidly as they ought to be). The data that was originally stored in a FileMaker Pro file is now converted to the rows and columns of a spreadsheet for proper number crunching, which somehow looks more formidable to the boss.

Choosing Your File Format

FileMaker Pro supports many file formats, which is great if you're using, for example, different spreadsheet programs and want to take advantage of exchanging data with Lotus 1-2-3 or Microsoft Excel. Table 19-1 gives you a pretty complete rundown of these various file formats and what you can use them for.

Table 19-1 FileMaker Pro File Formats Supported for Import/Export

File Format	*What You Can Use That Format to Do*
FileMaker Files (.FP3 or .FM extension)	Import data from a FileMaker Pro 3 or 4 file, or export that data to another FileMaker Pro 4 file.
Tab-Separated Text (.TAB or .TXT extension)	Exchange data with many other applications, including ClarisImpact. Use this file format if you're not certain which format to use.
Comma-Separated Text (.CSV or .TXT extension)	Exchange data with BASIC programs and some other applications, such as ClarisImpact. Also known as Comma-Separated Values (CSV).
SYLK (.SLK extension)	Exchange data with just about every spreadsheet program ever invented. This format is an industry standard and goes back a long way.
DIF (.DIF extension)	Exchange data with certain spreadsheet programs.
WKS (.WK1 or .WKS extension)	Exchange data with Lotus 1-2-3. Note that FileMaker Pro can import .WKS and .WK1 files but can only export to .WK1 files.
BASIC (.BAS extension)	Exchange data with Microsoft BASIC programs.
Merge (.MER extension)	Combine data in a Merge file with text. It's supposed to be equivalent to a Microsoft Word data source.
ClarisWorks Files (.CWK and .CWS extensions)	Import data from ClarisWorks 4 database files.
HTML Table (.HTM extension)	Save your data as an HTML table if you want to publish to your database on the Web with the Web Companion feature (new for FileMaker Pro 4).
DBF (.DBF extension)	Exchange data with Microsoft's Visual FoxPro, or with dBASE III and dBASE IV.
Excel (.XLS extension)	Import data from Microsoft Excel 4 through Excel 7, in addition to Excel 97. FileMaker Pro and Microsoft Excel form a powerful software combination for home, education, and business users.

Importing the Goods

The goods in this case can be files or data that you've created with another application. FileMaker Pro is very generous in what it allows you to bring in. Most of it is duty-free; you won't get stuck with any tariffs (at least none that I know of).

Using FileMaker Pro, you can

✔ Import files from another FileMaker Pro file, either from Mac or from Windows

✔ Import files from another application, such as ClarisWorks, HyperCard, or dBASE

✔ Import files from other sources, such as an SQL Server that uses the Data Access Manager (that's if you're really into high-power database importing)

✔ Import pictures or QuickTime movies into your files

Importing files from another database or another application is cool because you can combine your information from multiple files or sources into one all-inclusive file. From time to time, as you add more files or build new databases, step back for a moment and think about ways to consolidate those files. Importing files from one file into another is clearly a neat solution.

To import a file from another FileMaker Pro file or from another application, just follow these steps after you've opened the file that you want your data imported to:

1. Choose File⇨Import/Export⇨Import Records, as Figure 19-1 shows.

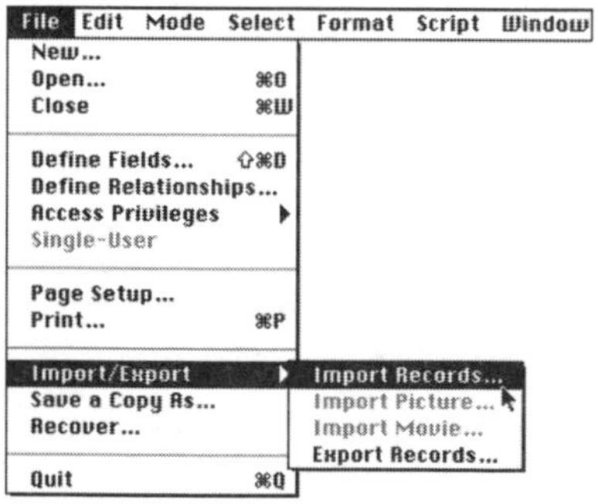

Figure 19-1:
The Import
Records
submenu
ready for
action.

File	Edit	Mode	Select	Format	Script	Window

New...
Open...   ⌘O
Close   ⌘W

Define Fields...   ⇧⌘D
Define Relationships...
Access Privileges   ▶
Single-User

Page Setup...
Print...   ⌘P

Import/Export   ▶   Import Records...
Save a Copy As...   Import Picture...
Recover...   Import Movie...
                     Export Records...

Quit   ⌘Q

2. In the dialog box that appears (which Figure 19-2 shows), click the file that you want to import.

Figure 19-2:
Ready to
import the
Bug Report.

In this example, I want to import the Bug Report into my Projects file.

If you click Show, you can see the number of different file formats that you can import into your FileMaker Pro file (Figure 19-3 shows these formats). This versatility is what makes FileMaker Pro a robust database program. You've probably heard that word *robust* in the computer world and maybe wondered what the heck people mean when they say that a particular software program is robust. Here's a good example: FilemakerPro allows you to import tab-separated text, Merge file formats, comma-separated text, BASIC, SYLK, DIF, WKS, DBF (which is the database format used with dBASE files), and even Data Access Manager files. That's robust!

Now the really cool thing here is that file format at the bottom of the screen in Figure 19-3, Microsoft Excel, a welcome addition to FileMaker Pro 4. With Microsoft Excel, you can import your Excel spreadsheets into a FileMaker Pro 4 database and build a database using the data from Excel. This new feature works with Excel 4.0 and 5.0 on the Mac, as well as Excel 4.0, 5.0, and 7.0 with Excel for Windows 95 and Excel 8.0 (Excel 97) with Windows.

3. The Import Field Mapping dialog box, shown in Figure 19-4, appears.

Try not to be overwhelmed by this dialog box (I confess: I was when I saw it the first time). I know that a great deal is going on. But all that FileMaker Pro is trying to do is bring the data from the file you're importing into the file that you're importing to. In this case, it needs to know where in the Projects file to put that Bug Report data.

The box on the right lists all the fields in your destination file, with arrows that point from the corresponding fields in your source file. It's as simple as that. If you want to change the order of those fields, click the field. A cursor appears that lets you move the fields up or down accordingly. If you don't want to change the order, FileMaker Pro maps the data in your source fields to the corresponding destination fields.

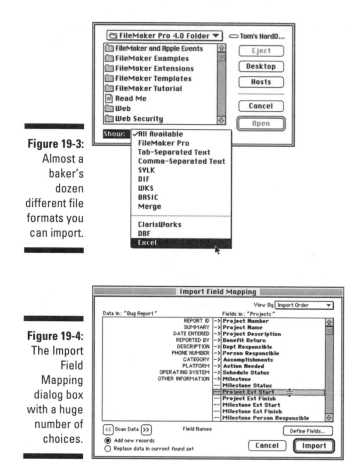

Figure 19-3:
Almost a
baker's
dozen
different file
formats you
can import.

Figure 19-4:
The Import
Field
Mapping
dialog box
with a huge
number of
choices.

Why would you want to reorder your fields? Well, say that you've inherited information from an older database where all the fields are in alphabetical order and your database is not. You've got problems, right? Not with FileMaker Pro — just match the fields, and you're golden!

4. Select the fields you want imported by clicking them, as shown in Figure 19-5.

Your cursor now turns into a check, with which you can click the box that separates the two large boxes on the left and right. By checking that box, you get this symbol: —>. It indicates that the data from the field to your left will appear in the field to your right. In this case, I'm mapping the ID numbers from my Bug Report to my Projects file so I can keep track of them better. Note that the default is set so that fields will import and have the —> symbol. By clicking the field, you deselect the field for import (- -).

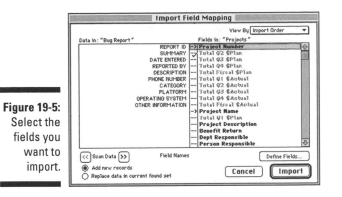

Figure 19-5:
Select the
fields you
want to
import.

5. Click Import if you don't want to make any changes to the matching order between your source file and your destination file.

Hold the mouse down and drag it down or up, as appropriate, if you want to select or deselect those fields quickly

FileMaker Pro is very generous about letting you do a variety of imports. But you need to follow a few rules so things go smoothly.

Rule #1: Importing to summary or calculation fields

If you think about it, importing data is pretty much equivalent to copying data from one source to another. FileMaker Pro lets you do that copying, except to calculation and summary fields, which means you can't copy your data or import it into either of those fields. Both the calculation and summary fields perform a mathematical or formula calculation to compute the values that you have in those fields. So you can't just drop imported or copied data into those fields because the fields are made up of formulas that you've defined in your definition of the field. Are you with me?

In essence, you can't import data directly into a calculation or summary field. There's no way.

Rule #2: Importing source layouts

When you import data from another source, FileMaker Pro copies that data into your fields, but it doesn't copy the original source layouts. Okay? I know that importing those source layouts in your destination layouts would be nice, but — wait a minute — the folks at Claris aren't going to let you down. You do have a way to copy the layouts and field definitions from one FileMaker Pro file into a new file. All you have to do is save a clone of the file:

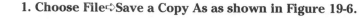
1. Choose File⇨Save a Copy As as shown in Figure 19-6.

Figure 19-6:
Ready for a
little clone
creation?

2. In the dialog box that appears (shown in Figure 19-7), choose Clone (no records from the Type box).

Figure 19-7:
Cloning my
address
book.

3. Click Save.

Saving a clone of the file preserves all the layout and field definitions of that file but strips out the data. It's like having a clean slate to start over with, but the layout and field definitions are still intact. Now you're ready to enter data or import data into this newly created clone of your database.

Rule #3: Converting FileMaker Pro

When you convert a FileMaker Pro 2.1 file or earlier FileMaker Pro file to FileMaker Pro 3 or 4, the latest versions, keep in mind that you're doing a form of import. In this case, FileMaker Pro is very forgiving because it lets you save the earlier version of the file before going ahead and converting it to the new version. FileMaker Pro generates an alert to rename the older file, and if you click OK, the program appends the suffix *Old* to that file. Still, remember that if you convert your old file to FileMaker Pro 4 but don't save it, you can't go back and save it later to that earlier version.

Exporting the Goods

You have some data in your files that you want to export out of FileMaker Pro into another application that can read the data. Piece of cake. Actually, the process operates just as you may expect: almost the reverse of importing data.

Exporting data is handy for several reasons:

- ✔ You may have times when you need to export your FileMaker Pro data to your word-processing program in order to send out a letter or do a mail merge.
- ✔ You may want to export files that you can use in a ClarisWorks or Microsoft Excel spreadsheet, or another application. In addition, you can create charts and diagrams from FileMaker Pro data with ClarisImpact or Microsoft Excel. It's way cool — and definitely worth checking out!

Rules for exporting

The rules for exporting data are simpler than for importing:

- ✔ You can export to another FileMaker Pro file. What happens is that FileMaker Pro becomes an option, creating a database that you can immediately use File➪Open to access.
- ✔ The file that you export is your *source file,* and the file you export to is the *destination file.*
- ✔ A new file is created that contains your exported data.
- ✔ When you do an export, the data that already exists in your destination file is written over — that is, replaced by the new, exported data.

When you're exporting a file, you want to be careful that another file with the same name doesn't already exist. Because if it does — whew! — you may be in trouble. FileMaker Pro replaces that file with the one that you're exporting. I confess that I've done this a couple of times before wising up and learning my lesson.

Doing an export

To export your FileMaker Pro data to another file format, here's what you do:

1. **Open the source file — for example, the Projects file you see in Figure 19-8 — and choose Mode⇨Find.**

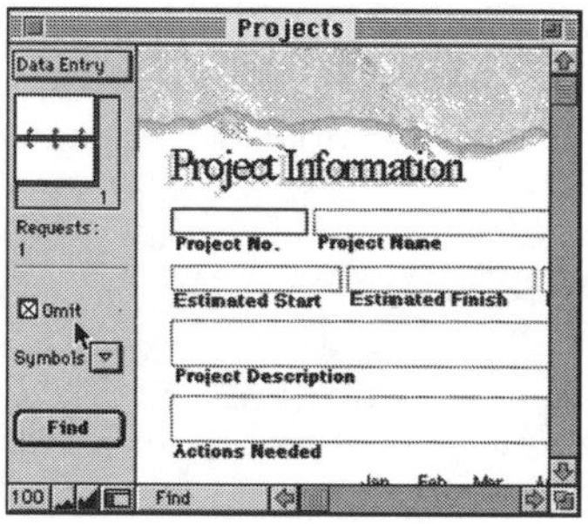

Figure 19-8:
A sample
Projects
file.

2. **Now in Find mode, click the Omit box to omit fields in your records that you don't want to export.**

3. **Switch from Find mode to Browse mode by choosing Mode⇨Browse.**

4. **In Browse mode, choose File⇨Import/Export⇨Export Records, as shown in Figure 19-9.**

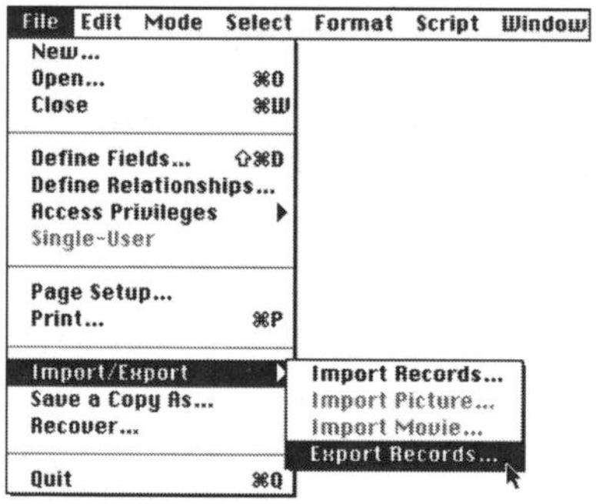

Figure 19-9:
Selecting
the Export
Records
submenu.

5. **Enter the name of the file you want to export in the Save As box, as shown in Figure 19-10, and click Save.**

Figure 19-10:
Name the
file you want
to export.

6. **To determine the order of fields you want to export, click items in the left box and then click Move. The selected text is highlighted, as shown in Figure 19-11.**

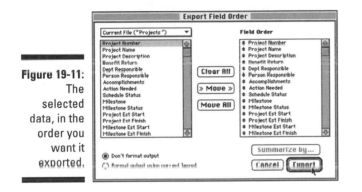

Figure 19-11:
The
selected
data, in the
order you
want it
exported.

7. **Click the Export button.**

The exported file now appears on the Macintosh or Windows Desktop as a simple text file, like the one in Figure 19-12. When you open it in SimpleText, WordPad, or another word processor, you get the information from your file in tab-separated text.

Figure 19-12:
The
exported
file's icon.

Project Numbers

Part IV
Advanced Stuff, OK?

The 5th Wave   By Rich Tennant

"Well, a relational database helps you seek out the connection between seemingly disparate items like, oh say, that tie you're wearing and this bowl of goat vomit."

In this part . . .

*L*ife advances forward, not backward; so do we all, whether we want to or not. Your work with FileMaker Pro ought to take you forward in the sense that, just by working through this book, you're going to know more.

Maybe you'll even want to know more than you already know. That's a possibility. If that's the case, you'll want to check out these chapters.

Chapter 20

Publishing Your FileMaker Pro Database on the Web

● ●

In This Chapter

▶ Thinking about why you want to publish on the Web

▶ Configuring the Web Companion dialog box

▶ Preparing your Web page's views for visitors

● ●

Depending on your perspective, the World Wide Web has changed a lot of the ways in which we live and work on the planet. So the fact that FileMaker Pro has changed with the times is only fitting, I guess; this program always keeps up with the latest. That's exactly what's happened from FileMaker Pro 3 (relational capability) to FileMaker 4 (Web publishing enhancements). Marketing folks like to call this kind of thing a *paradigm shift,* meaning that the purpose and power of the software has moved in a new direction.

Don't get too concerned about such a highfalutin term as paradigm shift, though. FileMaker 4 contains all the power and functionality of FileMaker Pro 3, plus this new, added capability. Incredibly, you really *can* publish your database on the Web using the Web Companion that comes with the program, if you have TCP/IP Internet access.

I'm devoting this chapter and the next to explaining how you can take advantage of this new capability in FileMaker Pro 4. Amazingly enough, you don't need any extra software: It's all right there for you to set up and work with in FileMaker Pro 4.

Maybe publishing your database on the Web is not for everybody, and that's why I've put this chapter in the "Advanced Stuff, OK?" part of the book. Maybe, on the other hand, you'll get inspired after reading this chapter and see how much fun Web publishing can be and want to give it a try. In any case, I walk you through the launch procedures.

In Chapter 21, I explain the intricacies of Web publishing and what you can work with in Table and Form views. That chapter also gets into searching and sorting of data, along with suggestions for custom Web publishing and modifying your home page. The entire Web publishing field just doesn't fit into one chapter.

Defining Your Project on the Web

For starters, you need to ask yourself the most fundamental question of all: Why? Why do you want to publish your database on the Web? What purpose does it serve? Network traffic is already pretty clogged up with tons of graphics, animated GIFs, sounds, and movies, making download times unbearably long and tedious. Most folks are probably suffering from some virulent form of information overload anyway.

Well, I think a good, solid, accessible database makes much more sense being on the Web than a bunch of screaming Java applets or monster GIF files, which take forever to download. You know that the people who access your FileMaker Pro database on the Web are seeking quality content — that is, data they can use for home, business, or education.

With FileMaker Pro 4, anyone with a Web browser (that is, Netscape Navigator or Microsoft Internet Explorer) and Internet or corporate intranet access can view, edit, sort, and search your valuable data. In addition, you can specify the level of access you want to allow to those folks who come to your FileMaker Pro database and search through its contents. Pretty cool, huh?

I mention all this stuff in advance of explaining how FileMaker Pro's Web Companion works because you should try to think now, if possible, about whom you want to access your database and what you want them to take away from it.

At any rate, I've come up with a set of possible uses for a database published on the Web. Some of these uses may surprise you, but they should start you thinking of things you can do.

- **Commercial catalog publishing.** The opportunities are obviously there to publish catalogs of various products on a Web site from which users can make credit card or other purchases.

- **Personal databases you may want to access while you're on the road.** Imagine accessing your own database on the Internet when you need to grab certain information but are in another city.

✔ **Company information, such as employee records and files.** Much of this information may be sensitive, but you have the advantage of limiting access to such databases on the Web by using passwords and other security protection.

✔ **Educational databases.** Information that you want to share with other students and teachers can be stored on the Web.

✔ **Collections of items, such as books, records, or memorabilia.** You may want to publish a database of items for sale from your home.

Well, those are just a few of the possibilities. I'm sure that if you put your mind to it, you can think of a dozen other uses for publishing on the Web. Let me know what they are.

Choosing among Various Ways to Publish

Once you've decided that you want to publish your FileMaker Pro database on the Web, you have three possible ways to tackle it: using Instant Web Publishing, using Custom Web Publishing, or modifying your home page.

The Instant Web Publishing route

Instant Web Publishing is the fastest and easiest method of publishing because you don't need to modify your existing FileMaker Pro database, use any software other than that bundled with your copy of FileMaker Pro 4, or even go through the motions of custom-designing special Web pages for your database. Using FileMaker Pro's Web Companion for Instant Web Publishing, you can specify all kinds of access and user privileges for visitors to your Web site, including privileges for viewing, editing, searching, and sorting your records. Visitors to your Web site and database see your database converted into a very cool-looking Web page. (Figure 20-1 shows my Contacts file as a Web page.)

Visitors have a choice of viewing your database in either Table or Form view. By clicking the Table View tab, they can see multiple records or a range of records at a single glance.

By clicking the Form View tab, they can see one record at a time, as Figure 20-2 shows.

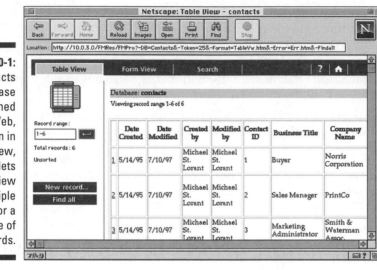

Figure 20-1:
A Contacts database published on the Web, shown in Table view, which lets you view multiple records or a range of records.

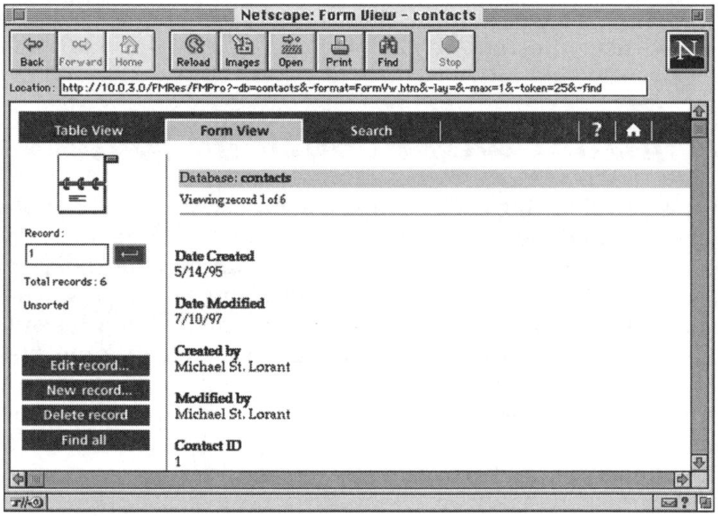

Figure 20-2:
A Contacts database published on the Web, shown in Form view, which lets you view one record at a time.

By clicking the Search tab, the visitors to your database on the Web can search for a particular record or a group of records, as Figure 20-3 shows. Visitors can specify the exact criteria by which they want to search on the Web page, and FileMaker Pro's search engine searches through all the records in your database and returns the results with the appropriate matches. Visitors can then see the results in Table view.

Figure 20-3:
A Contacts
database
published
on the
Web,
shown in
Search
view, which
lets you
specify
your search
criteria and
returns the
results of
your search
In Table
view.

```
┌─────────────────── Netscape: Search - contacts ──────────────────┐
│  ⟵    ⟶    ⌂      ⟳     ⊞     ⇧     🖶    🔍     ⬤           Ⓝ   │
│ Back Forward Home Reload Images Open  Print  Find   Stop           │
│ Location: http://10.0.3.0/FMRes/FMPro?-db=contacts&-max=1&-token=25&-format=Search.htm&-lay=&-view │
│ ┌──────────┬──────────┬────────────┐           ? │ ⌂ │          │
│ │Table View│Form View │   Search   │                              │
│                                                                    │
│  Total records: 6      Database: contacts                          │
│  Unsorted                                                          │
│                        Select search type, enter search criteria, then click Start search. │Search tips│
│  ┌────────────┐                                                    │
│  │Start search│        ◉ Match all words on page                   │
│  └────────────┘          (AND)              ○ Match any word on page (OR) │
│  ┌────────────┐                                                    │
│  │Clear fields│       Field          Type              Criteria    │
│  └────────────┘                                                    │
│                       Date Created    ┌──────────┐   ┌──────────┐ │
│                                       │ contains │   │          │ │
│                                       └──────────┘   └──────────┘ │
│                       Date Modified   ┌──────────┐   ┌──────────┐ │
│                                       │ contains │   │          │ │
│                                       └──────────┘   └──────────┘ │
│                       Created by      ┌──────────┐   ┌──────────┐ │
│                                       │ contains │   │          │ │
│                                       └──────────┘   └──────────┘ │
└────────────────────────────────────────────────────────────────┘
```

The Custom Web Publishing route

Custom Web Publishing is a more difficult method of publishing your database on the Web than the Instant Web Publishing route because you have to work with Claris Dynamic Markup Language (CDML) as well as Hypertext Markup Language (HTML) for best results. Custom Web Publishing with CDML tags allows you to customize your database's Web design to fit the needs of your visitors.

I recommend the Custom Web Publishing method *only if* you're a Webmaster, software developer, or heavy power-user with lots of HTML experience. While the custom method gives you more control over the look and feel of your database on the Web, you must delve fairly deeply into Web-page-programming stuff to bring it off. If this sounds like more of a challenge than you care to negotiate, stick with the Instant Web Publishing route as long as it serves your purpose.

Modifying your Web home page

If you've got some HTML programming or editing skills and you're using an HTML authoring tool, such as Claris Home Page or Microsoft FrontPage, you can use the HTML authoring software to integrate your FileMaker Pro database into a Web page. Web authoring software gives you more control over the look and feel of your pages, while insulating you from programming the HTML tags.

On a custom Web page that you author, you can add lots of neat things, such as

- ✔ Your company or business logo, as well as animated GIFs and other graphics

- ✔ Your e-mail address so that visitors to your Web site can get in touch with you

- ✔ Links to the databases you're publishing

Claris is coming out with a new version of Claris Home Page 3.0, which is designed to let you easily integrate your FileMaker Pro database with the pages on your Web site. This could be the answer to the prayers of users who want more control over their Web-database interface, but don't necessarily want to program in HTML or Claris Dynamic Markup Language. Stay tuned to the Claris Web site at www.claris.com for news of Home Page 3.0's arrival on the scene.

Preparing to Publish on the Web: A Brief Checklist

Before you can get rolling on publishing your database on the Web, you need to be sure that you've got the following things in order:

- ✔ Your FileMaker Pro 4 Web Companion software is installed properly on your Windows 95-compatible, Windows NT-compatible, or Mac OS-compatible computer. The Web Support files are installed automatically after you do a typical rather than a custom install on your machine.

- ✔ You've got access to the Internet or a company intranet.

- ✔ Your computer has at least a full-time dial-up connection to the Internet, but an ISDN, T1, or T2 Internet connection is preferable. Remember that your FileMaker Pro database is available to visitors on your Web site only when your computer is connected to the Internet or your company intranet.

- ✔ You've checked with your Internet Service Provider (ISP) or System Administrator to be sure that your system can handle Internet access to your database.

- ✔ You've prepared the files in your database properly, including layouts and fields that you want visitors to view, as well as specified passwords for access privileges. I explain a little later in this chapter what you need to do to prepare your files. Suffice to say that preparing your files should be an item on your checklist.

Determining your IP address number

If you don't know your IP address number, you can find out on the Mac by choosing ⌘⇨Control Panels⇨TCP/IP. In the TCP/IP dialog box that appears, you can see the IP Address Number. The figure below shows an IP Address Number of 10.0.3.0.

What FileMaker Pro 4 essentially does is operate as an HTTP (Hypertext Transfer Protocol) server. HTTP is designed as a common protocol running on many different types of computers — including Macintosh, UNIX, and even Windows — that lets Web servers and Web browsers talk to each other. FileMaker Pro 4 can then talk directly to Web browsers (and the folks using the browsers) when they request data or records from a FileMaker Pro database. These queries on the Web are sent to your database and are processed directly by FileMaker Pro 4.

Before anyone can visit your published database on the Web, however, you need to set up and configure the database as a hosting database.

To access FileMaker Pro over the Web, a visitor must enter a URL in his or her Web browser (either Netscape Navigator or Microsoft Internet Explorer), using the TCP/IP address or domain name of the computer that is running FileMaker Pro, such as http://mycomputer.somecompany.com or http://127.97.8.363.

FileMaker Pro then returns an HTML page, listing all the databases hosted for Web access. Visitors to your Web site can then just click a hyperlink to open your database in Table view in their Web browser.

```
┌─────────────────────── TCP/IP ───────────────────────┐
│                                                        │
│        Connect via:  [ Ethernet          ▼ ]          │
│  ┌─ Setup ─────────────────────────────────────────┐  │
│        Configure:    [ Using DHCP Server  ▼ ]         │
│                                                        │
│                                                        │
│        IP Address:    10.0.3.0                         │
│                                                        │
│        Subnet mask:   255.255.0.0                      │
│                                                        │
│       Router address: 10.0.0.1                         │
│                                            Search domains: │
│     Name server addr.: 10.0.0.3           [ vxtreme.com ] │
│                                                        │
│  ②                                                     │
└────────────────────────────────────────────────────────┘
```

✔ Your IP (Internet Protocol) address number, which should take the form of *xxx.xxx.xxx.xxx* (four numbers from 0 to 254). I suggest getting this number now and writing it down because you need it to launch FileMaker Pro's Web Companion and view your database locally on your computer before you let the world see your files. That way, you can make any changes and modifications to views, edits, searches, and sorts on your database.

Setting Up Your Web Companion for Action

Technically, you need to prepare your files before you can publish them on the Web. But that may be a little tricky to do at first without really setting up and configuring your Web Companion. That's the next step for both Mac and Windows users.

To set up your Web Companion:

1. **Choose Edit⇨Preferences⇨Application.**

2. **Click the Plug-Ins tab.**

3. **Click to select the Web Companion check box, as shown highlighted in Figure 20-4.**

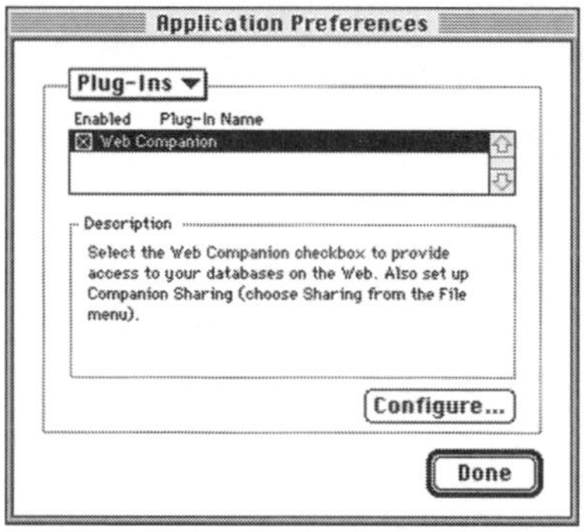

Figure 20-4:
The Application Preferences dialog box, with the Plug-Ins tab selected.

4. **Click Done.**

In Chapter 3, I talk about setting various preferences in FileMaker Pro. You may want to check out that chapter and be sure that you've set the other preferences you need as well.

Keep in mind that you need to set up the Web preference in the Plug-Ins tab one time only to enable the Web Companion plug-in to work for you.

Setting up your database for sharing

For each database that you want to publish on the Web, you need to set up that database individually for sharing. To prepare your database to be shared on the Web, follow these steps:

1. **Open the FileMaker Pro database that you want to publish.**

2. **Choose File⇨Sharing.**

3. **Click to select Web Companion in the check box from the Companion Sharing area of the dialog box, as Figure 20-5 shows.**

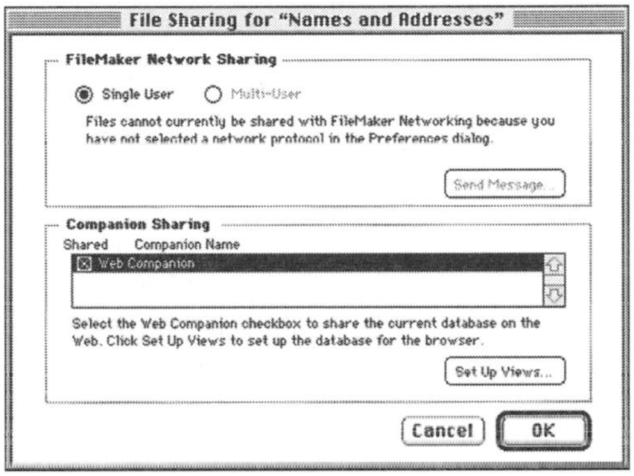

Figure 20-5:
The File
Sharing
dialog box,
where you
select Web
Companion.

File Sharing for "Names and Addresses"

FileMaker Network Sharing

◉ Single User   ○ Multi-User

Files cannot currently be shared with FileMaker Networking because you have not selected a network protocol in the Preferences dialog.

Send Message

Companion Sharing

Shared   Companion Name

☒ Web Companion

Select the Web Companion checkbox to share the current database on the Web. Click Set Up Views to set up the database for the browser.

Set Up Views...

Cancel   OK

4. **Click OK.**

The tricky thing here is to keep in mind that the settings you've specified are applicable only to the database that you have open right now. If you want to host other databases on the Web, you have to open them and perform the same sequence of steps for sharing.

Configuring your Web Companion

To finish with the setup and configuration of Web Companion, you only have a few more steps to take.

The Web Companion Configuration dialog box is the coolest dialog box in FileMaker Pro 4. I mean, once you've gone through this dialog box and checked out the items, you won't believe how easily you can publish your database on the Web. FileMaker Pro 4 practically does all the work for you. The default values in the Web Companion dialog box are perfect for most cases, so you usually don't have to modify the settings.

To change or verify the Web Companion configuration settings:

1. **Choose Edit⇨Preferences⇨Web Companion.**

2. **Click Configure, and you see the dialog box shown in Figure 20-6.**

```
╔═══════════ Web Companion Configuration ═══════════╗
║  ┌─Web Companion User Interface─┐ ┌─Log Activity─┐ ║
║  │ ☒ Enable Instant Web Publishing│ │ ⦿ None      │ ║
║  │ Home Page:   [(Built-in) ▼]   │ │ ○ Brief     │ ║
║  │ Language:    [English ▼]      │ │ ○ Extended  │ ║
║  └───────────────────────────────┘ └─────────────┘ ║
║  ┌─Remote Administration─┐ ┌─Security──────────────┐║
║  │ ⦿ Disabled            │ │ ⦿ FileMaker Pro Access Privileges│║
║  │ ○ Requires password: [    ]│ │ ○ Web Security Database│║
║  │ ○ Requires no password│ │                       │║
║  └───────────────────────┘ └───────────────────────┘║
║  TCP/IP Port Number: [80]                           ║
║                        [ Cancel ]  [  OK  ]         ║
╚════════════════════════════════════════════════════╝
```

Figure 20-6:
The ultra-cool Web Companion Configuration dialog box.

You see quite a few option lists, check boxes, text boxes, and option buttons in this dialog box in technical-sounding panels like Web Companion User Interface, Remote Administration, and Alter Spy Satellite Trajectory. If this puts you off, remember that the default settings are usually good enough. But in case you need to adjust one or more of these settings, I describe them in the following sections.

The Web Companion User Interface panel

The User Interface panel of the Web Companion dialog box allows you to set up the most fundamental items about your database's Web page: whether you want to use Instant Web Publishing, what you want to use for a home page for your database, and what language your home page uses.

- ✔ **Enable Instant Web Publishing check box:** Check this box if you're sure that you want to publish your database using the Instant Web Companion. If you want to go the route of custom Web publishing, don't check the box.

- ✔ **Home Page list box:** Pull this list down and click to designate a home page for your database. The default setting is the FileMaker Pro Web Companion's built-in home page for sharing your database on the Web (refer to Figure 20-7).

    I suggest taking a look at the built-in page, which may be adequate for your needs, before venturing out and creating your own home page. If you do want to create your own home page, you need to move it to the Web folder in the FileMaker Pro 4 folder. After you've created the page and moved it to the folder, you need to choose that home page from the Home Page drop-down list.

- ✔ **Language list box:** Just select the language you want your Web page to use.

The Log Activity panel

Log Activity is another panel in the dialog box which helps you keep track of how much activity your Web-published database is generating, such as the number of requests from visitors. Your options in this panel are None, Brief, and Extended. Depending on the radio button you check, FileMaker creates no activity log, an abbreviated activity log, or a detailed activity log. The log file is a text file named Web.log, which you can find in the same folder as the FileMaker Pro 4 software application.

The Remote Administration panel

Remote administration controls the uploading and downloading of database files to and from your Web folder by enforcing password access and protection. You have three options here: Disabled, Requires Password, and Requires No Password. In the Requires Password text box, you can set up the password that the Web user has to enter.

Claris recommends that you use only uppercase characters A through Z, numbers, or a combination of both when setting up your password.

The Security panel

The Security panel allows you to set up access privileges for your database. You have two options here in the Security panel of the dialog box: FileMaker Pro Access Privileges or Web Security Database. The Web Security Database gives you much more control over Web users' privileges to search, update, add, and delete the records you publish over the Web. I explain more about Web security databases in Chapter 21. For the moment, just leave the default FileMaker Pro Access Privileges option button selected.

Specifying the port number (or any port in a storm)

Depending on whether it's a Web or an FTP server, each server has a port number assigned to it. The *port number* specifies the way in which your Mac or Windows PC works as a Web server. Port number 80 is the Web server's port number, so that's the default. If port number 80 is already in use, you need to change it. Claris recommends changing it to port number 591, which has been registered with Internet Assigned Numbers Authority.

FileMaker Pro 4 is pretty smart about all this port stuff, thankfully. If it recognizes that port 80 is in use, it defaults to port number 591.

Now there's a catch here: If you specify port number 591, you need to make sure that visitors to your Web site who want to access your database append a colon followed by 591 to your IP address, so it looks like this: *xxx.xxx.xxx.xxx*:591.

Once you get the Web Companion Configuration dialog box settings right where you want them, all you have to do is click the OK button to accept your changes.

Working through the Views for Instant Web Publishing

The Instant Web Publishing tool eases you through the process of setting up views of your database for Web visitors. If you have already set up the Web Companion Configuration dialog box, you're ready to tackle the steps involved in establishing exactly how you want your files to be viewed in a Web browser. The Instant Web Publishing tool enables you to present the visitors to your Web site with the following views and capabilities when they arrive at the doorstep of your FileMaker Pro database:

- ✔ A very nifty Table view of your data, which lets Web visitors see and work with multiple records or a range of records
- ✔ An equally nifty Form view of your data, if they want to see or work with just one record at a time
- ✔ A Web page that lets visitors search the data in your published database, specifying search criteria
- ✔ A Web page that lets visitors sort the data in your published database

To set up all these possible options for visitors to your Web-published database, follow these steps:

1. **Choose Edit⇨Preferences⇨Web Companion.**

2. **Click one of the four tabs for the Web page you want to set up.**

   Figure 20-7 shows you the Web Companion View Setup dialog box with the Table View tab selected.

3. **In the Layout drop-down list, select the layout containing the fields that you want to display in various views. You can see the list of those fields below the drop-down list.**

4. **Click Done.**

This part is a bit difficult to get used to (at least it was for me) because you can't duplicate the exact graphical layout of your database on the Web. What you're doing is just specifying the fields that you want FileMaker Pro's Web Companion to display on the Web. The best thing to do is probably to go with the trial-and-error approach. Select the fields that you want to display, work through the Table and Form views, publish the database, and see what you think is okay in your Web browser. Chapter 21 explains more of this in detail.

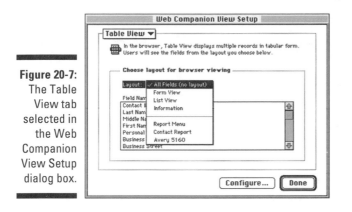

Figure 20-7:
The Table
View tab
selected in
the Web
Companion
View Setup
dialog box.

When you click the Form View tab, you can see a dialog box similar to the one in Figure 20-8, which lets you specify the layouts from a names-and-addresses database.

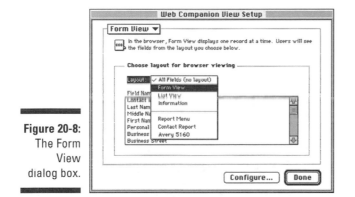

Figure 20-8:
The Form
View
dialog box.

Clicking the Search tab reveals a dialog box similar to the one in Figure 20-9, which lets you specify how a visitor to your Web site can search through a typical names-and-addresses database.

Clicking the Sort tab shows you another dialog box, similar to the one in Figure 20-10, which lets you specify the order in which data is sorted from a names-and-addresses database.

After you've taken the time to prepare your files and check through the various options available, you're ready to see the results of your labors.

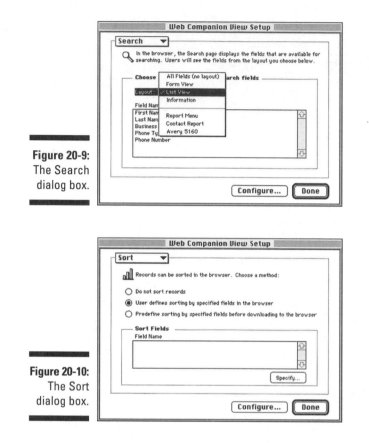

Figure 20-9:
The Search
dialog box.

Figure 20-10:
The Sort
dialog box.

It Doesn't Get Any Better than This!

There, I said it in the heading: Working with databases on the Web doesn't
get any better than the point at which you're ready to go to the Web like any
visitor and see your database in all its online glory. All you have to do is
open your Web browser, enter that IP address number in the location field —
in this case, `10.0.3.0` — and press the Return key. Magic! You're in business.
You see a Web page like the one that Figure 20-11 shows, in which I let
visitors select views from two databases (Contacts and Names and Addresses) that I've set up and configured with FileMaker Pro Web Companion.
The links to the those databases are already in place. Just go for it!

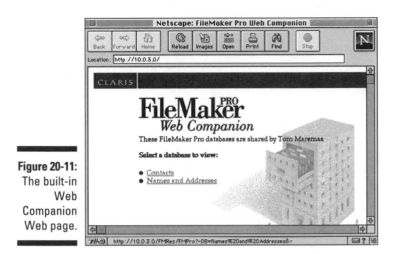

Figure 20-11:
The built-in Web Companion Web page.

Chapter 21

Publishing Your FileMaker Pro Database on the Web: The Sequel

In This Chapter

▶ Customizing how Web visitors view your database

▶ Getting more control over Web visitor access to your database

▶ Creating a home page for your database with HTML authoring software

*I*f you jumped into this chapter at random, looking for tips and strategies on how to publish your database on the Web, check out Chapter 20 first. That's where you find out how to set up your database files for publishing on the Web.

Now if you've arrived here fresh from Chapter 20, ready to go through the process of publishing your FileMaker Pro database on the Web, welcome. And I appreciate your sticking with me on the continuation of this Web publishing journey. There's a lot more here than meets the eye — hence, I call this chapter a sequel to Chapter 20.

As with any sequel, seeing the first part beforehand helps.

Starting Off on the Right Foot

To begin with, I've made a series of important assumptions:

- ✔ You've already decided that you want to publish your FileMaker Pro database on the Web, using FileMaker Pro's Web Companion, either for instant Web publishing or custom Web publishing.

- ✔ You have FileMaker Pro 4 (either for Windows or your Mac OS), along with the Web support files, properly installed on your system.

- ✔ Your Windows 95-compatible, Windows NT-compatible, or Mac OS-compatible computer has access to the Internet or a corporate intranet.

✔ You've gone through the setup and configuration procedures that I outline in Chapter 20 to prepare the files you want to publish on the Web.

✔ You've worked through the options in the Web Companion Configuration dialog box and made the appropriate choices for what you want enabled when your database is published on the Web.

If this list describes your setup and preparations, then you've come to the right place. If not, then retrace your steps and make sure you have everything in order.

Moving Ahead with Critical Steps

To move ahead and really figure out the ins and outs of database publishing on the Web, you may have to take one or two steps back just to make sure that you've got all the fundamentals down.

Any and all files that you place in your FileMaker Pro Web folder can be read and also copied by anyone who visits your Web site. Be extra careful about what you place there. If you've built databases containing proprietary or sensitive information, be sure that you move that information outside the Web folder.

Briefly, I want to bring your attention to two potential snags that may otherwise trip you up. I confess that they tripped me when I was figuring out the Web-publishing process. (We're all beginners in this world anyway until we get things in a groove.)

✔ Make sure that you've set the Web Companion preferences by checking that item in your FileMaker Pro Application Preferences Plug-in dialog box (that's a mouthful right there). You have to set these preferences only once to enable the Web Companion plug-in that lets you publish any FileMaker Pro database you want.

✔ After selecting the database to publish and opening it up, you need to specify that you want to share it on the Web.

Here are the steps you need to take:

1. **Open the database you want to publish in FileMaker Pro 4. Figure 21-1 shows a Music database.**

2. **Choose File⇨Sharing, as you see in Figure 21-2.**

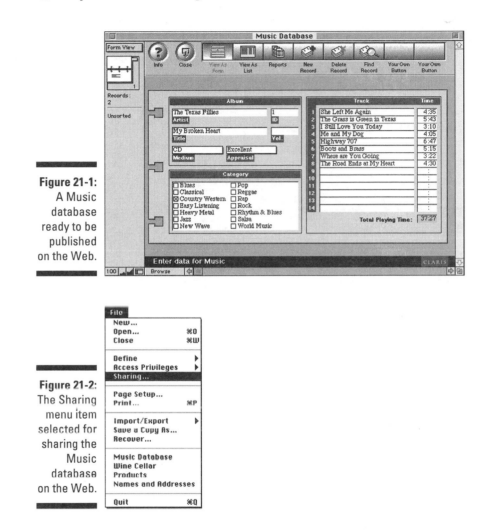

Figure 21-1:
A Music database ready to be published on the Web.

Figure 21-2:
The Sharing menu item selected for sharing the Music database on the Web.

3. **In the File Sharing dialog box that pops up, click Web Companion so that it's highlighted, as Figure 21-3 shows.**

4. **Click OK or click the Setup Views button.**

   If you click the Setup Views button, the View Setup dialog box appears, shown for the Music database in Figure 21-4, which lets you choose the layouts for Web browsing in either or both Table and Form views. Remember, you only have two choices with Instant Web Publishing: Table and Form views.

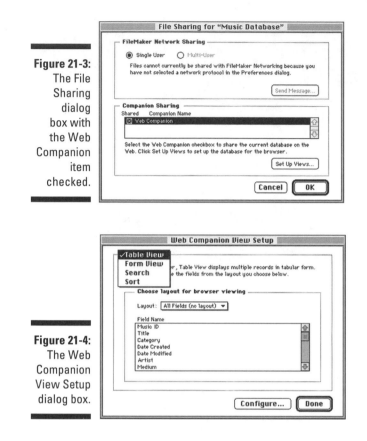

Figure 21-3:
The File
Sharing
dialog
box with
the Web
Companion
item
checked.

Figure 21-4:
The Web
Companion
View Setup
dialog box.

After you've followed this sequence of steps, you can open your Netscape Navigator or Microsoft Internet Explorer browser. Enter your IP address number and press the Return key. The FileMaker Pro Web Companion page appears, as shown in Figure 21-5, allowing you to access the databases that you have designed for sharing. The example shown shows three links in Figure 21-5: <u>Music Database</u>, <u>Contacts</u>, or <u>Names and Addresses</u>. Each link, when clicked, opens a database with the Table or Form view that you've configured.

Once you get in the groove with this sequence of steps, you can publish your databases easily and effortlessly, with a minimum of fuss and bother.

FileMaker Pro 4 performs the magic of creating Web pages with views of your database. If you've done any programming work with HTML, you'll appreciate this capability. Of course, you can create your own home page with links to your database by using good Web authoring tools such as Claris Home Page, Adobe PageMill, or Microsoft FrontPage (to cite a few examples). These authoring tools save you time, but you may have to do some HTML code tweaking for best results.

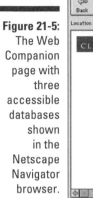

Figure 21-5:
The Web Companion page with three accessible databases shown in the Netscape Navigator browser.

Working with Table view

Figure 21-6 shows you the Table view of a Music database, which I got when I clicked the hypertext link on my Web Companion home page.

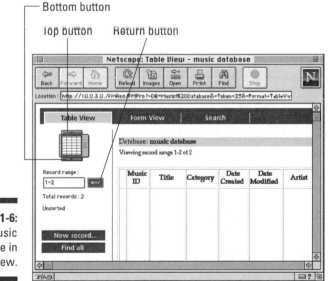

Figure 21-6:
The Music database in Table view.

To view multiple records at one time, you click the Table View tab in the upper-left portion of the browser window.

Just below that tab is a somewhat odd-looking icon. Don't despair — I couldn't quite figure it out at first, either. Technically, it's called a Record Range icon. The Record Range icon has a slider on the right-hand edge that, when you slide it up and down, enables you to view a range of records.

If you want to go to the first range of records, click the Top button; conversely, click the Bottom button for the last range of records. You can also specify the range of records you want to view in the Record range box and then press Return, or click the Return button shown in Figure 21-6.

Although the Music database here has only two records in it, you can add to it by clicking the New Record button. That button opens a new Web page that lets you enter data into the various fields in this Music database.

Table 21-1 shows you some of the cool things you and those visiting your Web site can do in Table view.

Table 21-1	Table View Buttons
Click This Button	*To Do This*
Sort	Rearrange the records in your database
New record	Add a new record to your database
Find All	Display the record range after a search
Number in the leftmost column	Edit a particular record in Form view
Home	Select another database

Working with Form view

To move from Table to Form view, you just click the Form View tab. You get a Web page, as shown in the Music database in Figure 21-7, which enables you to view one record at a time.

The Form View icon shown in Figure 21-8 seems pretty familiar. It's the FileMaker Pro Book icon, or is it? Well, it's not quite identical to the Book icon, but it lets you do the same things — namely, scroll through the records in your database by moving the slider up and down.

If you click the top portion of the Book icon, you can view the previous record in your database. Clicking the bottom portion of the Book icon lets you view the next record.

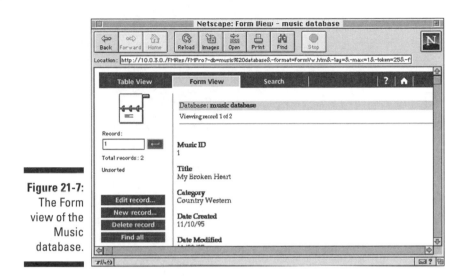

Figure 21-7:
The Form view of the Music database.

In the record, you can also type a record number and press Enter or Return on your keyboard, or click the Return button next to the record number field.

Figure 21-8:
Look closely. Is it the Book icon, or isn't it?

Use the slider to scroll through records

Choosing from the options in Form view

Table 21-2 shows you some of the cool things you and those visiting your Web site can do in Form View.

Table 21-2	Form View Buttons
Click This Button	*To Do This*
Sort	Rearrange your records
Edit	Edit or modify your current record
New Record	Add a new record to your database
Delete Record	Delete the current record
Find All	Display all the records in the database
Home	Select another database

Adding records

You can use the New Record page to add new records to your database.

To add a record:

1. **In Table view or Form view, click New Record.**

2. **On the New Record page, click in a field to type the new information. Press Tab to move between fields.**

   - To clear the new information you've typed, click Revert.

   - To return to Table view or Form view without saving a record in the database, click Back to View.

3. **When you finish typing the information into the fields, click Save Record.**

   The record is added to the database. You see a page confirming that you have created a new record.

4. **Click OK to return to Table view or Form view.**

Editing records

You can use the Edit Record page to permanently edit or modify a record in your database.

To edit a record:

1. **In Form view, click Edit Record.**

   In Table view, select the record you want to edit by clicking the hypertext number on the left of the record. Then click Edit Record in Form view.

2. **On the Edit Record page, click in a field to modify the information.**

   - To undo changes and return to the original field values, click Revert. You can't revert to the original values after you click Save Record.

   - To return to Form view without saving your changes, click Back to View.

3. **When you finish modifying the information in the fields, click Save Record.**

   You see a message confirming that you have edited a record.

4. **Click OK to return to Form view.**

Deleting records

In Form view, you can delete a record from the database. When you delete a record, keep in mind that you are permanently removing the data that you've entered in all the fields in a particular record.

To delete a record:

1. **In Form view, click Delete Record.**

   In Table view, select the record you want to delete by clicking the hypertext number on the left of the record. Then click Delete Record in Form view.

   You see a message confirming your request to delete the current record.

2. **Click Delete to delete the record. Or click Cancel to return to Form view without deleting the record.**

Searching for records

If you click the Search tab on either your Table or Form view page, you open up a Web page similar to the one shown in Figure 21-9 for a Music database.

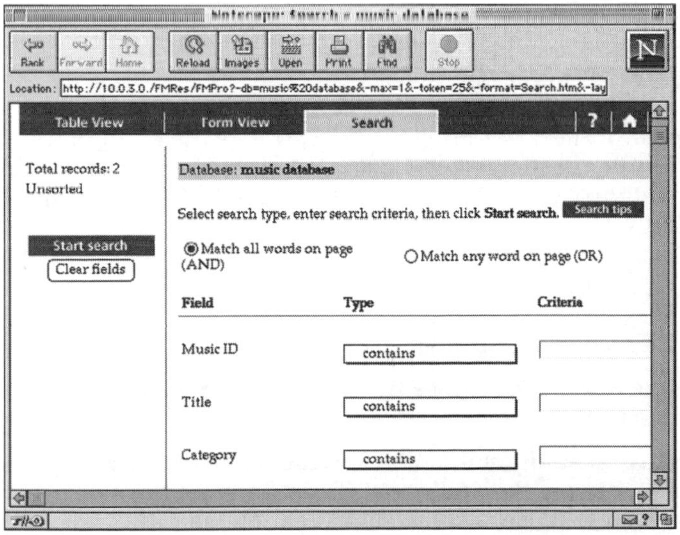

Figure 21-9:
The Search page.

On that Search Web page, you can look for a particular record or a group of records. To find records you want, you need to specify search criteria (that is, the values you want to find) on the Search page. FileMaker Pro 4 searches through all the records in your database and returns the search results — the set of records that matches your search criteria. These search results are then displayed in Table view.

To find a record or group of records, do the following:

1. **Click the Search tab.**

2. **Click Match All Words on Page (AND) to find values that match all the search criteria in the same field or across fields. Click Match Any Words on Page (OR) to find values that match one or more search criteria in the same field or across fields.**

3. **On the Search page, choose the type of search next to the field you want to search.**

4. **Enter the search criteria into the field you want to search.**

5. **You can repeat Steps 3 and 4 for as many fields as you want to search. (To reset the search criteria, just click Clear Fields.)**

6. **Click Start Search to search the database.**

   FileMaker Pro displays, in Table view, the record or records you searched for.

Sorting records

If you want to, FileMaker Pro lets you rearrange the order of the records in a database. You can sort records in ascending order, descending order, or a custom order based on a field's list of choices. You can sort on as many as four fields.

To sort records, follow these steps:

1. **In Table view or Form view, click Sort.**

2. **On the Sort page, choose the first field (for example, Last Name) and the sort order.**

3. **To sort on additional fields (for example, Last Name and then First Name), choose the additional fields. To reset the sort order or choose different fields to sort by, click Clear Fields.**

   Click Back to View to return to Table view or Form view without sorting the records.

4. **Click Start Sort.**

Database Security Issues

One of the most critical parts of publishing a database on the Web is the issue of security — that is, who has access to your database and how you control that access. In the Web Companion Configuration dialog box, you can choose from two types of security for your Web-published database: FileMaker Pro access privileges or Web security databases.

In Chapter 20, I advise you to leave the Security panel set to its default setting in the Web Companion Configuration dialog box. The default setting is the FileMaker Pro Access Privileges radio button, which means that for a specific file, users who open that database on the Web have the same access privileges as everyone else. All users share the same password and the same level of access to the database. FileMaker Pro access privileges on the Net are exactly the same as access privileges for opening the file on your computer or over a FileMaker Pro network. That's fine. And in most cases, it does the job.

However, if you want to restrict access to your Web-published database and control whether a person can search, update, add, or delete records, among other options, you can enable the Web security databases option in the Web Companion Configuration dialog box. Follow these steps to use the Web security databases option:

1. **Open the Web Companion Configuration dialog box. (Assuming that you have completed the steps in Chapter 20 to set up the Web Companion, choose File⇨Sharing, click Web Companion, click Set Up Views, and click Configure.)**

2. **Click to select Web Security Database in the Security panel.**

3. **Choose File⇨Open.**

4. **Double-click the FileMaker Pro 4 folder on your system; then double-click the Web Security folder.**

5. **Double-click the Databases folder and double-click Web Security, as shown in Figure 21-10.**

Figure 21-10:
The Web Security icon selected in the Databases folder.

6. **Choose Mode⇨New Record.**

7. **For Database Name, enter the name of the database you are establishing security for. Or you can type** All databases **to set privileges that apply to all the files you want to publish on the Web.**

8. **Enter information in the various fields for the access privileges you want to grant, as shown in the sample Employees database in Figure 21-11.**

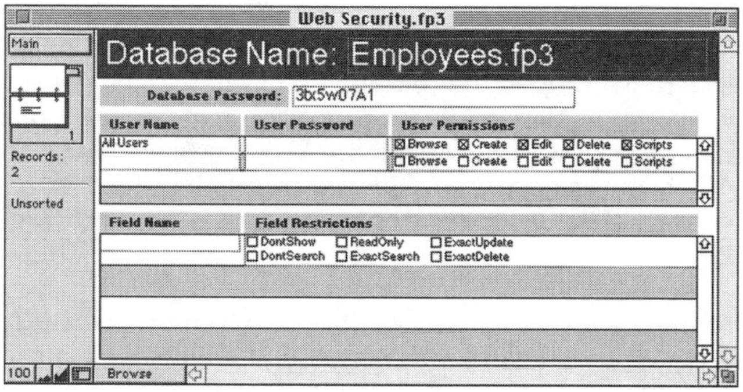

Figure 21-11:
The Web Security database for a database named Employees.

Web Security.fp3
Database Name: Employees.fp3
Database Password: 3bx5w07A1

User Name	User Password	User Permissions
All Users		☒Browse ☒Create ☒Edit ☒Delete ☒Scripts
		☐Browse ☐Create ☐Edit ☐Delete ☐Scripts

Field Name	Field Restrictions
	☐DontShow ☐ReadOnly ☐ExactUpdate
	☐DontSearch ☐ExactSearch ☐ExactDelete

9. **If the FileMaker Pro database has a password set up with FileMaker Pro access privileges, type that password in the Database Password field. If not, enter another password of your choosing.**

The database password overrides the Web Security database.

Handling Web security can be a tricky business. In most cases, you want to be sure that you've spoken to your System Administrator or the person in charge of assigning passwords and keeping track of access privileges to your FileMaker Pro databases.

Creating a Home Page Using Web Authoring Tools

Many folks have become overnight HTML hackers just by picking up and using some HTML authoring and editing tools, such as Claris Home Page, Adobe PageMill, or Microsoft FrontPage (to mention just a few). If you're comfortable with these tools, you can use them to host your FileMaker Pro database on your own home page. You need the following on your home page:

✔ A link to your published FileMaker Pro database, specifying the IP address of the computer hosting your database in this link

✔ A brief description of what your database contains, perhaps listing some of its most important features

✔ An e-mail address where visitors to the database can contact you if they have any problems or questions.

✔ A personal or company logo to identify your page

Chapter 22

The Magic of Scripting Your Commands

*I*n this book, I ask you to wear many different hats: designer, builder, graphic artist, recordkeeper, network person, and sorter of data, among other things. Now I have another hat I want you to wear: scriptwriter.

No, this isn't Hollywood. You don't have to write a movie script to work with FileMaker Pro.

Imagine having a library of scripts that you can pull out of a hat as if by magic. Imagine each of those scripts containing a little scenario, perhaps a set of commands to perform a sequence of actions, such as get me a letter, do a fax, or sort my records.

You're the movie director here (as well as scriptwriter, if you create your own script), and FileMaker Pro is at your command. Cool, huh?

Amazingly enough, all this magic starts with buttons.

Starting with Buttons

Buttons are cool; buttons are the way to go, right? Isn't pointing and clicking your way through a FileMaker Pro database easier than having to pull down a menu, click a menu item, and open a dialog box with more menus to pull down and click? No argument there.

One button ought to be able to do it all. You're right. That's what the folks at Claris thought, too, so they devised something so simple yet so powerful that it blows me away every time I mess around with it. Why not attach a script to each button, telling the button (in so many words) what you want it to do? Are you with me? This stuff is real, not Hollywood special effects.

A script consists simply of one command or a set of commands that tells FileMaker Pro to perform a series of actions. Scripts are cool because you get to automate things in your FileMaker Pro database. You can use a script to print your records, do a mailing, and move around to another file or layout. For example, you can create a script for finding, sorting, switching from one layout to another, previewing (with a pause) before printing, returning to Browse mode, or returning to your original layout.

In FileMaker Pro templates, you see buttons all over the place, in one layout after another, with labels on them, such as Find, Sort, Add Record, List, Envelope, and so on. When you click one of those buttons, FileMaker Pro goes into action to execute the command. The command may take you to another record, import a picture, change a password, scroll a window — well, I think you get the idea.

"Hey, where do I find these magic buttons?" you may well ask. You find them in Layout mode. Just choose Mode⇨Layout and then click the button tool from the FileMaker Pro toolset and drag it onto your layout. A dialog box pops up to let you specify the script that you want that button to perform. (For details on using the layout tools, check out Chapter 9.)

Creating a Dial-a-Phone-Number button

What's the coolest button to use in your FileMaker Pro database? That's a matter of personal preference, I guess, but I know one that would certainly save me time: a dial-a-phone-number button. In my personal address book file, that's a button I'd like to have. Well, my wish can come true with FileMaker Pro. (Maybe this is Hollywood magic after all.)

These steps show you how to create a Dial-a-Phone-Number button, but you can write a similar script that tells your button to perform any number of tasks.

1. **Open a FileMaker Pro database, either one you've started to build or an existing template, by choosing File⇨Open.**

2. **Choose Mode⇨Layout, or click the mode selector at the bottom of your layout and click Layout.**

3. **In the Tool panel to the left of your layout, click the Button tool, shown in Figure 22-1.**

Figure 22-1:
In this Tool
panel, the
Button tool
has been
clicked.

Button tool

Your cursor becomes a crosshair, and when you decide where you want
a button to appear, you simply position the button on your layout
where you think it is most useful and then click. By default, the button
is a rounded rectangle, as shown in Figure 22-2.

Figuro 22-2:
A new
button,
ready for
action.

If you don't particularly like a rounded button, you can change the
default button to a rectangle by choosing Edit⇨Preferences⇨
Application to open up the Layout Preferences dialog box, shown in
Figure 22-3. Then click the radio button for the shape of button you
want, and click Done.

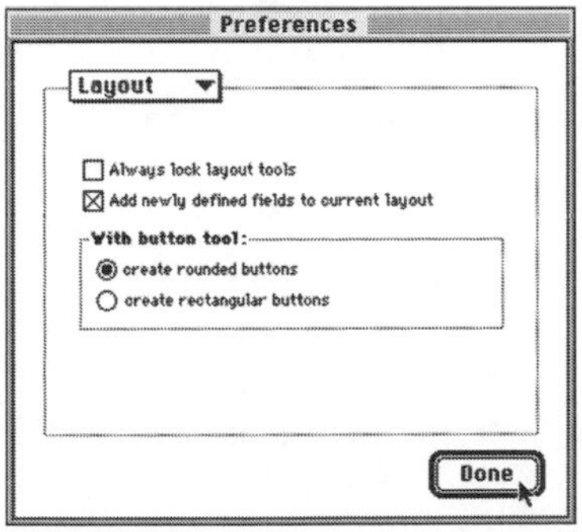

Figure 22-3:
Your
preference:
rectangles
or ovals.

Preferences

Layout ▼

☐ Always lock layout tools
☒ Add newly defined fields to current layout
┌With button tool:
● create rounded buttons
○ create rectangular buttons

Done

Simultaneously, as you drop your new button on your layout, the
Specify Button dialog box, shown in Figure 22-4, appears.

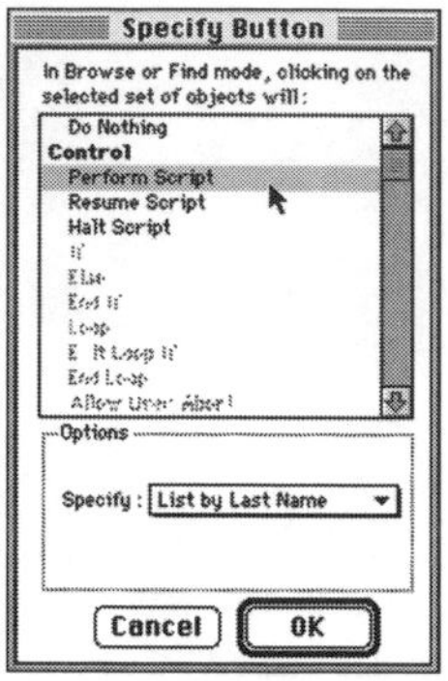

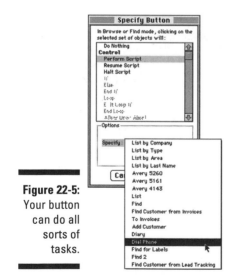

Figure 22-4:
What do
you want
your new
button to
do? How
about script
perfor-
mance?

4. In the Specify Button dialog box, under the Control subcategory, click Perform Script.

You want your button to perform a script — in this case, a script that dials a phone number.

5. In the Options section of the Specify Button dialog box, open the pop-up menu, click the script you want, in this case Dial Phone, as shown in Figure 22-5, and click OK.

Figure 22-5:
Your button
can do all
sorts of
tasks.

Now, keep in mind that Dial Phone is just one of many scripts you can get a button to perform. Figure 22-5 shows you a few of the possible scripts. I explain what the other scripts do later in this chapter.

Back in your layout, you may notice a blinking cursor on your newly created button. That cursor indicates that you ought to type in the name of your button. A good idea.

6. **Type the name you want for your button — for example,** Dial Phone.

7. **Choose Mode⇨Browse or choose Mode⇨Find to switch modes.**

Buttons are portable from file to file

In the Dial-a-Phone-Number example, I installed a Dial-a-Phone-Number button in my Contacts database in the Data Entry file. Of course, because it's a button and therefore a graphic object, you can cut, copy, and paste it to another layout, if you want. That's the exciting part about buttons: They're portable. Once you've attached to the button a script specifying what actions you want the button to perform, you can take that button along with its accompanying script to another FileMaker Pro file. All you have to do is copy that button while you're in Layout mode by choosing Edit⇨Copy or pressing ⌘+C on the Mac or Ctrl+C in Windows; then open a new or existing file and paste that button onto the layout of the new or existing file. The button retains its script and performs what it's scripted to perform. Is that way cool, or what?

The Scripting Business

You're not quite in the scripting business yet. By taking a button and selecting from a list of scripts you want that button to perform, such as dialing a phone, you've passed the test of being at least a junior FileMaker Pro scriptwriter. Jumping from specifying buttons to writing scripts isn't, however, an enormous leap. FileMaker Pro makes it much easier than you may expect.

Right up there next to the Format menu on the FileMaker Pro menu bar is the Script menu. That's where your scripts are added as pull-down menu items. That's also where FileMaker Pro's scripting engine lives. It's called *ScriptMaker,* and when you select it, a big Define Scripts dialog box jumps into view. I discuss the dialog box's script-definition options later in this chapter, in the section "Hello, ScriptMaker."

Okay, if buttons already have scripts attached to them that FileMaker Pro has specified, how else can you get a script to perform the actions you want in your FileMaker Pro database? Well, I'm glad you asked. After defining a script — for example, one that returns you to Find mode — you find that script added as a pull-down menu item in the Script menu, along with a keyboard equivalent to the right of it. Figure 22-6 shows you what I'm talking about. There, you see the Dial Phone script that I've defined for a button, along with scripts for List, Find, and Show Message, as well as their keyboard equivalents.

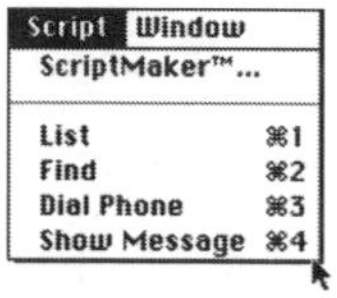

Figure 22-6:
Adding your
scripts to
the Script
menu.

Script	Window
ScriptMaker™...	
List	⌘1
Find	⌘2
Dial Phone	⌘3
Show Message	⌘4

Are you getting itchy to write some scripts of your own? I hope so. Scripting can be fun and can save you time because, with just a couple of mouse clicks, you can get FileMaker Pro to do boring, repetitive tasks for you — such as finding, sorting, and printing — while you kick back and enjoy other things in life. Read on.

You can even create *subscripts,* which, as you may figure, are scripts within a script. (Programmers love this kind of *nesting,* as it's called, and you don't have to be a programmer to like it, too.) What a subscript essentially does is let you break down a very complex task or set of actions into ever smaller and more manageable tasks or actions.

For example, if you want to get fancy, you can get one script to perform a second or third script, even if that second or third script is in a different file.

Here are just a few scripts that I want to introduce to you in an effort to show you how powerful and useful scripting can be:

- ✔ You can get a script to perform a start-up sequence for you where FileMaker Pro opens a new record for data entry each time you launch the program.

- ✔ Printing is always painful, as far as I'm concerned, so anything that helps automate that process is a bonus for me. With a neatly defined printing script, for example, you can just click a print button, and the script prints your records or layouts exactly the way you want.

- ✔ You can do an exit script so that when you're done with the work on your FileMaker Pro database, you can exit gracefully and without a lot of good-byes.

These scripts are just a few of your options. Once you get into scripting, you'll come up with your own favorites.

The world is an imperfect place. Now that I've introduced to you all the cool things you can do with scripts and buttons, I ought to spell out one of the limitations of scripting. It comes down to this: You can't use any of your scripts with FileMaker Pro Web Companion, which you use to publish your database on the Web. (Check out Chapters 20 and 21.) I won't get into the technical reasons for this.

But all is not lost. You can build, for example, a script that launches your Web browser and displays a particular URL, or another script that lets you send Internet mail, if you've got an e-mail account.

Giant Steps Are What You Take . . .

FileMaker Pro understands life better as a set of steps. Don't ask me why, but it does. Steps are the commands that you use in your script. Steps tell FileMaker Pro what to do. "Step here, step there," you may bark as a Script Director, but unless FileMaker Pro understands what you're talking about, I'm afraid it's going to be stubborn, even disobedient. It simply won't execute the script you want.

Guess what? You don't actually have to write or type out these steps as you would if you were writing a movie script in your favorite word processor. FileMaker Pro provides you with a list of steps for your script, which you can then point at and click and subsequently add to your own list of actions that you want a script to perform. But you need to know what the steps are that FileMaker Pro understands.

The following sections provide listings of the different categories of steps for you. You need to use these steps if you want FileMaker to do its magic and — presto! — perform for you.

Rather than list all these steps somewhere back in an appendix in this book, I chose to include them here, even before you move to the next level of actually assembling these steps into a script. I think that you should get your wheels turning a bit now so you can begin to see all the possibilities of using different scripts.

The steps in one of these categories, of course, can be added to the steps in another category to perform a series of actions. Hollywood was never this easy. Giant steps are what you take walking on the moon, incidentally. But before you can take those giant steps, try out these smaller steps on Earth.

Control steps

Control steps determine how you want your scripts to perform in general — indeed, whether you want them to perform at all. It's kind of the boss of the scripts; in Hollywood, you might call this set of steps the *producer.*

Perform Script	Performs a subscript or external script
Resume Script	Resumes a script that is paused
Halt Script	Stops performing all scripts
If	Performs steps if a calculation is True (not zero)
Else	Performs another set of steps if a calculation is False (zero)
End If	Marks the end of an If statement
Loop	Repeatedly performs a set of steps; you can use this step to define a script that repeats itself
Exit Loop If	Exits a loop if a calculation is True (not zero)
End Loop	Marks the end of a loop
Allow User Abort	Allows users to stop a script; this can also be set to prevent users from stopping a script
Set Error Capture	Turns error messages on or off when performing a script

Navigation steps

Navigation steps are great for defining where you want to move around in your FileMaker Pro layout. Call these *gofer scripts,* to continue with the Hollywood analogy.

If you move around from layout to record and back, or perform any other sequence of steps, these navigation steps help out. Figure 22-7 shows you the navigation steps you can choose from.

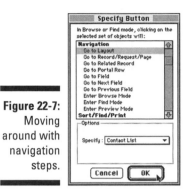

Figure 22-7:
Moving
around with
navigation
steps.

Go to Layout	Views the specified layout
Go to Record/Request/Page	Moves to a record in the found set in Browse Request/Page mode, a find request in Find mode, or a page in Preview mode
Go to Related Record	Moves to the current related record in the related file
Go to Portal Row	Moves to a portal row or to a specified field in a portal row
Go to Field	Moves to a field on the current layout
Go to Next Field	Moves to the next field on the current layout
Go to Previous Field	Moves to the previous field on the current layout
Enter Browse Mode	Switches to Browse mode
Enter Find Mode	Switches to Find mode
Enter Preview Mode	Switches to Preview mode

Sort/Find/Print steps

You can use these scripts for tedious, repetitive tasks, such as finding certain records or printing. Call them *grunt scripts* because if you have to perform the tasks, you'll probably grunt while doing them. Incidentally, I find the Page Setup step incredibly useful.

Figure 22-8 shows you the Specify Button dialog box with the Sort/Find/Print steps. Here's what they can do for you:

Sort	Orders records in the found set
Unsort	Restores records to the order in which they were created
Find All	Finds all records in the file
Find Omitted	Finds the records omitted from the found set
Omit	Leaves the current record out of the found set
Omit Multiple	Leaves a number of records, starting from the current record, out of the found set
Perform Find	Finds records that match the find request(s)
Modify Last Find	Changes the last find request(s)
Page Setup	Sets Page Setup options, such as horizontal or vertical orientation
Print	Prints information from the current file

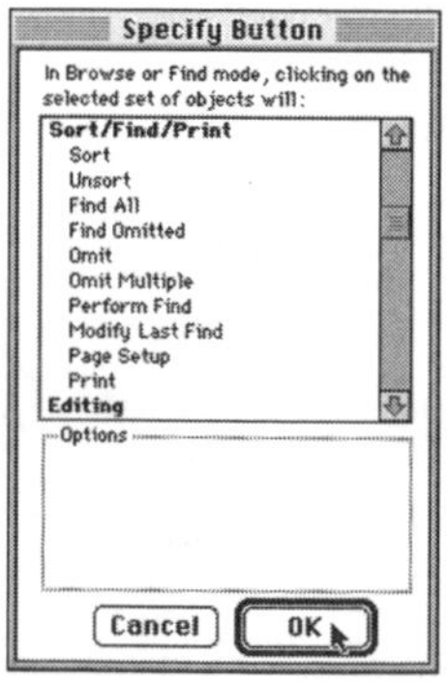

Figure 22-8:
Some very useful scripting steps.

Editing steps

I like editing steps because, again, if you include them in your FileMaker Pro database, they save time in doing mundane chores, such as cutting, copying, and pasting. Back in Hollywood, these steps would be *cutter scripts,* what those film editors do in darkened rooms with miles of celluloid cut to ribbons on the floor.

Figure 22-9 shows you the editing steps you can use. Here's what they do:

Figure 22-9:
Simplify
some
editing
tasks with
these
scripting
steps.

Note that FileMaker Pro performs editing steps on fields that show up in the current layout only.

Undo	Reverts to the action before the last action
Cut	Deletes the contents of a field and puts them on the Clipboard
Copy	Places the contents of a field on the Clipboard but doesn't delete from the field
Paste	Places the contents of the Clipboard into a field
Clear	Deletes the contents of a field without copying the contents to the Clipboard
Select All	Highlights the entire contents of a field

Field steps

If you want to do things with fields, or have fields do things for you, field steps are what you use. I especially like the whole set of pasting steps for automating the creation of a particular layout. For example, you can paste in the current time and current date or the results from a calculation into a field. A good script composed of these steps is a time-saver, indeed.

Figure 22-10 shows you field steps in the Specify Button dialog box. If you use these steps, FileMaker Pro performs the following commands:

Figure 22-10:
Use these scripting steps when working with fields.

Set Field	Replaces the contents of a field with the result of a calculation (the field doesn't have to be on the current layout)
Paste Literal	Pastes a text string into a field
Paste Result	Pastes the contents of a field or the results of a calculation into another field on the current layout
Paste from Index	Pastes a value from the index into a field
Paste from Last Record	Pastes data from a field in the last active record into the same field in the current record or find request
Paste Current Date	Pastes the system date into a field
Paste Current Time	Pastes the system time into a field
Paste Current User Name	Pastes the name of the current user into a field

Records steps

You're always working with records and more records, once you get rolling with FileMaker Pro. So these steps are a godsend when you add them to your script. Figure 22-11 shows you the steps you use if you need to get FileMaker Pro to perform things with your records.

Figure 22-11:
Steps to help
you work
with records.

New Record/Request	Adds a record or find request
Duplicate Record/Request	Copies a record or find request
Delete Record/Request	Permanently deletes the current record or find request
Delete Portal Row	Deletes the current portal row
Revert Record/Request	Returns the current record or find request to the way it was before you added or changed its data
Exit Record/Request	Exits the current record or find request; use this step to finish entering data, update a calculation, or click outside a field
Copy Record	Places the contents of the current record on the Clipboard
Copy All Records	Places the contents of the found set on the Clipboard
Delete All Records	Permanently deletes all records

| Replace | Changes the contents of a field in all records in the found set |
| Relookup | Updates a lookup value in the records being browsed |

Import/Export steps

If you're doing a great deal of importing and exporting of data or graphic images, here are the steps you need to know about:

Import Picture	Imports a graphic into the current field
Import Movie	Imports a QuickTime movie into the current field
Import Records	Brings data into the current file
Export Records	Saves data in a format you can open in another application

Windows steps

Windows steps are cool because you get to do scripts that control what's displayed on your screen in each file. Here are the steps:

Freeze Window	Stops updating the window; use this step to hide actions from users
Refresh Window	Redraws the screen, or resumes updating after Freeze Window
Scroll Window	Scrolls the window up, down, or to the current selection
Toggle Window	Shows, hides, or sets the size of the window
Toggle Status Area	Shows or hides the status area
Toggle Text Ruler	Shows or hides the text ruler
Set Zoom Level	Sets a zoom percentage to zoom in or zoom out
View As	Views one record or a list of records

Files steps

I like steps for files because, with just a click of a button using these scripts, you can get FileMaker Pro to open and close your files, change passwords, or save copies. Here are the files steps:

New	Creates a file
Open	Opens an existing file
Close	Closes a file
Change Password	Changes passwords
Set Multi-User	Turns network access on or off for the current file
Set Use System Formats	Uses date, time, and number formats saved with the current file, or uses the system formats
Save a Copy as	Saves a copy of the current file
Recover	Recovers a file

Spelling steps

FileMaker Pro even includes steps to check your spelling. That's certainly a bell and a whistle. Here are the spelling steps:

Check Selection	Checks the spelling of text in the selected field
Check Record	Checks the spelling of text in the current record
Check Found Set	Checks the spelling of text in all fields of all records in the found set
Correct Word	Displays the Spelling dialog box, where you can correct a misspelled word; the Spell As You Type feature must be on for this option to be enabled. Check Chapter 3 for details on setting this as preference.

Spelling Options	Displays the Spelling Options dialog box
Select Dictionaries	Displays the Select Dictionaries dialog box
Edit User Dictionary	Displays the Edit User Dictionary dialog box

Open Menu Item steps

FileMaker Pro also provides you with scripts that let you open certain menu items in the program. These are designed to save you a lot of time, particularly with actions that you may perform over and over. Here they are:

Open Application Preferences	Displays the Application Preferences dialog box
Open Document Preferences	Displays the Document Preferences dialog box
Open Define Fields	Displays the Define Fields dialog box
Open Define Relationships	Displays the Define Relationships dialog box
Open Define Value Lists	Displays the Define Value Lists dialog box
Open Help	Displays the FileMaker Pro Help system contents window
Open ScriptMaker	Displays the Define Scripts dialog box; FileMaker Pro stops performing a script after this step because it takes you to the ScriptMaker option.
Open Sharing	Displays the File Sharing dialog box

Miscellaneous steps

FileMaker Pro comes with a few extra steps (notably in defining relationships) that don't quite fit in the other categories. Check these out:

Show Message	Displays an alert message
Beep	Plays the system beep sound
Speak	Produces speech from text

Dial Phone	Dials phone numbers
Open URL	Launches a Web browser and displays a URL (Uniform Resource Locator). This step is new to FileMaker Pro 4.
Send Mail	Allows you to use "To" and "CC" fields for mass or bulk mailings of e-mail. This step is new to FileMaker Pro 4 and works on both Mac and Windows versions of the program.
Send Apple Event	Sends an Apple event to other applications
Perform AppleScript	Performs AppleScript commands
Comment	Adds notes to describe a step
Flush Cache to Disk	Saves the FileMaker Pro internal cache to disk
Quit Application	Closes all files and quits FileMaker Pro

The Business of Defining Scripts

Even the magic of Hollywood (I shudder to think) is a business. You're in business with FileMaker Pro when you begin defining scripts by picking and choosing the steps you want. Here's where you've got to make some smart choices and figure out what you really want your scripts to do.

Throw the following questions at yourself or your colleagues at home, work, or school:

- ✔ When do I want my scripts to begin?

- ✔ What do I want them to do? How can I break the task of a script down into smaller increments or steps?

- ✔ Am I going to work with just one file or many files? How are my scripts going to perform over many files?

- ✔ Do I want to use scripts for printing, importing, finding, sorting, or page setup?

- ✔ How will I navigate through my fields with these new scripts? What navigational steps do I need?

- ✔ How should the script finish? Where do I want it to end up?

Once you've thought things through and come up with answers to some of these questions, you're ready to swing into action. Lights, camera, action! All right, this isn't Hollywood, but why not just pretend for a moment?

Hello, ScriptMaker

Before you get the lights and cameras rolling, you ought to know a few things about FileMaker Pro's incredible ScriptMaker feature, which lets you produce custom scripts.

If you're going to define a script for printing, importing, exporting, finding, or sorting, you need to store the settings for the script. That way, FileMaker Pro simply grabs the settings when it executes the script for you.

So a little legwork is in order. You need to choose File⇨Page Setup; in the dialog box that appears, select the settings you want, and click OK. Do the same thing for Print Options: Select the settings and click Print. FileMaker Pro saves those settings for you, so when you execute a script, it has retained those settings and is able to access them easily.

Follow this same procedure for storing your settings if you're planning to use import, export, find requests, and sort order in your scripts.

A script has some limitations; for example, it can store only one type of setting at a time. If you have to use more than one setting, you have to define a subscript to get the action you want.

Now you're ready to get moving on the set. Proceed this way:

1. **Choose Script⇨ScriptMaker.**

    The Define Scripts dialog box for a sample database such as My Address Book appears, as shown in Figure 22-12.

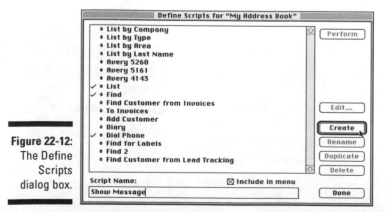

Figure 22-12:
The Define
Scripts
dialog box.

Define Scripts for "My Address Book"

- • List by Company
- • List by Type
- • List by Area
- • List by Last Name
- • Avery 5260
- • Avery 5161
- • Avery 4143
- ✓ • List
- ✓ • Find
- • Find Customer from Invoices
- • To Invoices
- • Add Customer
- • Diary
- ✓ • Dial Phone
- • Find for Labels
- • Find 2
- • Find Customer from Lead Tracking

Perform

Edit...

Create

Rename

Duplicate

Delete

Script Name: ⊠ Include in menu

Show Message

Done

2. In the Script Name text box, enter the name of the new script you want, and click Create.

The Script Definition dialog box appears, as Figure 22-13 shows. In the column on the left, you have a list of the available steps, outlined earlier in this chapter, at your disposal.

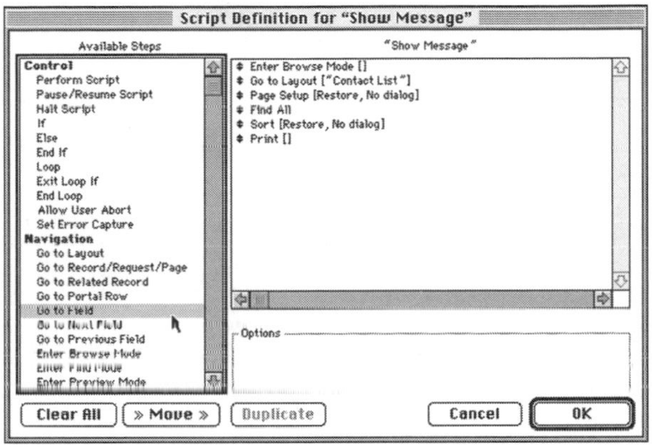

Figure 22-13: The Script Definition dialog box.

3. Click to select the steps you want, and click Move after each selection.

The steps you select are now added to the set of steps in the right column of the dialog box. You can rearrange the order of the steps by clicking the items in the list. Or, if the steps are in the correct order, you don't have to rearrange them at all.

To eliminate a particular step from your script, click the Clear button. You can also click Clear All and start from scratch, selecting the available steps from the list on the left and then moving them to the list on the right.

4. After you've selected the steps and the sequence in which you want them performed, click OK.

If you're brave enough to go to the subscript level here, don't click OK just yet, but follow the rest of these steps. If you want to stop here, click OK.

5. In the available steps list, click Perform Script.

That step now appears in the right column of the Script Definition box.

6. You can click in the Options box near the bottom of the screen in the Perform Sub-scripts box and then select an option such as Find from the Specify pop-up menu, as shown in Figure 22-14.

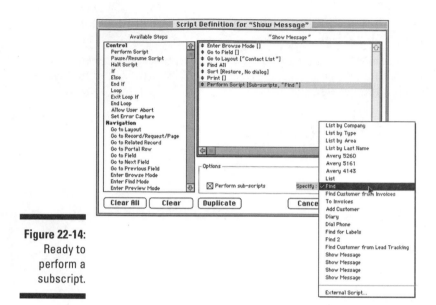

Figure 22-14:
Ready to
perform a
subscript.

7. Click OK.

The subscript is now part of your script, which you can see in
Figure 22-15.

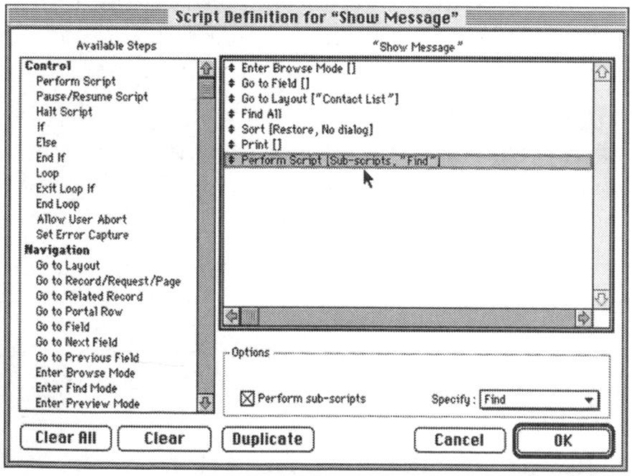

Figure 22-15:
Finding a
subscript in
your script.

8. By clicking OK, you return to the Define Scripts dialog box. In upper-right corner of that dialog box, click Perform, as shown in Figure 22-16.

If you click the box that says Include in Menu, that script then appears on the Script menu on your menu bar with a keyboard equivalent to the right of it.

Congratulations! You're in the scripting business! Is the real Hollywood next?

Figure 23-16:
When finished, your newly created script appears in the Define Scripts dialog box.

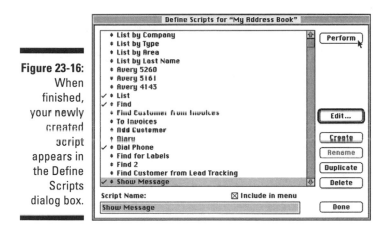

Chapter 23
All That Relational Jazz

*I*s FileMaker Pro truly relational? Is it not? I won't get into a debate here about that issue. And ultimately, does it really matter in the great cosmic scheme of things? Well, that's another, more philosophical debate. Time to stop debating and get to work.

Some years ago, the experts in the database field put forth a set of criteria by which a database would qualify in theory as *relational*. I'm not sure how many of those criteria FileMaker Pro meets. Nor do I think it really matters for this book's purposes. From a practical point of view, if FileMaker Pro has so-called "relational" capabilities, why not take advantage of them? Am I making sense, or not?

If you've been using a version of FileMaker Pro prior to Version 3, perhaps 2.0 or 2.1, you'll be delighted to see how the new relational stuff works. In fact, you'll probably want to convert some of your existing FileMaker Pro 2.1 files to FileMaker 4 just so you can take full advantage of the relational capabilities now offered to you.

In Chapter 5, I introduce you to what I called the "relational boogie," which I explain in two parts: defining the relationships you want between files and then specifying the fields that you want to be related in your FileMaker Pro layouts. You may want to flip to Chapter 5 if you're reading for the first time about FileMaker Pro's relational features. In this chapter, I move from boogie to jazz, from a few dance steps to making relational music.

Defining the Relational in FileMaker Pro

A *relational database* lets you take the data from one file and use it in your current file, after you've defined the nature of the relationship between the data. You don't have to just copy your data from one file to another — which leads to that dreaded phenomenon: duplication. I mean, you're going to have a certain amount of duplication in whatever type of database you use. But there is a limit, no?

In the relational world, your data belongs to your original file, so when you change or update it — for example, adding new values — the data in your new file changes, too. How? Funny you should ask. It's accomplished simply by defining the relationship you want between the two files, one of which is your *master file* and the other your *related file.* (Both are explained in the next section in this chapter.) FileMaker Pro takes care of the rest.

In Chapter 5, you find out about defining the relationship between two particular files — using a Personal Address Book and a Contacts database — whose fields contain common data, such as last and first names, addresses, and phone numbers. The example in that chapter defines a one-to-one correspondence between the data in a master file and the data in a related file.

This chapter extends some of the concepts introduced in Chapter 5 and shows how you can easily establish one-to-one relationships between data in master and related files by using the Field tool in Layout mode. In addition, I want to introduce you to the Portal tool, which lets you establish a one-to-many correspondence between the data in your master file and the data that resides in your related file. The Portal tool is unique to FileMaker Pro 3 and 4 and is very handy for displaying all the related fields, as well as related records, in your layouts.

Some key terms you need to know

Before you swing into action, you need to know some key terms:

- ✔ **Master file:** The file that accesses and displays your data from another file. You use this master file to allow data from another, related file to be displayed. You don't have to copy that data into your master file. Whew! That data in your master file changes and gets updated whenever the values in your other file change.

- ✔ **Related file:** The file containing the data you want to access and display in your master file. Are you ready for this now? A related file and a master file can be the same file. Go figure. I won't try to explain that just yet.

✔ **Match fields:** This one shouldn't be all that difficult to figure out. Match fields occur when the fields in the master file and fields in the related file contain values that you want to use to find matching records. In the relational world, the values in the match field have to be equal to each other.

Some other important things you need to know

You need to know just a few other things before you get started defining relationships between fields in your FileMaker Pro 4 files.

✔ Relational stuff does not work with files created in FileMaker Pro 2.1 or earlier. Of course, if you convert a FileMaker Pro 2.1 file to a 3 or 4 file, you can take advantage of the program's relational features. Each converted file then becomes a potential candidate for setting up and building a relationship to another file. You just have to decide among the various files as to which ones you want to use to build relationships.

✔ Before you can define a match between related fields, you have to index those fields. Indexing speeds up the matching between data in related fields and is necessary before you actually start using the relationship in your FileMaker Pro database.

✔ If you have two or more files from two or more databases that you want to establish as related, you need to open each file separately and turn on the indexing feature for each of the fields that you want to match.

✔ Admittedly, turning on indexing may *not* be the most intuitive way to work in building a FileMaker Pro relational database, because indexing is usually a step that you think about later rather than sooner in the process. That's okay. You can save the indexing of the matching fields until you've completed the whole process of establishing the relationships among different fields. In other words, indexing has to be done, but not right away.

To index fields in your relational database, follow these steps:

1. **Choose File➪Define➪Fields.**

2. **When the Define Fields dialog box appears, select the fields that you want to match, and click Options.**

3. **When the Entry Options dialog box appears, click the Storage Options button at the bottom of the dialog box.**

The Storage Options dialog box shown in Figure 23-1 appears with the options available for indexing the field you've selected.

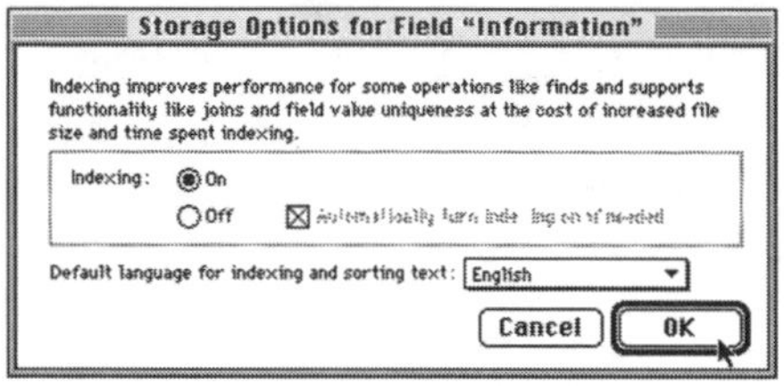

Figure 23-1:
The Storage
Options
dialog box,
ready to
index.

Storage Options for Field "Information"

Indexing improves performance for some operations like finds and supports
functionality like joins and field value uniqueness at the cost of increased file
size and time spent indexing.

Indexing: ◉ On
                ○ Off   ☒ Automatically turn indexing on if needed

Default language for indexing and sorting text: English ▼

Cancel   OK

4. **Click the On radio button to turn on indexing for the field, and click OK.**

5. **In the Define Fields dialog box, click Done.**

You can place a related field in your layout either by itself or in a portal. In the layout of your master file, that related field name appears as `Relationship name::Related field name`, or as simply `::Related field name`.

Portals? What am I talking about here, a ship at sea? Actually, it's not a bad way to describe this unique feature in FileMaker Pro. A *portal* is a representation of the correspondence of related fields between records in your master file and another database. It is represented on your layout by an icon. Whew! I know that may be a bit much to digest all at once. But when you see a portal in action containing more than one related field from a list of all the related records in another database, you'll get the hang of it. In fact, when portals contain more than one related field, you see the data in those fields displayed in rows, with each row displaying one separate record.

Figuring Out Which Files to Relate to — This Is No Blind Date!

The hard part about working with a relational database is just figuring out which files from one database you want to relate to which files from another database. You don't have any easy formula to work off of. The main question to ask is, What data exists in common among your different database files? That's a head scratcher, all right. But it has to be the start for any relational database work that you do with FileMaker Pro.

For example, in a small business, you may have data in your Invoice files that match the data in your Customer Contacts file. Matching the data from one file to the other saves you the time of having to look up, for example, which of your customers have paid their invoices.

At school, you could set up a relational database that lets you match the fields from a file that contains the dates of certain historical events for your history class with a file that contains the dates of major political campaigns for your political science class. The matching files would let you keep track of the dates of both without having to look up the data in each file separately.

If you work at home, you may want to build a relational database in which the data from your Projects file is displayed in a field in your Billing file. That way, when billing out a project, you don't have to copy and paste the information from your Projects file to your Billing file. It's already there for you to work with, which saves time if you have to document the hours on a particular project in order to bill out your work.

The ideal relational database contains a set of matches, or *correspondences,* between files. Determining these matches is something you have to think out carefully. You can't really build a good relationship here on a blind date. You need to see what data matches or doesn't match among the files in various FileMaker Pro databases. In order to accomplish this feat, you may want to take out pencil and paper and draw up a list of fields in the files you want to relate. You may be surprised to find more possible matches than you think.

The first place to look for a match between related files is any field that contains an identification number. ID number fields are always used as examples of typical fields you can match from one file to another. For example, in a business, you may have an Employee file with ID numbers in fields for each of your employees. At the same time, you may have another file in your business that lists vacation and other days off for your employees, also with an ID number. Both files are good candidates for establishing a relationship. In your Employee file, which you designate as the master file, you can display related files that list the vacation periods for your employees. FileMaker Pro performs a match for you by finding all the records for your employees' vacations based on the matching ID numbers. Cool, don't you think?

The advantages of going relational are significant. Because each occurrence of your data is stored in only one file at a time, you avoid duplication of information and can manage your FileMaker Pro database much more efficiently than if you had to constantly update the data in multiple files.

After Selecting Your Master and Related Files, You're Ready to Dance

Chapter 5 uses the example of matching a few common fields from a Personal Address Book file with the fields in a Contacts file as a good illustration of how you establish master and related files. Because my Personal Address Book file was smaller and contained fewer fields, I wanted to use that as my master file, where I could specify the related fields from my larger Contacts database file. Establishing a relationship between the two files made sense mainly because one was for business while the other was for personal use. Not all the names in one would occur in the other.

This chapter takes you to the next level and shows you a few tricks I've picked up in the course of working with FileMaker Pro's relational capabilities, so I've selected some examples that illustrate some of these finer points. If you're a little uneasy with the concepts here, you can find out about the fundamentals of relational database design in Chapter 5.

After some brainstorming and diagramming of files and fields on paper, I have identified three separate files that I can use to establish my relational database. The first file is what I call my Publications Organizer. I essentially use this file to catalog the work I'm doing, whether it's a book, magazine article, or piece for publication on the World Wide Web. I'm sure you have a similar organizer, a database that's like a central clearinghouse for your work. Check it out and see whether you can use it as your own master file.

A good candidate for a master file is the file that you use most often in your database work — the one that typically stores your most important information. If you look through your own files, you can identify that file fairly easily because it's often the file that you come back to again and again. It stares at you a lot. It's the file that, essentially, keeps your house in order.

Figure 23-2 shows you the main entry screen from my Publications Organizer. Basically, it's one great big Rolodex with fields for titles, categories, and brief descriptions of published and unpublished work. Nothing too fancy here. At the bottom of the Publications Organizer is a set of buttons that let you move forward or backward one record at a time in the file, as well as to the first or last record. I tried to keep things simple and easily accessible so that I know what I'm producing and where it's going.

The second file that I use a lot is my FileMaker Pro To Do database. I customized this database from a shareware template and found it very useful for setting up priorities, categories, and deadlines for the various things on my to-do list. I like it because it's strictly no nonsense: just the facts, Jack. I add a new record and enter in the deadline to complete the work, as well as its priority in my life and the category (Business or Personal). Figure 23-3 gives you a look at this very bare-bones, not-too-fancy To Do file.

Figure 23-2:
The main
entry
screen
from a
Publications
Organizer,
ready to
serve as a
master file
in building a
relational
database.

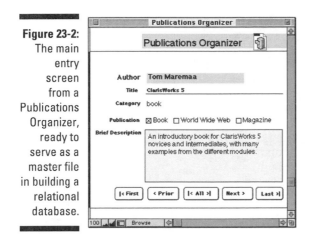

Now, my To Do file has one field that, when I think about it, ought to be a good candidate for a related field. It's a field that may be useful to have in my Publications Organizer: the Deadline field. Nowhere in my Publications Organizer do I see anything about deadlines! And every author I know lives and, dare I say it, dies by deadlines. Of course, I could just go ahead and add that field, right? But then I would be duplicating a field I already have in my To Do file. Are you with me on this train of thought?

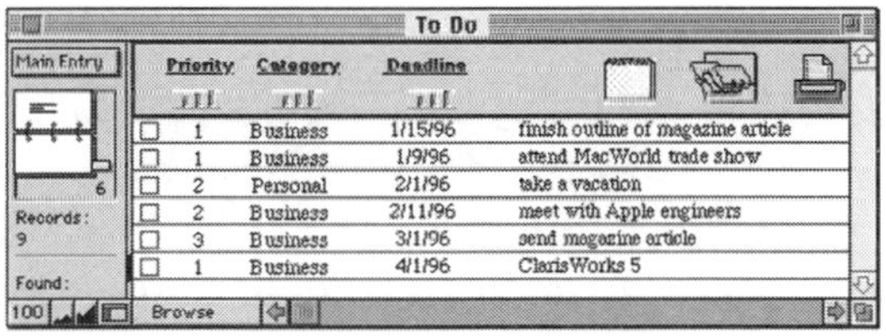

Figure 23-3:
A bare-
bones
To Do
database
file, but
one with
potential for
related
fields.

Now, the third file that I want to relate to my master file is a file called Tom's Projects. I've modified this file from one of the FileMaker Pro templates and plugged in my own data. Figure 23-4 shows you a screen from Tom's Projects. I've set up fields for Project Number, Project Name, Schedule, Project Description, Estimated Start Date, and Estimated Finish Date. Again, nothing too fancy here.

Figure 23-4:
Tom's
Projects,
another file
with
potential for
related
fields.

But look closely for a moment at the screen for Tom's Projects. You can see fields for starting and finishing a project. Those fields aren't included in my To Do file, nor are they in my Publications Organizer. Hmmmmmmm. Well, I think I have some good candidates here for related fields, don't you?

Now that I've surveyed the scene, and perhaps found a few wallflowers at the party, I think I may be ready to dance — and who knows, if I play my cards right, maybe even go out on my first big date.

The First Big Date

Sooner or later, after you've flirted and danced with your partner and perhaps exchanged phone numbers, you ought to be ready for that first big date. In the database world, the first big date comes about by matching fields. Here's how you proceed:

1. **Open your master file — in my example, it's the Publications Organizer — by choosing File⇨Open and selecting your file.**

2. **Switch to Layout mode by choosing Mode⇨Layout, or by selecting Layout from the mode selector at the bottom of your FileMaker Pro screen.**

3. **In Layout mode, click the Field tool and drag it to a place where you want to position a field in your layout.**

    The Specify Field dialog box appears on-screen.

4. **In the Specify Field dialog box (see Figure 23-5), click the Current File pop-up menu and click Define Relationships; then click the Create Field Label check box and click OK.**

Always check the Create Field Label box because it helps you keep track of the new fields you've added to your layouts. If you don't want to use that field label, which basically just names the field for you, you can always delete it later on.

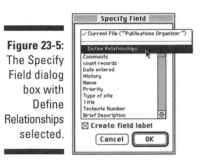

Figure 23-5:
The Specify
Field dialog
box with
Define
Relationships
selected.

After clicking OK, the big but empty Define Relationships dialog box for
your master file appears, as shown in Figure 23-6 for the Publications
Organizer.

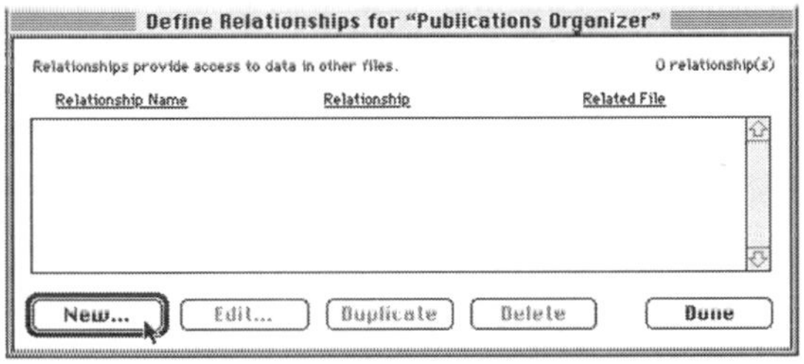

Figure 23-6:
The big but
empty (for
now) Define
Relationships
dialog box.

5. Click New.

Don't worry. You can add to this empty dialog box soon. You should
note the three important categories here: the Relationship Name, the
Relationship itself, and the Related File. The categories are important
because, for each relationship you define, you want to be sure that your
relationship name is appropriate and that you've decided which file is
master and which is related.

After you click New, FileMaker Pro asks you which file you want to
specify as a related file. In this example, I've selected from a folder on
my Desktop the To Do file as the first of my related files. Notice that
FileMaker Pro does not actually open the file you select but rather
displays, in the Edit Relationship dialog box, a list of the fields in that
file (see Figure 23-7).

6. Enter the Relationship Name you want.

FileMaker Pro defaults to the name of the file you specify as related. But
you may enter any name your choose. I recommend going with the
default name.

7. **In the list boxes, select the field you want to match from your master file (Publications Organizer) with a field from your related file (To Do).**

In Figure 23-7, I've selected the Title field from the current, or master, file and the To Do field in the related file.

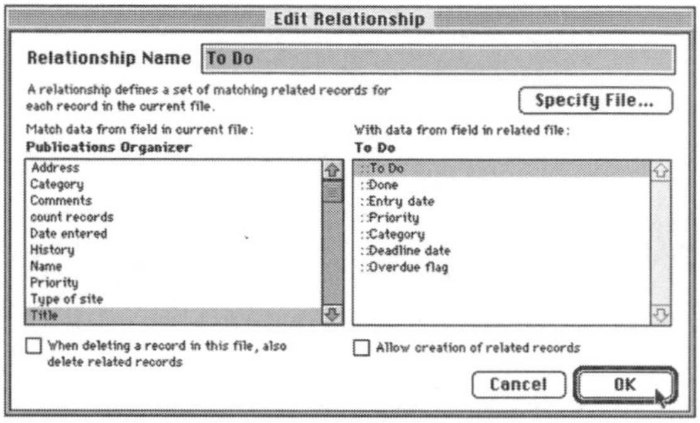

Figure 23-7:
The Edit
Relationship
dialog box
with fields
you can
match.

> **Edit Relationship**
>
> **Relationship Name** | To Do
>
> A relationship defines a set of matching related records for each record in the current file.   [Specify File...]
>
> Match data from field in current file: With data from field in related file:
> **Publications Organizer**   **To Do**
>
> Address | ::To Do
> Category | ::Done
> Comments | ::Entry date
> count records | ::Priority
> Date entered | ::Category
> History | ::Deadline date
> Name | ::Overdue flag
> Priority
> Type of site
> Title
>
> ☐ When deleting a record in this file, also   ☐ Allow creation of related records
>   delete related records
>
> [Cancel]   [OK]

At the top of the dialog box, FileMaker Pro defaults in the Relationship Name box to the name of the related file — again, in this case, the To Do file. You can enter any name you want for the relationship, or simply use the default name. In the list box to the right, FileMaker Pro indicates the matching related fields with a double colon (::).

8. **Click OK to return to the Define Relationships dialog box, where you see the Relationship Name (To Do), the Relationship (Title= ::To Do), and the Related File (To Do) all selected. Then click Done.**

Figure 23-8 shows you the Define Relationships dialog box for this example. Congratulations! This step is the first big kiss on your date.

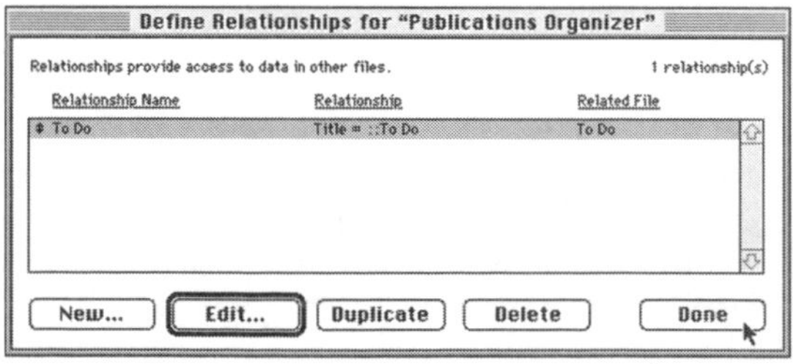

Figure 23-8:
The
updated
Define
Relationships
dialog
box for
Publications
Organizer.

> **Define Relationships for "Publications Organizer"**
>
> Relationships provide access to data in other files.   1 relationship(s)
>
> Relationship Name   Relationship   Related File
>
> # To Do   Title = ::To Do   To Do
>
> [New...] [Edit...] [Duplicate] [Delete]   [Done]

If you click the Edit button, you can go back to the previous Edit Relationship dialog box and make any changes you want. Clicking Duplicate lets you duplicate the relationships you've already established. Those duplicated relationships appear in the Define Relationships dialog box just below the first relationships you've established. The double arrow to the left of the selected To Do field lets you move the fields up or down in the order you want when you've established more than one relationship.

Switching from Layout to Browse mode in your master file reveals the related To Do field with the data displayed right there on-screen, as Figure 23-9 shows. In my example, this field matches the data in my Title field (ClarisWorks 5). It's like having a database within a database, but with only those fields that are relevant to your master file. With this relational match, you can keep track of things in your To Do file just by clicking in the Title field of your Publications Organizer. FileMaker Pro is at your service and brings them right up!

Figure 23-9:
The related To Do fields, in this case matching the Title field in the Publications Organizer.

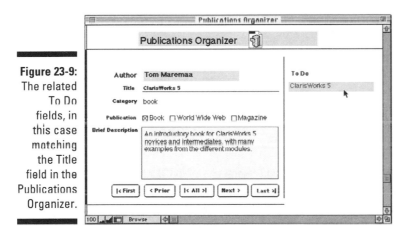

The Second, Third, and Fourth Dates: Are We Going Steady Yet?

Why just one set of matching fields? Why not add a few more that are relevant? Now that I'm on the road to building a meaningful relationship — aren't all relationships meaningful when they start? — I want to add new matching fields. Here's how:

1. **In Layout mode, if you've already established the initial relationships by matching your first fields, select the Field tool and drag it on your layout.**

The Specify Field dialog box appears. Note that while you're working in Layout mode in your master file, FileMaker Pro is bringing you a list of the fields that are in your related file. Pretty clever, I'd say.

2. Select another field you want to relate to your master file, check the Create Field Label check box, and click OK.

Guess what? You're hot; you're smokin'! If you return to Browse mode in your master file, you see the new field where you've placed it on your screen. Figure 23-10 shows that I placed the Deadline Date field from my To Do file just below the To Do field.

Figure 23-10:
The Deadline Date related field in my Publications Organizer.

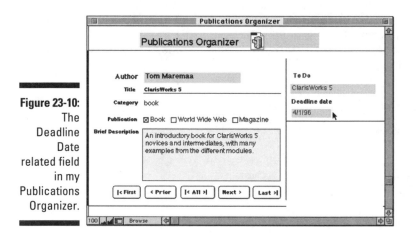

Now, I want to add a few new To Do items to my To Do file, just to make things interesting. Figure 23-11 shows you that I've added a new record, with *FileMaker Pro article* as the data in my field, along with the deadline of 5/1/98.

The idea here is that, in practical terms, you're going to be adding new records over time to your related files. You won't just be working with your master file — in this case, the Publications Organizer. The To Do file is handy, as I mentioned before, just because you can add projects to it quickly and pin down an immediate deadline for a particular project you have to complete.

Now, when I return to my Publications Organizer and enter **FileMaker Pro Article** into the Title field — presto! — the same name appears in my To Do field, and right below that the new project's deadline date (see Figure 23-12).

I think you get the idea now that just by typing in what I have to do, in this case a FileMaker Pro article, I automatically get the deadline date to appear in my Organizer. This is way cool.

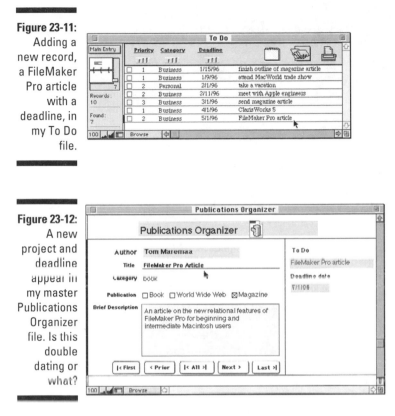

Figure 23-11:
Adding a new record, a FileMaker Pro article with a deadline, in my To Do file.

Figure 23-12:
A new project and deadline appear in my master Publications Organizer file. Is this double dating or what?

But wait a minute. What happened to Tom's Projects? Remember that file as one of the three potentially relational files I started with? I'm not talking about a love triangle — just a good old-fashioned romance after some steady dating.

The Romance Begins with the Portal Tool

In the file Tom's Projects, shown in Figure 23-13, you see fields for project name, project number, project description, schedule status, and, right below schedule status, estimated start and estimated finish dates. After some thought, I can see that in my Publications Organizer, I sure could use those last two fields, and maybe even see a list of all the related records from that Projects file.

Figure 23-13:
Estimated
Start and
Estimated
Finish Dates
are two
possible
fields
relating
to my
Publications
Organizer.

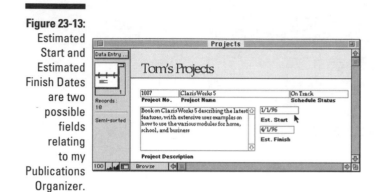

Imagining a romance beginning with a Portal tool may be hard, but why not? I don't want to strain the limits of this romance metaphor that I've been using to describe how you build relationships between matching fields in FileMaker Pro. Bear with me. I had to figure out a way to introduce you to this nifty tool that lets you view a list of one or more records from a related database file.

Figure 23-14 shows you the Portal tool that appears on the Tool panel when you're in Layout mode. You use the Portal tool to draw a rectangle that holds all the fields you want to show from a related file.

Sounds simple, right? Well, you can't quite imagine the programming power that this little tool unleashes for you. With just a couple of point and click actions, you're able to open up a window (I guess that's what portals really are) onto another world of related files and records.

Are you ready for some action? I mean, I'm getting romantic, okay?

Figure 23-14:
The Portal
tool, up
close and
personal.

1. **In Layout mode, select the Portal tool from the Tool panel and drag the tool onto your layout as you would if you were using the Field tool to place a field on your layout.**

   The Portal Setup dialog box appears. You want to show the records from Tom's Projects by using this portal capability.

2. **Click the Show Records from Pop-Up menu, click Define Relation-ships (as shown in Figure 23-15), and click OK.**

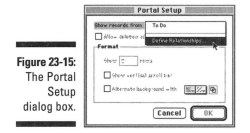

Figure 23-15:
The Portal
Setup
dialog box.

The familiar Define Relationships dialog box appears.

3. **In the Define Relationships dialog box, click New.**

The Edit Relationship dialog box, shown in Figure 23-16, appears.

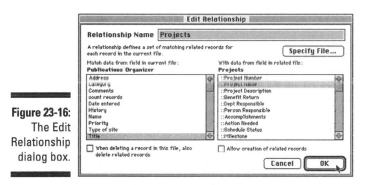

Figure 23-16:
The Edit
Relationship
dialog box.

This time, the Edit Relationship dialog box lists fields from my Publications Organizer and Projects files.

4. **In the Edit Relationship dialog box, give a name to your new relation-ship, select the fields you want to match from each side of the dialog box, and click OK.**

In Figure 23-16, notice that I've selected the Title field from my master file (Publications Organizer) and the Project Name field from my related file (Projects).

The Portal Setup dialog box reappears (see Figure 23-17) to let you display the records from the related file in your master file. You can specify how you want to display your related records in your master file.

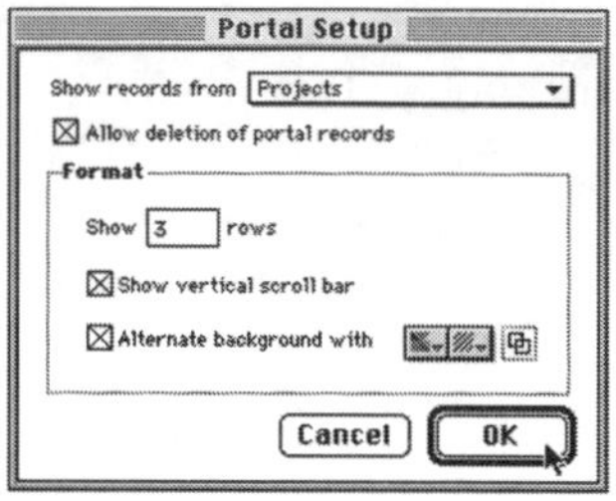
Portal Setup
Show records from
Projects
Allow deletion of portal records
Format
Show 3 rows
Show vertical scroll bar
Alternate background with
Cancel
OK

Figure 23-17: Specify how to display your related records.

5. **In the Portal Setup dialog box, you can tell FileMaker Pro how many rows you want to display.**

   You can also choose to include a vertical scroll bar and an alternating background display for your portal. You should also check the box to allow deletion of portal records. After you've set up your portal the way you want it, click OK.

   Switch back to Layout mode to see the portal added to your layout. In Figure 23-18, I've displayed a three-row portal to the lower right of the layout with a vertical scroll bar and alternate background colors.

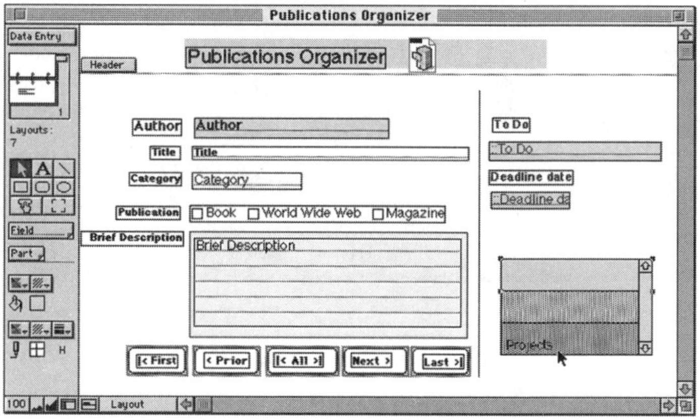
Publications Organizer
Data Entry
Layouts:
7
Header
Publications Organizer
Author
Author
Title
Title
Category
Category
Publication
Book
World Wide Web
Magazine
Brief Description
Brief Description
To Do
To Do
Deadline date
Deadline da
Projects
Field
Part
|< First
< Prior
|< All >|
Next >
Last >|
100
Layout

Figure 23-18: The portal for the Tom's Projects records now showing in the Publications Organizer.

6. **To add fields to your portal, return to the Specify Field dialog box, select the field you want, and click OK.**

7. **In Layout mode, place your new matching fields in your layout portal.**

   For best results, place the fields in rows of alternating backgrounds, as shown in Figure 23-19.

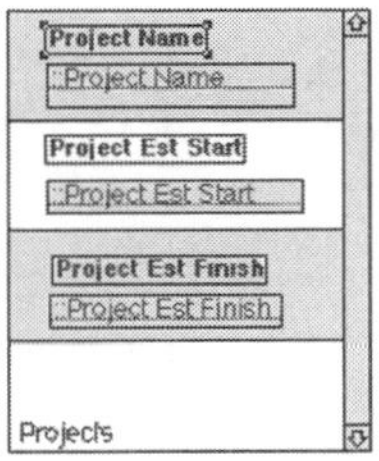

Figure 23-19:
Placing
matching
fields in
your layout
portal.

8. **Switch from Layout mode to Browse mode to find those fields included in the portal on your master file.**

Figure 23-20 shows the complete relational setup with the related fields from my To Do file and my Projects file. In the portal, you can also view a list of all the related records from the Projects file.

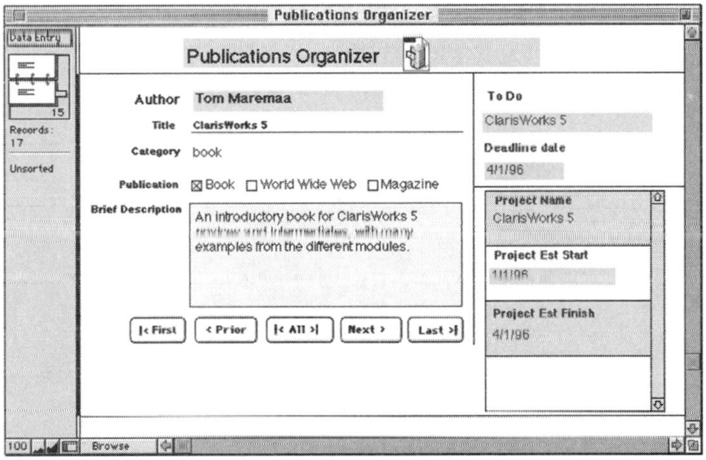

Figure 23-20:
The
Publications
Organizer
with related
fields from
two files
and a
portal.

Well, there you have it! A relationship in the making: from first dance to first date to first kiss to the thrill of romance. Who said creating a relational FileMaker Pro database couldn't be fun?

Part V
Things That Didn't Quite Fit Elsewhere

The 5th Wave   By Rich Tennant

"FOR US, IT WAS TOTAL INTEGRATION OR NOTHING. FOR INSTANCE, AT THIS TERMINAL ALONE, I CAN GET DEPARTMENTAL DATA, PRINTER AND STORAGE RESOURCES, ESPN, HOME SHOPPING NETWORK AND THE DISNEY CHANNEL."

In this part . . .

The world is an imperfect place; not everything fits where it's supposed to fit. Same goes for this book. There are some things that I just couldn't quite squeeze into other parts, so they're here for you. These chapters ought to enhance your FileMaker Pro experience, with tips on going online, doing neat tricks with graphics in your layouts, and looking at some things that can go wrong. Give it a shot.

Chapter 24

Online with the Folks Who Brought You FileMaker Pro

● ●

In This Chapter

▶ Dealing with updates and the point release

▶ Listening to my online spiel

▶ Thanking the folks at America Online

▶ Providing you with a list of phone numbers in case of emergency

● ●

*F*olks in the computer world often say that software is never finished. Whenever I hear that, I always chuckle and shake my head. It's true. As good as FileMaker Pro 4 is — and if you've been reading this book, you know that I think it's pretty darn good, even great — it's not perfect. No software program is. Programs always have little things that may be broken and need minor fixing or tweaking. Despite the extensive testing and debugging that most software goes through when it's released, you inevitably find bugs or glitches (things that don't work quite correctly) that need fixing.

Don't be upset if you come across these problems. Remember: No software program is ever perfect. If the folks at Claris happen to find any minor bugs after releasing a program like FileMaker Pro, you can bet your sweet banana they're going to do everything possible to fix them. What happens after the fixes are made? Read on.

Updates and the Point Release

After its initial release, a program like FileMaker Pro goes through another round of testing and debugging, this time by you and the community of FileMaker Pro users. If you or these folks find anything wrong, it's important that you report it to Claris, and, in turn, Claris will employ its army of software engineers to mend the problem. After that, Claris releases an update, or *point release,* of the program.

Ever wonder about those strange numbers that follow a version number of a software program, like 1.1b, or 1.0.1? I've never quite been able to figure them out myself — and I work in the computer industry. Whatever their exact meanings, you get the general idea that, for example, FileMaker Pro 4.01 is not quite the same as FileMaker Pro 4.0. Typically, it's an update with a few minor fixes to the release version. How many you don't really know, nor can you find out, because that information is usually kept under wraps.

In any case, I wouldn't be too worried about a 4.01 version. It probably means that some computer geek found a bug when opening 10,000 records at midnight while drinking his 25th can of Coke and searching for the *n*th occurrence of G*o*d in a calculation field. And driven by this finding, he reported the "problem" to the programming gurus at Claris, who promptly swung into action and fixed (or *patched*) the problem, which was only reproducible once in every 5 million cases. The geek slept better at night (or day) knowing that he had saved the world from the tyranny of this bug. Such is life.

You should get concerned a bit, however, if you see or hear of FileMaker Pro 4.1 or 4.2. That's a version undoubtedly with more than just a few minor fixes. It may actually have some new features added or a fix to a very nasty crash bug that happened to slip through all the heavy-duty testing and debugging. A 4.1, 4.2, or greater version is one you ought to have. The question is, How do you get it? That's what the rest of this chapter covers.

My Online Spiel

Here it comes — my online spiel. Please lighten up and listen. Just because you're starting out with FileMaker Pro, and getting the basics down so that you get up to speed, it doesn't mean you should be disenfranchised from the computer world and feel like an outsider looking in. As a matter of fact, when working with FileMaker Pro or any other program, you need to be on top of things. In six words, *you need to be plugged in.* It's as simple as that.

Suppose Claris releases another version of FileMaker Pro, fixing a problem that you've been having. How do you get that version? Well, you can call up Claris, request Customer Service, bounce around the automated phone messaging service like a pinball, and eventually place your order with Claris. Then wait two, three, or four days to get the update in the mail. Then install the update on your computer. Makes sense, right? Wrong.

You can get an update of FileMaker Pro or any Claris product as fast as you can make a phone call, press a few buttons, and download the software over your phone lines right into your computer. Compare 20 minutes with four days. Which do you prefer?

You gotta do it, my friend. Take the plunge. Buy a modem and check the computer magazines for special online offers. Gosh, just check your mail. America Online, to which I've been a loyal subscriber for years, is still sending me computer disks and even CD-ROMs trying to entice me to join up. Unless you live on an exotic island in the Pacific, you've probably been bombarded as well. To repeat myself: Take the plunge.

Thank You, America Online

America Online is my online service of choice. You may have a favorite of your own; some folks love CompuServe, which has now merged with America Online. Whatever your choice, you won't go wrong in getting the latest product news and updates from Claris.

These days, everybody in the computer world and elsewhere talks about having _resources,_ but what are they really saying? I think they're saying that in order to get the job done — for example, working with a database program like FileMaker Pro — you need to tap into all the resources and all the necessary information you can get.

Claris has an online forum on America Online. An online forum is like a bulletin board in cyberspace where folks exchange news and information. It's one of the coolest places you can go to get the latest news, product updates, and FileMaker Pro shareware and templates. It's a super resource. And it's yours for the asking.

Claris also has a World Wide Web site, at `www.claris.com`, but I prefer the America Online forum because it's easier to download shareware, templates, and other goodies than from the Claris Internet home. Claris does a heckuva job managing and regularly updating the information that appears on this forum, so you're bound to get the latest software updates and product news straight from the horse's mouth.

You can save yourself a lot of time that you may spend making calls to technical support or customer service by cruising the Claris forum online.

What's the keyword?

After you've logged onto America Online, for example, you get to the Claris forum fast by simply using a keyword shortcut. What's the keyword? That's a big secret that I'm going to share with you if you promise not to tell anybody. It's — here comes the drum roll — **Claris**, as shown in Figure 24-1.

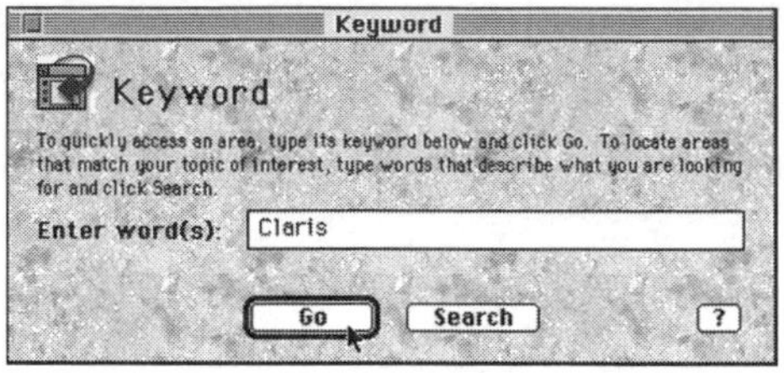

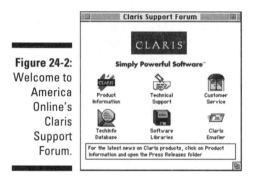

Figure 24-1: The quick and easy way to access the Claris forum on America Online.

Just type in the magic word **Claris**, and you're off to the races. You see the Claris Support Forum screen, as shown in Figure 24-2.

Figure 24-2: Welcome to America Online's Claris Support Forum.

You can click the Product Information, Technical Support, Customer Service, TechInfo Database, Software Libraries, or Claris Emailer icon. If you click the TechInfo Database icon, you see the dialog box shown in Figure 24-3.

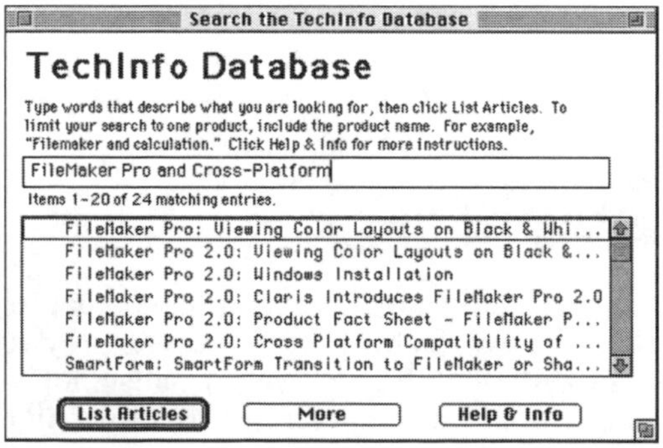

Figure 24-3: A search database is available on America Online.

Just enter a query, and America Online searches the database for you. This option is handy stuff because it lets you search and retrieve key information that relates to a specific problem you may be having.

If you click the Software Libraries icon, you see the screen shown in Figure 24-4.

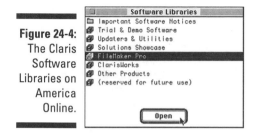

Figure 24-4: The Claris Software Libraries on America Online.

Click FileMaker Pro and then Open to bring up the screen (shown in Figure 24-5) listing all the FileMaker Pro shareware, demos, and templates that FileMaker Pro builders and designers have uploaded for your viewing and working pleasure.

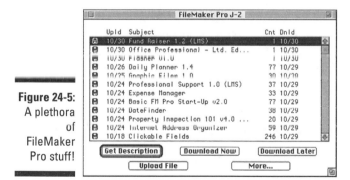

Figure 24-5: A plethora of FileMaker Pro stuff!

The joys of FileMaker Pro shareware

America Online's FileMaker Pro software library offers plenty of shareware choices, as you can see from the screen in Figure 24-5. I highlighted the file Fund Raiser just to show you where you can start. From there, you can download a Daily Planner, an Expense Manager, and an Internet Address Organizer, among other shareware programs.

You can get a brief description of the shareware program by double-clicking the name, which opens up a text file. Then after that's over, you can decide if you want to take the time to download it. Lots of FileMaker Pro database builders and designers lovingly post their creations here and offer them at bargain-basement prices. Some even give them away. I can't begin to tell you what a valuable resource (there's that word again) this library is for us ordinary folks.

Just by downloading a few of these sample FileMaker Pro databases, you get a feel for what's out there and for what can and cannot be done with the magic of this program. I'm always learning something new, for example, whenever I download the latest NAT. NATs are the subject of the next section.

What's a NAT?

Thought you'd never ask. It's the most common, simplest database you can build with FileMaker Pro, the one that everybody should build at least once. It's simple and easy enough to construct in less than an afternoon. It's a NAT — you know, a FileMaker Pro database that consists of only three great fields: Names, Addresses, and Telephone numbers.

After you've built your NAT, you can upload it to the Claris forum on America Online and share it with the world. I hope you'll do that, because if you do, I'll be sure to download it and save it in my library of NATs. Happy NATing!

More icons from the Claris Support Forum

If you click the Technical Support icon in the Claris Support Forum, you can dig into a folder with FAQs (frequently asked questions), as Figure 24-6 shows.

Figure 24-6:
Frequently asked questions, answered online.

If you click the Customer Service icon, you can open up the Customer Service Forms folder and do the following:

- ✔ **Change your address and update any changes in your address online for all of your Claris software:** Use the Address Change form located in the Order Forms folder.

- ✔ **Order a software upgrade:** Any upgrade to your software is bound to have major changes. Just order your upgrade online.

- ✔ **Order a trade-up:** *Trade-ups* are upgrades offered to owners of competitive products, such as other database programs. You need your Visa, MasterCard, or American Express credit card number and expiration date, along with the serial number of the competing product to do a trade-up.

- ✔ **Order or download the latest software updates:** Technically, an update is what's called a *maintenance* release of the program. You can read that as bug fixes, maybe a few itty-bitty enhancements. Updates are there for you in the Claris Resources software library to download.

- ✔ **Request that the update disks are shipped to you:** To order those disks, you use the Place an Order form.

- ✔ **Connect with Claris Customer Service about an order or question:** Send e-mail to the screen name `CLARIS CR`.

Claris recommends that you channel your technical support questions to the product message boards in the technical support area. Well, that's what the company literature says. I recommend that you keep this book handy whenever you work with FileMaker Pro.

Pitching a FileMaker Pro digital 'zine

A really cool FileMaker Pro magazine is published online. Check it out. It's called *ISO,* or *Interactive Support Online.* You can find it under Claris Solutions Alliance (CSA), or at `http://www.iso-ezine.com/indes.php.`, if you're on the Web. It contains a whole set of articles, troubleshooting tips, and tricks of the trade aimed specifically at the FileMaker Pro community of users. It's a great resource for all folks who work with FileMaker Pro. Enjoy!

Tech Support

Claris has excellent tech support if you need it. Lines may be busy at peak hours, but you ought to be able to get through most of the time. The tech support people are friendly and knowledgeable. You should get an answer to your question right away, or at least within an acceptable time frame.

Before you call, though, you ought to get your ducks in a row and make a list of all the things you want to ask, plus any information that's relevant about the Macintosh or Windows computer you're working with and its memory configuration or system extensions.

Here are the numbers:

- **For technical support:**
  - Macintosh technical support: 408-727-9054
  - Windows technical support: 408-727-9004
  - Hearing impaired support (TDD): 408-987-7312
  - FAX answer line: 800-800-8954
- **Times (all times Pacific):**
  - English-language hours: Monday to Thursday, 6 a.m. to 6 p.m.; Friday, 6 a.m. to 2 p.m.
  - French-language hours: Monday to Friday, 10 a.m. to 1 p.m.
- **For customer assistance:** 408-727-8227 (Hours: Monday to Thursday, 8 a.m. to 5 p.m.; Friday, 8 a.m. to 2 p.m.)
- **For dealer locations (in the United States):** 800-3-CLARIS (325-2747)
- **For dealer locations and product upgrades (Canada):** 800-668-8948

Chapter 25

When Things Go Wrong

● ●

● ●

*F*rom time to time, things go wrong. It's a law of nature, I guess. Contrary to the prevailing view that computers are incapable of making errors or mistakes, you'll find that most often just the opposite is true. Computers make so many mistakes that you wonder how they ever got through third-grade math.

It's the nature of the beast — the programming beast. Programmers, being human, make errors or find that, after fixing a dozen mistakes (called *bugs*) in the software, they've created another dozen, just in their fixes. That's why any work on software is never finished; errors multiply like compound dividends in your savings account. As you fix a few, another batch appears. The more you beat on it, the more bugs you'll shake out.

None of this bug stuff should worry you, particularly with FileMaker Pro. The honchos at Claris are very, very thorough about testing their product before it hits the market — in other words, before you get your hands on it. FileMaker Pro is a rock-solid product.

On the other hand, you may get an occasional error message when you work with the program. Sometimes, these errors (or *error conditions,* as computer geeks call them) are not repeatable, and that can be a source of frustration. Newly released software programs feature a great deal of unexplained behavior as par for the course. As a matter of fact, the world in general features a great deal of unexplained behavior.

Encountering Error Messages

If something isn't working right, FileMaker Pro is gracious enough to give you an error message. These messages pop up on-screen and alert you to a condition or situation that's going on with your program.

Don't panic if you get an error message. Everybody gets these messages at one time or another. Read them through carefully before you act, or before you click a button. Error messages are there to give you a path out of your problem or to alert you to choices.

The problem with error messages is that they're sometimes cryptic or misleading. Often these messages are written by the programmers who write the code that makes FileMaker Pro work. These programmers, if they're good, have to learn how to write in a language that is not English. So, when they write a message in real English, it comes out sounding like geekspeak.

Be tolerant here. A lot of programmers flunked freshman English or never took a writing class, but that doesn't make them bad. I know that error messages can be frustrating — the logic is sometimes twisted or, worse, incomprehensible. They weren't written by PR departments or political spin doctors. These messages are buried in the heart of every software program, including FileMaker Pro, and you need to make an effort to understand them.

One of the most common error messages

Here is one of the most common error messages you may find in FileMaker Pro.

```
The application has unexpectedly quit.
```

This means that FileMaker Pro has run out of memory. You need to increase the memory size that you've allocated to FileMaker Pro. To do so, click the FileMaker Pro icon on your Desktop and then choose File⇨Get Info in the Macintosh Finder. In the Get Info dialog box, you can enter a larger amount of memory in the Memory requirements box. Chapter 3 explains this procedure. FileMaker Pro's *memory footprint,* or the RAM taken up by the application, is actually quite small (unlike many applications), so you won't encounter this error too often. In any case, it's always a good idea to add as much RAM to your Mac or Windows system as you can afford.

A catalog of common messages with their solutions

Table 25-1 contains an alphabetical list of the most common FileMaker Pro error and alert messages that you may encounter when working with the program. Don't panic if you get one of these messages. And don't be intimidated by the wording and language of the message. Just stay calm and accept the fact that you may have to read a message two or three times to figure it out.

Table 25-1	FileMaker Pro Error Messages
Message	*Suggested Solution*
Access to this layout is not currently available. Therefore this change will be made only to your temporary local copy.	You don't have access privileges to the particular layout. You can change the layout temporarily, but the changes won't be saved. To change the layout permanently, get the password from your system administrator. Check Chapter 18 for a discussion of access privileges.
Communication with the host was interrupted and could not be reestablished.	This is a network problem, which you won't encounter unless you're on a network. Click the Quit or Exit button to quit FileMaker Pro; then restart the program. Reopen the file from the network.
\<Filename\> cannot be opened because it would exceed the host's capacity. Try again later.	Again, a networking problem. The file is currently in use by the maximum number of guests allowed. You have to wait for someone else to close the file.
\<Filename\> is currently in use and could not be opened. The file is single-user, or the host could not be found on the network.	Another networking problem. You need to contact the host to open the file not as a single-user file but as a multi-user file.
FileMaker cannot host or be a guest of a file because NetWare for Windows is not installed (-9118)	You aren't running the NetWare driver, or the NetWare server isn't available on the network. See the FileMaker Pro Installation Guide for how to solve the problem.
Network synchronization error.	Click the Quit or Exit button to quit. Restart FileMaker Pro and reopen the file from the network.

(continued)

Table 25-1 *(continued)*

Message	Suggested Solution
Some time field values could not be recognized as valid times. You can find these by searching for "?."	FileMaker Pro can't recognize the format of the time values you've imported. Search for invalid date values that aren't in the standard format of *hh:mm:ss* by entering the ? operator in a find request.
Sorry, this file is badly damaged. Please use the Recover command.	Choose File⇨Recover to reconstruct the file immediately. Hopefully, it's still salvageable.
Sorry, FileMaker is unable to read the disk. Click Retry to try again, or click Quit and copy the file to another disk. (Error *n* at *n*)	Your disk is full, or the file is damaged. If you're unable to open the file after clicking Retry, copy the file to another disk.
Sorry, FileMaker is unable to update the disk. Click Retry to try again, or click Quit and copy this file to another disk. (Error *n* at *n*)	FileMaker Pro can't save the file to your disk because of a disk error. Follow the instructions in the message carefully to save the file to a different disk.
Sorry, there is not enough memory to complete this operation.	Close all other files and applications and try again.
Sorry, *<filename>* could not be imported. There may be a problem in the file.	Make sure that the file is in a format that FileMaker Pro recognizes. Then try again.
Sorry, FileMaker is unable to continue printing. (Error *n*)	Make sure that your printer is properly connected to your computer and (obviously) switched on. You may also want to troubleshoot the problem by checking the Windows 95 Wizard, which is found at Start⇨Help. For network printing, make sure that you're properly connected to the network and that the network is currently functioning right. Check with your system administrator about the network printer's setup.

Message	Suggested Solution
The field `<field name>` in the lookup file `<filename>` has been defined to have *n* more repetitions than the field `<field name>` in this file. As a result, some data may not be copied when a lookup is performed. Proceed anyway?	A lookup file has more repetitions than the matching field in the current database. Redefine the field in one of the files so that the field in both files has the same number of repetitions.
There may not be enough disk space to complete this operation. FileMaker will not be able to open the file if this operation fails. Proceed anyway?	Just click Cancel; then copy the file to a disk with free space and give the operation another try. Proceed with caution.
Waiting for response from `<guest>` All other guests must wait until the problem is resolved or `<guest>` is disconnected.	One of the guests on the network has accidentally lost the connection with the file's host or is busy with another application. Ask the guest on the network to make sure that FileMaker Pro is connected to the net.
You cannot replace the found set because your password does not allow you to edit records or the file is multi-user.	You're importing records that you don't have access privileges to edit. It's a password problem. Contact your network administrator to work out your access privileges for editing records.

The Attack of the Killer Virus

Viruses were a plague on the software industry a few years back; I can't think of anybody who didn't get attacked by one and go screaming in agony out of his or her office. Strangely enough, almost 70 percent of the viruses out there were written by programmers in Eastern Europe with nothing but smuggled PCs and time on their hands, not by disgruntled U.S. programmers out to get revenge on the boss. Thankfully, many of these viruses have stopped immigrating to the West.

Still, from time to time, you're going to run into a virus if you're not careful. A virus may strike without warning (in the dead of night, as in a good mystery novel), or you may get some advanced notice.

Built into FileMaker Pro are some cautionary mechanisms that detect the presence of a possible virus. Heed these warnings and take the appropriate action that I describe here.

It's a Saturday night; rather than going out on the town, you're getting to work on a cool FileMaker Pro database that you want to knock out in your spare time this weekend. Suddenly, when you boot up your copy of FileMaker Pro, you get this message on-screen:

```
Your copy of FileMaker Pro has been corrupted or modified
by another application or a virus. Please make a new copy
from locked master disks.
```

Eeeeech!

Stay cool. The end is not near. Yes, there's something wrong, but you're not helpless. More than likely, your copy of FileMaker Pro has been infected by a computer virus.

What you need to do is get the latest version of Disinfectant, the virus-stomping software available from various online services, such as America Online, CompuServe, and Prodigy. This program was graciously produced by John Norstad, who offers it as freeware to the world. You must have a copy if you have a Macintosh; the program is not virtually indispensable — it's indispensable, period! (Check out Chapter 24 for information about down-loading software, such as Disinfectant, from various online services.)

Of course, you can get commercial virus-protection programs, such as those from Symantec, out on the market as well, but you may want to start with Disinfectant.

On Windows, my tech editor recommends Dr Solomon's for virus protection if money is no object (Dr Solomon's Software, Inc., 1-888-DRSOLOMON). On a budget, ThunderBYTE Anti-Virus for Windows 95 is, like Disinfectant, a shareware program. You can find out more about the program at http://www.thunderbyte.nl.

Viruses are mostly spread by floppy disks. They can also spread virulently on a network, but your network manager is usually hip to this possibility and has installed some form of virus-protection software onto each computer on the network. Or if the program was uploaded to an online service or bulletin board, you can bet that it was run through Disinfectant or another program first to scan for and detect any possible viruses. But despite all the protection, some viruses still get through.

If you get an on-screen message about FileMaker Pro having been corrupted or modified, get to work right away checking for any possible viruses. Make sure that you run Disinfectant on your hard drive or on any floppies that you suspect may be culprits. Although Disinfectant is for Mac-only users, such antivirus programs run pretty much the same on Windows computers.

Don't be shy about using Disinfectant. Everybody, at one time or another, runs into a virus on his or her system. And if that virus has infected your copy of FileMaker Pro, you need to take action.

After Disinfectant has checked your files and folders and stomped any viruses it may have found, you see a screen similar to the one in Figure 25-1, reporting to you with the results of its mission.

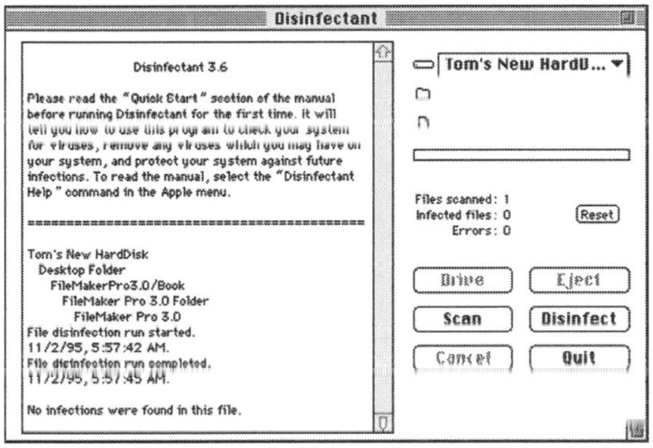

Figure 25-1:
Disinfectant's
report card.

If Disinfectant does find a virus, your best plan of attack is to trash any of the infected FileMaker Pro files or the application itself and replace them with new, clean copies from your locked master disks. *Locked master disks* are disks that you've write-protected by moving up the little button on the upper-left corner of your disk. Nothing, not even the deadliest virus in the computer world, can attack it because the disk can't be written to. Creating a locked master disk is standard operating procedure.

Check any floppy disks that are passed on to you from unreliable sources or people you don't really know before you install the floppy's contents to your hard drive. The same caution holds true for files that you download from online services or bulletin boards. Use Disinfectant to scan and disinfect those files.

Your copy of FileMaker Pro needs to be healthy and happy to function properly. It doesn't have time for a winter cold or flu bug.

The lesson is a simple one: Don't take any chances with software that you think may be infected with a virus.

Chapter 26
Some Neat Tricks of the Trade

This chapter is a kind of grab bag; it's a collection of odds and ends, little tricks of the trade that ought to help you build better databases with FileMaker Pro. I've culled these goodies from my travels on the road with FileMaker Pro and want to share a few with you. I'm sure you can come up with your own FileMaker Pro tricks, once you put your mind to it.

Don't Forget Monitor Size

In designing a FileMaker Pro database and working with your layouts, think in pixels as well as inches. You may well ask, "Why?" Because thinking of the monitor on which your database will run and its size in pixels is helpful. If you're designing the database just for yourself, well, the answer is pretty obvious. You design the layout to fit your monitor size. On the Mac, that's typically a 13-inch, 16-inch, or 20-inch monitor, while on most PC compatibles, it's a 14, 15, 17, 20 or 21-inch monitor.

In fact, I once built a nifty FileMaker Pro database that fit perfectly on my 20-inch monitor. Guess what? Not everybody in the office was blessed with a 20-inch monitor. So using my database, everyone else had to scroll down on the file just to see the forms. I had to redesign the darn thing, scrunching it down to fit those smaller monitors.

The tip is simple:

1. Go into Layout mode by choosing Mode⇨Layout.

Note that you need to have a file active. You can't really do these steps before you start designing a database.

2. Choose Show⇨Graphic Rulers, as shown in Figure 26-1.

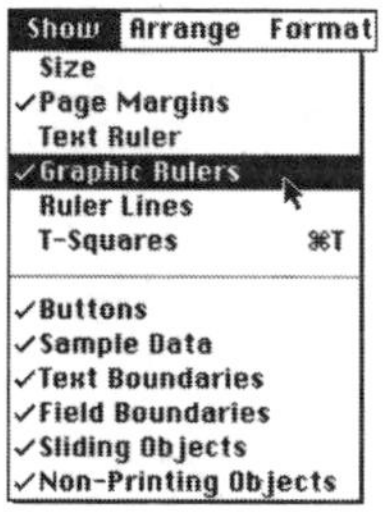

Figure 26-1:
Getting ready to size up your database.

3. On your layout, in the upper-left corner where you see *inches,* click twice until you get px, which is short for *pixels* (see the sample layout from My Address Book shown in Figure 26-2).

Figure 26-2:
Changing your graphic ruler to pixels.

Instead of inches, you see the measurement of your layout in pixels. A long ruler extends vertically and horizontally to indicate pixels.

Why the heck do you need pixels, anyway? The answer is quite simple: That's the way your computer display, or monitor, is measured. The screen has a resolution in pixels. Typically, a 14-inch color monitor has a resolution of 640 x 480 pixels — that's 640 pixels horizontally and 480 pixels vertically. Most people will be working with *at least* that screen resolution.

I work with a 17-inch Multiple Scan Display, and it has a switch that lets me change resolutions from 640 x 480 pixels to 832 x 624 pixels to 1024 pixels x 768 pixels. That's three different resolutions on just one monitor! You can't please everybody with your database design, so I'd stick to the 640 x 480 pixels as your measurement.

Alternatively, you can do the following:

1. **While in Layout mode, choose Mode⇨Set Rulers, as shown in Figure 26-3.**

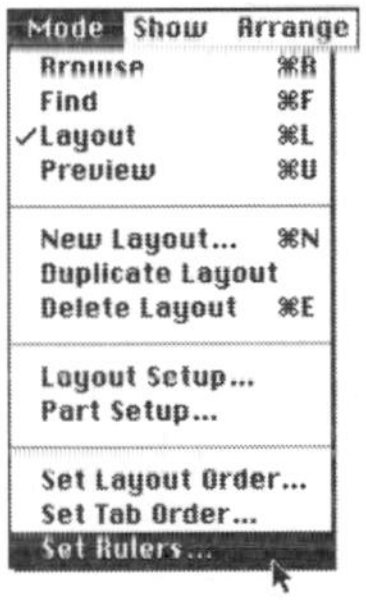

Figure 26-3.
Another way to change how your ruler measures up.

2. **In the Set Rulers dialog box shown in Figure 26-4, open the Units pop-up menu and click Pixels.**

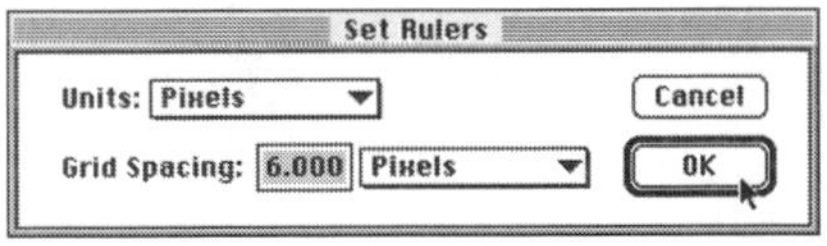

Figure 26-4:
Using a dialog box to specify units of measure.

You may want to consider doing multiple layouts designed for different monitors, one for those smaller (13–15-inch monitors), with a button that lets your users toggle between those versions. Even though you may have to compress your layout to fit those smaller monitors, the folks who use them will thank you in spades.

Indexing Text Fields to Search

Most people who use your database have one concern and one concern only: finding data fast. As a database grows, with new records getting added every day, searching becomes all the more important. If the users of your database need to search text, for example, you can speed things up by indexing the text in a particular field. Unfortunately, the way you do that is a bit clunky from my point of view. The process may be a little tricky to figure out at first because the indexing capability appears almost hidden, like a mask. Yet that mask, like the one Jim Carrey wore in the movie *The Mask,* makes things happen for you. So once you index the fields in your files that you think will be most heavily searched, you'll be smokin', as Jim Carrey said in *The Mask.* Here's how:

1. **Choose File⇨Define⇨Fields.**

   Note that you can define a field for indexing after you have created it.

2. **In the Define Fields dialog box, enter the name and type of field you want to define; then click Options.**

   The Entry Options dialog box appears, as shown in the example in Figure 26-5.

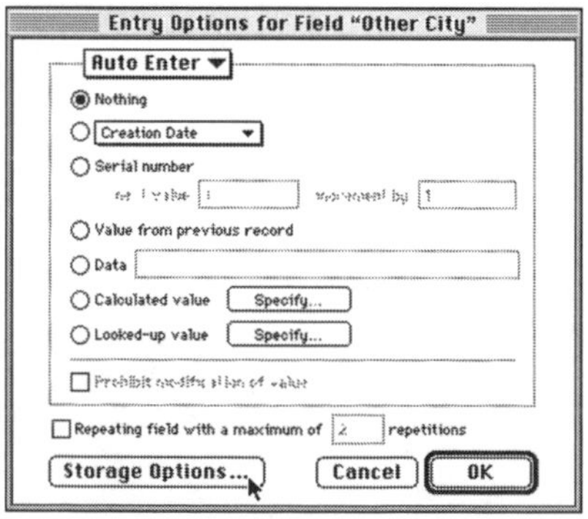

Figure 26-5:
The Entry
Options
dialog box.

Entry Options for Field "Other City"

Auto Enter ▼

● Nothing
○ Creation Date ▼
○ Serial number
  next value: 1   increment by: 1
○ Value from previous record
○ Data
○ Calculated value   [Specify...]
○ Looked-up value   [Specify...]

☐ Prohibit modification of value

☐ Repeating field with a maximum of 2 repetitions
[Storage Options...]   [Cancel]   [OK]

3. Click Storage Options at the bottom of the dialog box.

Another dialog box appears, as shown in Figure 26-6, allowing you to activate indexing.

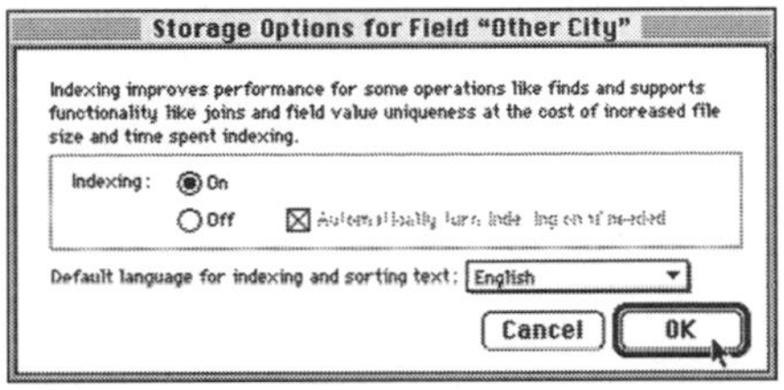

Figure 26-6:
Indexing is
as easy as
clicking a
button.

Storage Options for Field "Other City"

Indexing improves performance for some operations like finds and supports functionality like joins and field value uniqueness at the cost of increased file size and time spent indexing.

Indexing: ● On
○ Off   ☒ Automatically turn Index ing on if needed

Default language for indexing and sorting text: English

Cancel   OK

4. Click the radio button to turn on the indexing option.

5. Click in both the Storage Options and Entry Options dialog boxes.

6. Click Done in the Define Fields dialog box.

Now when you search on a particular field, you'll find that just by entering a word or phrase, you can retrieve the records you want. That's a pretty good return on your investment, I'd say. Check out Chapter 18 for more information on searching and finding.

Locking Those Layout Tools

Layouts are tricky because you've got to juggle lots of tools, moving back and forth from one tool to the other according to the demands of your design. Now, if you want to keep the selected tool active, you can preset that option in your Preferences dialog box. Here's how to lock the tools you work with in your active layout:

1. Choose Edit⇨Preferences⇨Application.

2. In the Preferences dialog box, open the pop-up menu on the Mac or the tab in Windows and click Layout, as shown in Figure 26-7.

3. Click the check box Always Lock Layout Tools.

What happens now is that the tool you're working with becomes black and remains selected until you select a different tool or press Enter. Check out Chapter 3 for more details on locking your layout tools.

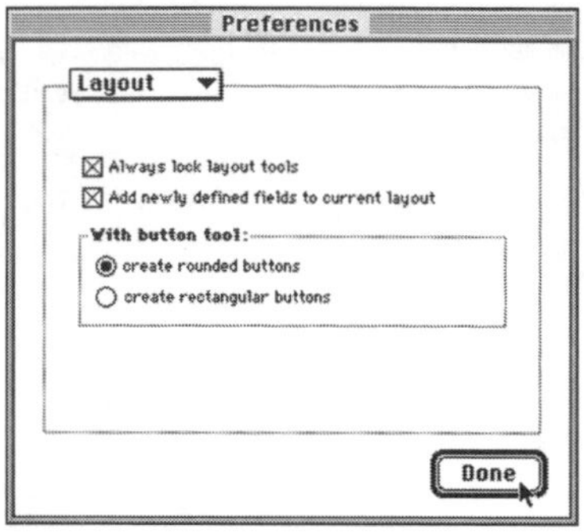

Figure 26-7:
Set your
layout
preferences
in this
dialog box.

Have You Checked Your Alignment Lately?

Getting the proper alignment for the graphic objects in your layouts can be a real pain, unless you try every trick in the book. If you try to line up your objects in a horizontal or vertical row by "eyeballing" them, as graphic designers say, you'll find yourself pushing the limits of your patience. Working that way can be a frustrating business.

Here's a much easier way to do alignment:

1. **In Layout mode with a layout active, click the Pointer tool.**

2. **Drag the Pointer tool to the fields that you want to line up.**

3. **Select the fields you want to group together and align, as shown in the example in Figure 26-8.**

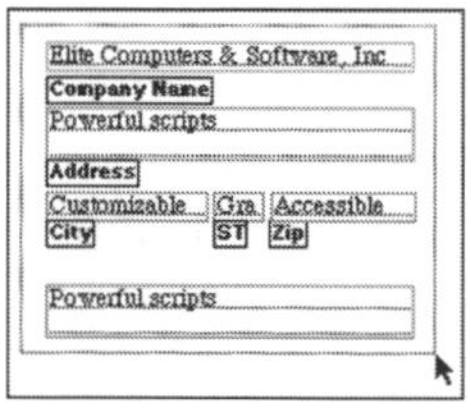

Figure 26-8:
A group of
fields,
selected
and ready
for
alignment.

To select and group the fields you want to align, you need to click around all the fields with the Pointer tool. Just point and drag around the outside corners.

A dotted line appears around the selected fields.

4. **Choose Arrange⇨Group.**

   Magic! You see all the grouped fields now highlighted. That way, you know they've been selected and will work together. You can now move the group as one piece to any position you want on your layout.

   The most precise way to move those grouped fields or graphic objects is by using the arrow keys. Each keystroke left, right, up, or down moves the objects 1 pixel in that specified direction.

5. **Choose Arrange⇨Set Alignment.**

   The dialog box shown in Figure 26-9 appears, giving you a set of choices in terms of aligning those objects from top to bottom and left to right.

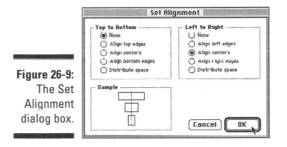

Figure 26-9:
The Set
Alignment
dialog box.

This alignment setting is very handy to have and ought to save you much time and effort that you may have spent otherwise if you tried to do the precision alignment just by eyeballing the objects.

Grouping Those Buttons

Buttons are one of the coolest things in FileMaker Pro, but gosh, they're sometimes hard to control. I mean, you have to work hard to get them to do what you want. After you've gone through the procedure of defining a button, you want to tag it, label it, and enter a name on that button, which is okay. But sometimes you want to layer that button or add a color or texture to create a 3-D effect in your layout. Now things get more complicated.

If you layer a button with another graphic object, you end up playing cat-and-mouse with the Bring to the Front and Send to the Back commands in the Arrange menu when you're in Layout mode. Then after you've layered the button with a cool color or texture you like, you're ready to move it to the desired position on your layout — and whoa, you end up moving the button in pieces. See Chapter 22 for more details on how you can script buttons to do amazing things.

This tip is simple enough: After you've created the button effect you want, stop what you're doing and click and drag the Pointer tool over the whole button. Then choose Arrange➪Group. The layers of the button are now grouped together.

I can't begin to tell you how many times I've not done that. And suffered the consequences: scattered buttons all over my layout. Drat!

Command-dragging — that is, holding down the ⌘ key on the Mac or Ctrl key on Windows while dragging the mouse — selects an object or field that the selection rectangle touches. This way, you don't have to drag around the objects. Keep in mind that Command-clicking a field or text object resets the default font to match the selected object, saving you time in layouts when you've got multiple fonts to work with.

Do-Nothing Buttons — for Now

I suggest that you use the Button tool in Layout mode to place your buttons where you want to them to appear on your layout. But when the Specify Button dialog box appears on-screen, asking you to define an action for that button, stop and catch your breath and then select the Do Nothing option (see Figure 26-10).

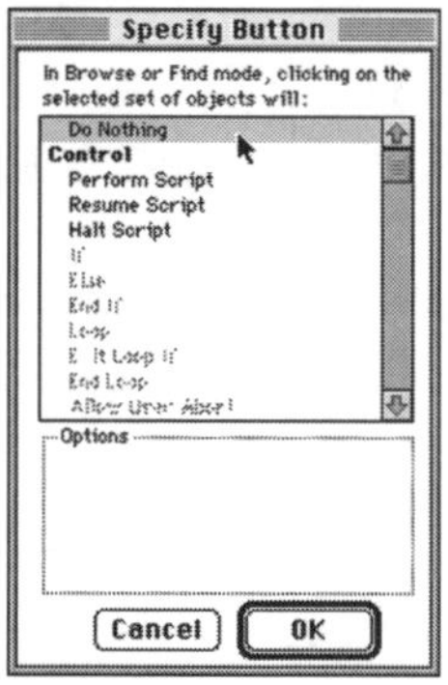

Figure 26-10:
Don't you wish your life had an option like Do Nothing that you could choose occasionally?

Specify Button
In Browse or Find mode, clicking on the selected set of objects will:
Do Nothing
Control
Perform Script
Resume Script
Halt Script
If
Else
End If
Loop
Exit Loop If
End Loop
Allow User Abort
Options

Cancel   OK

That's right: You don't want your button to do a darn thing right now. I understand the temptation to scroll down the list and select something, anything, even if you're not sure what exactly you want your button to do just yet. A button that does nothing seems like a button not worth its bits and bytes.

If you can, resist the temptation to define the action for your new button. Wait until you have your buttons sized and resized, colored, textured, layered, labeled, grouped, and positioned (whew!) where you want them on your layout — then move into action, as far as having them perform for you.

When you're ready to spring those buttons into action, choose Format⇨Button, as shown in Figure 26-11, and that very same Specify Button dialog box appears with all those wonderful choices of what you can get your button to do.

Format	Script	Window
Font		▶
Size		▶
Style		▶
Align Text		▶
Line Spacing		▶
Text Color		▶
Text...		
Number...		
Date...		
Time...		
Graphic...		
Portal...		
Button...		
Field Format...		⌥⌘F
Field Borders...		⌥⌘B
Sliding/Printing...		⌥⌘T

Figure 26-11:
Your path back to the Specify Button dialog box.

Oh, Those Undocumented Keystrokes

Here are some keyboard commands that you won't find documented anywhere in FileMaker Pro. Don't ask me why. Life is full of mysteries, ain't it?

✔ While you're in Layout mode, press the Enter key to toggle back and forth between the last layout tool you've selected and the Pointer tool. Very handy indeed, because typically when doing a layout, you're doing a lot of toggling between various tools in the Tool panel.

✔ When you're cruising through dialog boxes on the Mac, press ⌘↑ or ⌘+↓. This shortcut lets you move up or down each item listed in a dialog box, if you're in ScriptMaker or doing layout stuff. (You can't use just the arrow key to do the job.)

✔ When you're flipping through your records one at a time in Windows, press Ctrl+↑ or Ctrl+↓. I like this shortcut because of the proximity of the right Ctrl key and the arrow keys: they're almost next to each other. Once you get used to working with these keystrokes, you can move through your records without even looking at the keyboard.

Using That Spell Checker Wisely — with a Button

Use the spell checker that's built into FileMaker Pro but turn off the questionable-spelling indicators listed in the Spelling Options dialog box, as shown in Figure 26-12. Nothing is more annoying than having your Macintosh beep or flash at you every time you type a "questionably" spelled word. How does it know what's questionable and what's not? Who had the idea of implementing such a feature? If you click a radio button telling your computer to beep or flash at you, good luck. I guarantee that you'll drive yourself nuts in no time at all.

Nevertheless, you don't want to neglect your spelling entirely. After you're done inputting data into your records, a good habit to get into is to choose Edit⇨Preferences⇨Document, then select Spelling.

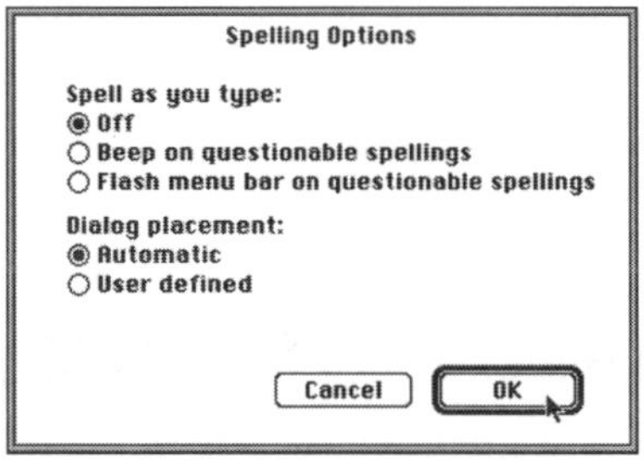

Figure 26-12:
The Spelling
Options
dialog box.

> **Spelling Options**
>
> **Spell as you type:**
> ⦿ Off
> ○ Beep on questionable spellings
> ○ Flash menu bar on questionable spellings
>
> **Dialog placement:**
> ⦿ Automatic
> ○ User defined
>
> [Cancel] (OK)

Or if you really want to be cool, you can drop a button on one of your layouts with a script attached to it that, when you click it, automatically checks the spelling of a record or a selection.

1. **Drop a button onto your layout. The Specify Button dialog box pops up.**

2. **Scroll down the menu item in the Specify Button dialog box until you come to Spelling.**

3. **Select the Spelling script you want for that button in your layout from the options listed in Figure 26-13.**

The options for spell checking include the following:

- ✔ Check Selection
- ✔ Check Record
- ✔ Check Found Set

✔ Correct Word

✔ Spelling Options

✔ Select Dictionaries

✔ Edit User Dictionary

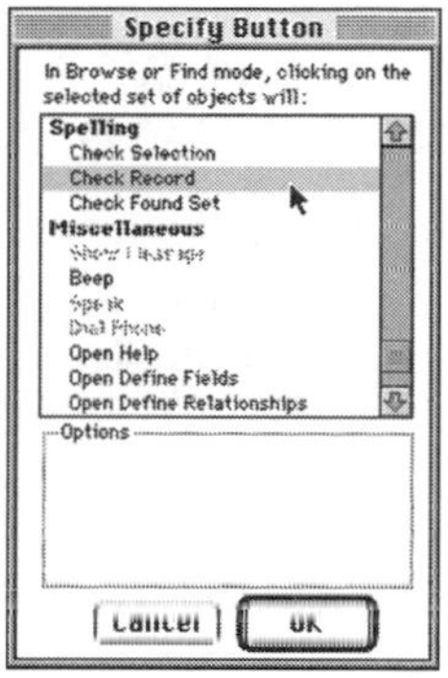

Figure 26-13:
Writing a
script to
automate
your spell
checker.

Adding a button is a useful reminder if you think you're prone to making many spelling errors while inputting data into your records, or if you think that data you're importing from elsewhere may be full of spelling errors.

Remember that FileMaker Pro has a spell checker with over 100,000 words in its library. Use it.

The Joys of Multiple Finds

And find this and find that or find this or that. . . . Oh, there's logic to it. Actually, there's nothing too complicated about using the *and* criterion to do a multiple find. For example, say that you want to find all the Bobs who live in California and work for Widgets, Inc. Luckily, unlike with some database programs in which you have to type the word *and* until you're blue in the face, you don't have to be so particular in your search criteria with FileMaker Pro. Just follow these steps to do a multiple find:

1. Open your file.

For example, to find all those California Bobs at Widgets, Inc., you may want to search a Contacts file with a listing of names, addresses, and companies.

2. **In Find mode, just click through the fields that correspond to the data you want to find.**

3. **Enter the text you want to find.**

   In my example, you want to find all the Bobs in California working at Widgets, Inc.

4. **In Find mode, click the New Request menu item.**

   This action lets you find all the records that contain *Bob* in the Name field, *California* in the State field, and *Widgets, Inc.* in the Company field. Piece of cake.

Now guess what? The New Request command lets you work with more than one find request at a time. What this means is that your multiple-find requests can also act like an *or* criterion.

This feature lets you, for example, find all the records that contain either *California* or *Ohio* in the State field, if you're not sure whether Bob lives in California or Ohio, working for Widgets, Inc. What you do is generate two requests: the first request lists *California* in the State field, and the second lists *Ohio*. Cool, huh?

Part VI

The Part of Tens

"OH THOSE? THEY'RE THE SEAT-CUSHION-MOUSE. BOUNCE ONCE TO ACCESS A FILE, TWICE TO FILE AWAY—KEEPS THE HANDS FREE AND THE BUTTOCKS FIRM."

In this part . . .

What would any *...For Dummies* book be without the Part of Tens? This is an absolute must. Here you've got ten cool things about FileMaker Pro, ten suggestions for resources you can look to when in need of help, and ten helpful and productive tips for manipulating your database, whether you're a mouse person or a keyboard person. (I'm a keyboard person myself, but I can relate to you mouse folks, too.) Just your everyday, run-of-the-mill, Part of Tens collection of goodies. Enjoy!

Chapter 27

Ten Best Keyboard Shortcuts

· ·

In This Chapter

▶ Undoing mistakes with ⌘+Z or Ctrl+Z

▶ Sorting with ⌘+S or Ctrl+S

▶ Cutting, copying, and pasting with ⌘+X or Ctrl+X, ⌘+C or Ctrl+C, and ⌘+V or Ctrl+V

▶ Selecting everything with ⌘+A or Ctrl+A

▶ Selecting objects in a layout by type with ⌘+Option+A

▶ Defining fields with ⌘+Shift+D or Ctrl+Shift+D

▶ Creating a new record, new layout, or new request with ⌘+N or Ctrl+N

▶ Going to the next record, next request, or next layout with ⌘+Tab or Ctrl+↓

▶ Printing with ⌘+P or Ctrl+P

▶ Quitting with ⌘+Q or Alt+F4

· ·

*F*ileMaker Pro is so loaded with keyboard shortcuts that picking just the ten best is hard. More like the top 25 would be in order. So my list here is pretty subjective, though it is based on actual use — in other words, the keystroke combinations I actually use to get the job done.

You may come up with your own list, as you master FileMaker Pro. So be it.

I confess: I'm a diehard keystroke man, stemming from the days when I worked with computers that had no mouse. An old-time word-processing program called WordStar challenged every digit on every hand, but once you mastered it, you could keystroke your way through the most complex editing chores.

Now keystrokes are there as an alternative to pointing and clicking with your mouse. But if you learn them, they'll save you a lot of time. One, two, bang on the keyboard, and you've got it done, faster than a mouse can sprint across your living room floor. Speed is the name of the game here.

Okay, for those of you who are counting, this chapter features 12 keyboard shortcuts. I couldn't resist adding a couple extra. Note that for each item, I've put the Mac keyboard shortcut first, followed by the Windows keyboard shortcut.

⌘+Z or Ctrl+Z to Undo

All right, nobody's perfect. We all make mistakes. In life, undoing mistakes is sometimes hard; in the world of FileMaker Pro, you've got a keystroke combination right there at the bottom of your keyboard that lets you undo the last thing you did. (But only the last thing, not a bunch of things before that.) Use it, and use it often. Remember that FileMaker Pro is set to save automatically for you (unless you tell it to do otherwise in the Memory Preferences dialog box, where you can set saving to occur every 10, 15, or 30 minutes, or once every hour). So don't wait too long to undo something. Undo it *now*.

Figure out what combination of thumb and finger works for you to get this keystroke combination cooking. Thumb and forefinger? Thumb and middle finger? Pinkie and thumb? Once you groove it, like a good backhand on the tennis court, you know you can go to it in times of need — and times of undo.

⌘+S or Ctrl+S to Sort

I had a heckuva time getting used to this command because it's the same keyboard command, in other programs, for saving your work. Because FileMaker Pro saves automatically, or in intervals you specify, there's no Save command in the File menu or available to you as a Save shortcut on the keyboard.

There's no save command in FileMaker Pro, either on the Mac or under Windows. You have the option to set the frequency of your saving in the Memory Preferences dialog in 10, 15, or 30 minute intervals, or in one full hour intervals. The option is to let FileMaker Pro save during idle times, that is, when you've lifted your keys from the keyboard or your hand from the mouse. The reassuring thing here is that you know the records in your database are not going to be lost because you got up for a cup of coffee and your computer went down because of a power loss in the building. The program is working behind the scenes to make sure your valuable data is being saved.

But the ⌘+S or Ctrl+S command is for sorting. And you do quite a bit of sorting when your FileMaker Pro database grows and blossoms with a thousand records. Think of sorting as a way of harvesting your fields, or at least seeing how the rows line up. When in Browse mode, this command takes you right to the Sort Record dialog box, where you can choose what you want to sort as well as specify the sort order for those items.

⌘+X or Ctrl+X, ⌘+C or Ctrl+C, ⌘+V or Ctrl+V to Cut, Copy, and Paste

Whatever you're doing, you live and die by the Cut, Copy, and Paste commands. They're your lifeblood. I must use them a thousand times a day in whatever program I'm in. When you're doing layouts in FileMaker Pro, these keystrokes are a must. Learn them and save the time you would otherwise use to go up to the Edit menu with your mouse, select the Copy, Cut, or Paste item in that Edit menu, and then click the item.

I have an unorthodox style of attacking these keystrokes — namely, crossing over the keyboard with my right hand and pressing the combination with my forefinger down on the ⌘ key on the Mac or the Ctrl key in Windows and my middle finger on the appropriate *X, C,* or *V* key for a Cut, Copy, or Paste. But the style works for me. You'll probably figure out a style that works for you, too.

⌘+A or Ctrl+A to Select All and ⌘+Option+A on the Mac to Select Objects (in Layout) by Type

Why change one when you can change all? I use this keystroke almost as much as I use the Cut, Copy, and Paste combinations. When you're editing, you sometimes need to select all and make global changes (to your layouts, for example).

I use the thumb down on the ⌘ key and my forefinger pressed on the A key. But I can't do it without looking.

⌘+Option+A on the Mac is a very awkward but highly useful keystroke combination. It's awkward because you have to press down with your left forefinger and middle finger to get the ⌘ and Option keys and then cross over the keyboard with your right forefinger to hit the A key. (I'm sure other finger, hand, and thumb combinations are possible, but I bet they're all awkward.) In any case, the effort is worth it, particularly if you want to change all the fonts to the same font size or style in your graphic objects. This keystroke combination does the job nicely.

⌘+Shift+D or Ctrl+Shift+D to Define Fields

If you like to define fields and fill up your FileMaker Pro database with lots of them, you'll come around to using this keystroke shortcut sooner or later. Again, it's one of those triple combinations that are a bit awkward to use until you get the hang of them. But I wouldn't leave home without it.

Fields must be defined, and you've got to meet the challenge of that imposing Define Fields dialog box with all those things to enter and choose. This keystroke combination takes you there, pronto. The rest, as they say in kindergarten, is up to you.

⌘+N or Ctrl+N for New Record, Layout, or Request

In the world of databases, nothing quite matches the thrill of adding a new record. (Of course, if you have to add a thousand new records in one day, the thrill may get old fast.) In any case, ⌘+N or Ctrl+N does it for you instantly. A new blank record screen, with lots of fields to fill, pops up. Or a New Layout if you're in Layout mode, or a New Request if you're in Find mode.

If you like new things — adding new things, I should say — you'll be happy with this keyboard shortcut. If you like old things . . . sorry, FileMaker Pro doesn't offer a keyboard shortcut for adding old things to your database. You're stuck with the new here.

⌘+Tab or Ctrl+↓ for Next Record, Request, or Layout

This keystroke, which works in Browse and Layout modes, is awkward to learn because it involves using your left thumb to press the ⌘ key and your forefinger or middle finger to press the Tab key. But man, it's powerful. You move with this keystroke combination — move from one record to the next or from one request or layout to the next. This keystroke is, in a word, hot. Once you start using it, you'll feel your fingers begin to sizzle.

⌘+P or Ctrl+P to Print

Using ⌘+P or Ctrl+P is a very satisfying way to order FileMaker Pro to print the records in your database when you're ready to print. For some reason, in every Macintosh and Windows program I've ever worked with, I always use ⌘+P or Ctrl+P when printing. Don't ask me why. Maybe it has to do with the psychology of wanting to give a printer commands rather than wimpy mouse and menu clicks. You know, printers are stubborn beasts, and unless you boss them around — muscle them around, in fact — they won't obey. Am I right about this, or what? Or is it just a guy thing?

⌘+Q or Alt+F4 to Quit

Like ⌘+P or Ctrl+P for Print, I always use this command when quitting FileMaker Pro (or any other Macintosh program, for that matter). There must be something about finality here — a philosophical imperative about using a couple of keystrokes rather than mouse points and clicks to wrap things up for the day. You want to be in charge. You want to command your program to quit. You want to get the monkey off your back.

I'm sure some computer scientist has it figured it all out and is ready to publish a Ph.D. dissertation on the subject. I'll keep you posted.

Chapter 28
Ten Useful Things to Click

- -

In This Chapter

▶ Button tool

▶ ScriptMaker

▶ Recover

▶ Book icon

▶ Portal tool

▶ Mode selector

▶ Pointer tool

▶ Fill tool

▶ Find button

▶ Part tool

- -

*K*eyboard shortcuts, if you're not all thumbs, let you do some things faster and more efficiently in FileMaker Pro than the mouse does. No argument about that. But you can perform some actions only with mouse clicks. And these actions deserve recognition, not just because you need to mouse-click them but because they're useful and cool. Here is a list of my top ten favorites.

Button Tool

I've sung the praises of this tool in previous chapters, so I'll try not to repeat what I've said before. This tool lives in the lower-left corner of the Tool panel in Layout mode. Click it, and your cursor becomes a crosshair until you place the crosshair down on your layout. When that happens, you get a button. The button can be a rounded rectangle or just a plain rectangle, depending on your choices in the Layout Preferences dialog box.

Once that button is placed down on your layout — all with just one mouse click — a whole world of possibilities opens up for you. You can get that button to perform a script for you, which means that clicking the button does just about anything, from performing simple finds to speaking the Gettysburg Address. Mastering the possibilities is up to you.

ScriptMaker

One click in the Script menu (Script⇨ScriptMaker), and ScriptMaker opens its arms — and its big Define Scripts dialog box — to you. The thing I like about this feature is the awesome power available to you with just one mouse click. ScriptMaker is like another full-blown application tool built right into FileMaker Pro that lets you choose from a set of commands or scripts that you can attach to buttons and dialog boxes in your database. It's a kind of visual programming language that's easy to learn and use. And its power is there for the asking — or clicking.

Recover

Things go bad from time to time. It's a law of nature, I guess. Most software programs — like other programs in life — don't give you much time to recover anything when disaster strikes. They're not very forgiving. In FileMaker Pro, a simple mouse click in the File menu (File⇨Recover) gets you an immediate option to recover a damaged file. It's like having your own File Doctor right there with you — and not a generic File Doctor, but one that's specific to FileMaker Pro, with the necessary diagnostic and repair tools to save the life of your valuable files.

Book Icon

 I'm not sure what exactly to call the Book icon. Is it a book? A mini-Rolodex? A hanging spiral-bound notebook? But it's been there for years (since the first release of FileMaker Pro several centuries ago), and it does the job. With just a mouse click, you can flip through the records, the layouts, and the finds in your database. By looking at the Book icon, you know right away the number of records or layouts that you've got and where you are — record number 12, for example — in the order. It's a perfect icon for clicking. It highlights when you click it, and it moves you from one record or layout to the next.

In the course of my FileMaker Pro lifetime, I must have clicked this icon a million times. And it's still as much fun as the very first click.

Portal Tool

This tool made its first appearance in FileMaker Pro 3. It sits right next to the Button tool in the lower part of the FileMaker Pro Tool panel when you're in Layout mode. I liken this tool to the genie in Aladdin's lamp. This tool unleashes the power to define relationships among the various files in your FileMaker Pro database. With a single mouse click, you can establish and build a new set of relationships from one file to another.

Mode Selector

When you're working with FileMaker Pro, you inevitably switch back and forth from one mode to another, from Browse to Layout and back, or from Layout to Find and back. If you had to go to the menu bar at the top of your screen and choose a mode from the Mode menu every time, you'd find it quite tedious. Not that some folks who work regularly with FileMaker Pro don't do just that. I'm sure they do. But life is much simpler with one mouse click on the mode selector at the bottom of your screen. A little pop-up menu appears right there for you with all four modes to choose from. You can scroll through them almost instantly and switch from one mode to another in the blink of an eye. Now *that's* clicking.

Pointer Tool

What would you do without this tool? The thing is, it's not there just for pointing but also for performing other chores when you're in Layout mode, such as resizing and modifying fields, buttons, or other graphic objects. I've often wondered why this tool points left, not right or center, but that's a philosophical (or maybe a political) issue, I guess. Suffice to say, with just a mouse click, you activate a powerful little puppy here. It lets you take charge of your layouts, boss those graphic objects around, and plant new fields of almost any size you want.

Fill Tool

I didn't use this tool for a long time, because most of my files were in black and white. But one day I got fill-bucket crazy and began pouring globs of color into my graphic objects and fields. I was like a kid finger-painting for fun. Now I use the Fill tool, which lives just below the Part tool in Layout mode, all the time. With just a click of the mouse, I've got a color palette to choose from or, next to the color palette, a palette of patterns in various shades of gray. I can add spice to my layouts and make them visually exciting. With this tool, the days of boring database designs are over.

Find Button

[Find] I'm still amazed to think that you can switch to Find mode and, sitting right there on the left, see a button labeled Find that lets you search and find like you've never searched and found before. It's the most obvious button in the world. With a mouse click, you can find records that match a particular request you've made. Working with a database doesn't get any easier or better than this.

Part Tool

[Part] The Part tool isn't *part* of a tool, but rather a tool that lets you set up the parts you want in a layout. With just one mouse click, many doors open, with many choices. You get to define the parts of the layout where you want to put your fields. You get to choose title headers, headers, body parts, footers, footer titles, subsummaries, trailing grand summaries — all with this tool. After you click, your cursor becomes a hand, and you can move that hand anywhere you want on your layout. A dialog box pops up to let you define what you want that part to be — for example, as a header, where the information repeats at the top of every record in your file. You've got an unbelievable amount of power built into a little tool that becomes a hand when it moves across the open spaces of your layout.

Appendix
Installing FileMaker Pro 4

• •

In This Chapter

▶ Off the shelf and out of the box: taking your puppy home

▶ Preliminary RAM check

▶ Going for it

• •

*I*f your Macintosh or Windows computer is a part of a network, you'll need the help of your network guru to make the right installation. Ask him or her to help set you up properly. Network installs are beyond the scope of this book.

If you're upgrading from an earlier version of FileMaker Pro, you've been there before, so installation ought to be a snap. There are some things, however, that you ought to be aware of, if you're a Mac user, such as having enough RAM and hard disk space, or where to position your copy of FileMaker Pro on the Desktop if you're using drag and drop. Check out the details in this chapter.

Off the Shelf and out of the Box: Taking Your Puppy Home

The FileMaker Pro box comes loaded with manuals, disks, and registration cards, as well as promotional flyers and other goodies. After you tear off the shrink wrapping and pull out the disks, be sure to save the packaging, at least for a little while. You want to be sure that you received everything with your copy of FileMaker that you were supposed to get.

Don't hesitate to cuddle that box as if it truly were a new puppy you'd brought home from the pet shop. It's a natural human reaction. Software likes to be cuddled, properly cared for, and fed. Remember that your software contains the collective efforts of hundreds, if not thousands, of workers at Claris and elsewhere. It's the result of a lot of hard labor and zillions of hours of midnight programming. Treat it with the respect it deserves.

Preliminary RAM Check on the Mac

Before you get rolling, you want to be sure on the Mac that you've got enough memory or RAM to keep your new puppy happy.

FileMaker Pro 4, at least in the version I've been working with, takes up 1.1 megabytes (MB) of disk space and needs at least 4MB of RAM, that is, 4,096 kilobytes (K), to do its magic. The Get Info box, shown in Figure A-1, which you can access from the Macintosh Finder's File menu, tells you the story.

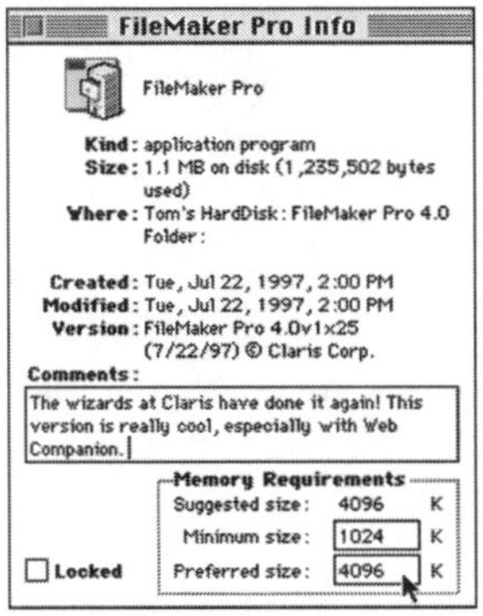

Figure A-1:
This info box shares what you need to know about FileMaker Pro's memory requirements.

```
▓▓▓▓▓▓      FileMaker Pro Info      ▓▓▓▓▓▓

   📦    FileMaker Pro

        Kind : application program
        Size : 1.1 MB on disk (1,235,502 bytes
               used)
       Where : Tom's HardDisk : FileMaker Pro 4.0
               Folder :

     Created : Tue, Jul 22, 1997, 2:00 PM
    Modified : Tue, Jul 22, 1997, 2:00 PM
     Version : FileMaker Pro 4.0v1x25
               (7/22/97) © Claris Corp.
    Comments :
    ┌──────────────────────────────────────┐
    │The wizards at Claris have done it again! This│
    │version is really cool, especially with Web   │
    │Companion.|                             │
    └──────────────────────────────────────┘
              ┌─Memory Requirements──────────┐
              │ Suggested size :  4096     K │
              │ Minimum size :   ┌1024┐    K │
              │                  └────┘      │
    □ Locked  │ Preferred size : ┌4096┐    K │
              │                  └────┘ ▶    │
              └──────────────────────────────┘
```

If you're running on a system with 16MB of RAM, you should be fine. The only thing I'd recommend is checking your System folder to be sure it's not bloated with too many fonts or extensions that aren't really necessary or that you don't use very often. Trim down your system, if possible, to 8MB or less. That way you'll be able to run FileMaker Pro and one or two other applications without getting too close to your 16MB ceiling.

If you have a Macintosh with 8MB of RAM, consider upgrading and adding another 4MB to your system. Your Macintosh will thank you profusely and reward you with many happy hours when you don't have to stare at a "Not Enough Memory" error message on your computer screen.

Of course, the more memory you have on your system, the better. You'll be able to run FileMaker Pro and as many other application programs as your memory allows. Life will be easier. You'll smile and whistle while you work.

Going for It

Now you're ready to rock 'n' roll:

1. **Count your blessings that installing FileMaker Pro on your Macintosh or Windows computer may be one of the easiest things in life that you'll ever do.**

   Remember, ease of use is a God-given (or whichever divine being you wish to credit) right for all computer users. Difficulty, particularly when it comes to installation, is a very bad thing. This is not an Olympic diving contest where degree of difficulty actually counts in your point total.

2. **Take a deep breath and stay cool.**

   Installation on your Mac or Windows computer is not a big deal. Thousands of people before you have done it successfully; thousands after you will do it successfully, too.

   Remember, though, you're unique, just like everybody else.

3. **After unwrapping the disks and turning on your computer, go for it: Begin feeding those floppies or CD-ROMs to your computer.**

4. **After you've inserted Disk 1 into your Mac, you ought to get a FileMaker Pro folder shown in Figure A-2, all opened up for you. On Windows, you'll get the same identical folder, also opened.**

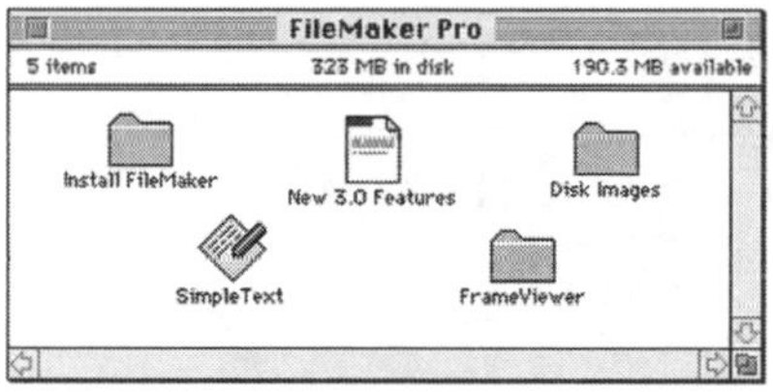

Figure A-2: Your new FileMaker Pro folder.

5. **Click that Start FileMaker icon.**

   You see the Start icon, shown in Figure A-3. You're launching the installation program that will install FileMaker Pro and its accompanying files on your system.

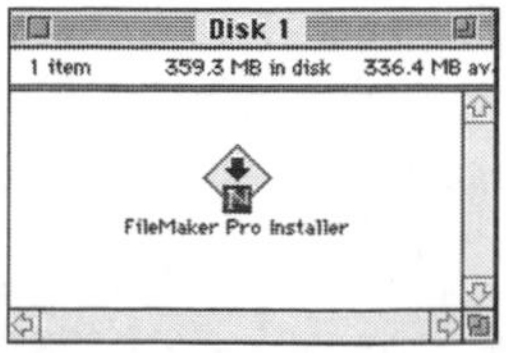

Figure A-3: Ready to install FileMaker Pro?

6. **The License Agreement dialog box appears, as shown in Figure A-4. After you've read over the agreement and are ready to abide by its terms, click Accept.**

Figure A-4:
The
installation
is at hand.

You're on a roll now.

7. **The FileMaker Pro Installer screen, shown in Figure A-5, appears.**

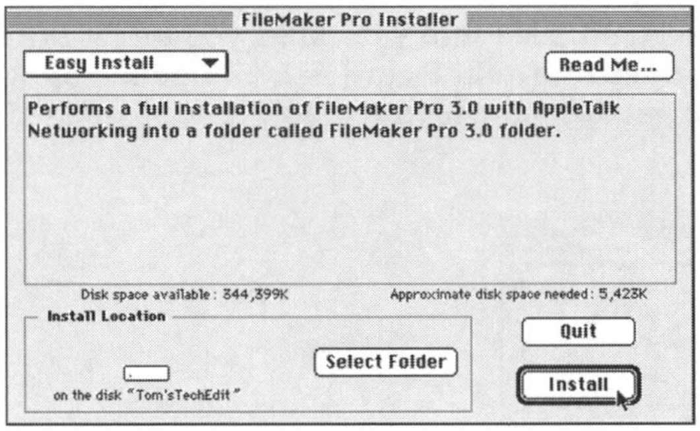

Figure A-5:
Choose
your
installation
weapon.

At this point, basically, you've got two options: Easy Install or Custom Install. I would go with Easy Install, if you're sure that you've got enough RAM on your system. You also need to be sure that you've got enough hard disk space. FileMaker Pro 4 requires about 40MB.

8. **If you want to go with the Easy Install option, make sure the pop-up menu in the upper left of the screen reads Easy Install and click the Install button.**

The installation program prompts you for the disks that need to be installed on your system.

If you want to do a Custom Install, as shown in Figure A-6, you have the option of clicking the items you want installed. Again, though, I don't recommend a Custom Install right now.

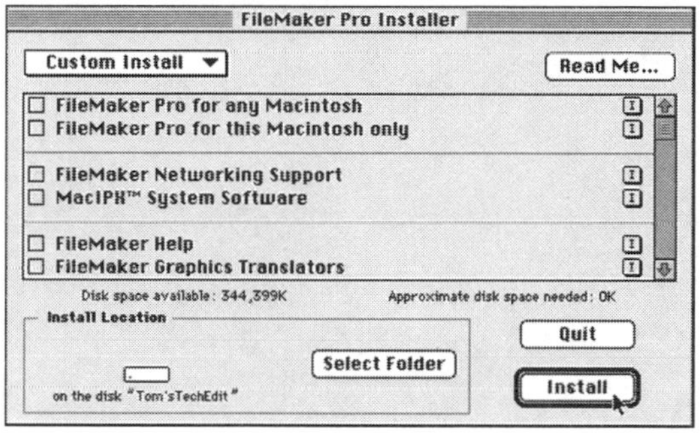

Figure A-6:
The daunting task that awaits you if you choose a Custom Install.

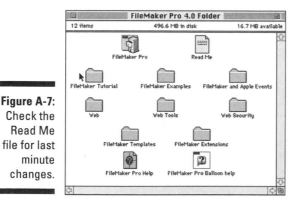

If you insist on doing a Custom Install, you'll still be prompted for the disks you need to insert into your Mac or Windows computer.

9. **Kick back, relax, and let the installation do its thing.**

   FileMaker Pro does the rest for you. It places the application and its related files in the appropriate folders. And when the installation is complete, FileMaker Pro will let you know.

10. **On the start-up screen, you'll get to enter your name and the name of your organization, as well as the serial number from your package.**

   Now if you look in the FileMaker Pro 4 folder on your Mac or Windows computer, you'll see all the files and folders shown Figure A-7. For starters, check the Read me file for any last minute changes or additions to the program.

Figure A-7:
Check the Read Me file for last minute changes.

Congratulations on a successful application launch! You're now in business. Enjoy!

Index

(continued)

(continued)

(continued)

• *N* •

(continued)